PARADISE
FOUND

The musings of a distinguished psychiatrist and
author that pull a lifetime's experiences together in
an attempt to answer questions that concern
us all.

PARADISE FOUND

Reflections on Psychic Survival

by

Arthur Guirdham

TURNSTONE PRESS LIMITED
Wellingborough, Northamptonshire

First published 1980

British Library Cataloguing in Publication Data

West, Peter
    Biorhythms.
    1. Biological rhythms
    1. Title
    612'.014   BF637.B55

ISBN 0-85500-128-3
ISBN 0-85500-135-6 (Pbk)

Typeset by Ad'House, Earls Barton, Northampton.
Printed and bound in Great Britain by
Biddles Ltd., Guildford, Surrey.

Contents

Introduction

The other day when walking down a lane an iron cage tightened round my breastbone. The tide of life went out. My psyche, pulsating in a thin wavelet on the shore, resisted the suction of the ebb tide. I had had another and sharper attack of angina. I sat on a stone and let it pass. It was a still day with a touch of autumn in the air. I wondered if, in the seasons of my soul, it was later than autumn. Because of this closer intimation of mortality it seemed to me that the day was come when I should summarise what I have learnt in my passage through this world. It seemed that by so doing I might return, dressed in another garb, to my vocation as a doctor, because what I have to say is both realistic and reassuring. Though it starts off with the proposition that we endure the worst here in this world, we end with the knowledge that we achieve a peace not of annihilation and unending sleep, but something of which we are conscious.

The evening of my attack I insisted on going to a small dinner given by a woman whom I had appointed to her first job forty-three years ago and who wished for the presence of her first chief. I was very happy. It was obvious that my hostess had given and received much affection from the staff she had directed. There was such a harmony of love and gratitude that I was loathe to leave the party early. Inside the well lit room with its white walls my psyche was loosened from my personality. The psyche is the immortal and mature element of our nature which enters us at conception. The personality is what we fabricate slowly from the conspiracy between our genes and our environment. My liberated psyche relived those earlier days when the high trees deadened the traffic past my house, when what is now a park was a field glistening with buttercups and with the cuckoo calling from beyond the high elms on mornings of May. Because of my soul's ephemeral freedom from the chains of personality I was joined to the psyches of those around me. This is a deeper, rarer and briefer experience of love than what we mean by the word which conveys too often possession smeared with the anodyne of beautiful sensations. Out in the dark streets it was different. I could, because I was still living in my psyche, enjoy the iridescent green of the leaves near the street lamps and the shape of the trees, their branches raised in imploring arms to a starlit but inscrutable sky.

Then the spell was broken. I wondered how it was with those with whom I had dined, when they went home and whether, like me, they shunned the hostile frontiers of night beyond the street lamps; whether, alone, at home, they reverted to a sense of their own solitude, recollecting that in the end, at death and often years before it, we are so often alone as far as contact with other personalities are concerned. Sometimes in dying we are able to smile at arms raised to welcome us by psyches still watching over us. Nevertheless it was a dark thought to think of the light room and the unity of love within it, and to recall that, away from others, away from such rare harmonies, away even from the coarser consolation of the tribal instinct, so many of us are frightened and alone.

It is for this reason that I begin to write this book which tries to answer questions we all ask, of others if we are honest, of ourselves if we bluff. Where do we come from and what are we here for? What happens after death and what, if any, is the purpose of life? There will be little theorising. I leave that to the theologians and scientists who constitute the two sides, one dulled, the other unnaturally burnished, of the same worn penny. What I write expresses not only my philosophical attitude but is the story of my inner life. The two motives are inseparable. All philosophy is the muted story of one man's struggle with the universe. In writing this record I will not discard the weapons of intuition and logic which served me well enough in the practice of medicine. The older I grew the more I relied on the former for diagnosis and the latter for its justification. Nor will I reject those deep and sudden convictions which pierced me like lightning when, as a boy in Cumberland, on the road to Loweswater, walking between hedges frothing with honeysuckle, its odour borne towards me by the soft sea wind, I was stabbed to the heart by my sudden realisation of the changeless, grocer's shop prescriptions of Christianity, of the special allowance which would be undoubtedly made (provided the representations to God were suitably phrased) for blacks and other zoological embarrassments who had never heard the Word. In these moments I was tiptoeing cunningly past the elastic and rapidly expanding frontiers of hell; but the seawind was blowing, the roses were blooming. By Loweswater it was all heaven and no wind and the silence and beauty were unbroken by the mutterings of hell expressed in the echoes of theological ideas. In this hell I had walked in heaven. Such sudden convictions which fill the gulf created by a missed heartbeat are of great importance. I will speak also a little of the truth implicit in beauty, and which I felt in my childhood and boyhood as a total experience to be lost with age. In adult life I was still transported by beauty, but its manifestations were more external and I was not wholly engulfed by it. But what I am most concerned with is revealed truth because, without pride or humility and mostly with regret, I accept that I have been given the capacity to hear those who speak truth from worlds where this life is seen, not in its fullness, but in its very littleness as the ripple of a breath on the waters of the Cosmos. I have also learnt truth directly from a memory extending over millennia and which includes an immensity of pain.

For those for whom to communicate with the ones we call dead spells imbalance and hysterical suggestibility, it should be said that my approach to revealed truth was logical and progressive. It began with the intensive verification of minute historical data, and proceeded onwards through psychic synchronisations to direct communications from the dead who, in speaking of past lives, fulfilled the dictum of Plato that truth and wisdom are merely memory, provided the latter extends beyond the confines of a single life. I learnt what I know not in the timeless half-dream, half-death of life as a lecturer in philosophy at an Oxford College, but in psychic warfare extended over decades; when people took their lives because they could not penetrate the mystery of the hell about them, and in which, at peace for a moment watching the tapers of the almond blossom hastening the dispersing mists of winter, I was suddenly aware of someone in need and hastened to find them at the point of suicide.

1.

God, Suffering and Beauty

This book is not one of those charming productions for children of all ages. It is not a plot on the part of writer and reader to convince each other of their fundamental niceness. It starts from the premise that this life is the first encounter in a long war, a battlefield rather than a golden opportunity. Can it even be called an opportunity if it is given to us all? The adjective golden is hard to interpret by those born blind or spastic or those dying of cancer.

To all of us, when we are depressed, it seems a predicament rather than a potential paradise. Profounder minds than our own have regarded it as such. It has always intrigued me that the education of an English gentleman was based until recently on the Greek and Latin classics and the principles of the Anglican Church. He acquired from the better teachers of the classics the illumination of a lost autumn, of a serenity which in some vague way led up to Christianity but failed to stay the course for unspecified reasons. Yet many classical philosophers regarded this life as a purgatory in which the soul was imprisoned in matter and that the worst thing of all was to be born. From the Anglican Church impressionable youth deduced that on this earth we might suffer a little — it said so in the hymns — but that in the next world we reaped the harvest of our good works here by entering a heaven which was all too often the refinement of our life here below and in which we re-encountered our loved ones without incurring responsibility for them or being driven mad by their idiosyncrasies. Fortified by this academic exercise in schizophrenia, by this alchemistic fusion of the pagan and the Christian, privileged youth managed to confront life with a fortitude which was attributable not to

God or his instructors but to his own staying power.

What are the facts of life as I have seen them as a doctor? A young married woman from a clean house in a mean street smiles humbly at what reassurance the nurse can give her as they wheel her into the operating theatre. She has three young children, a drunken husband and an inoperable cancer. The surgeon will make an incision into her abdomen to see the secondary growths of the liver he has palpated already. The incision will be closed by sutures and she will return home to die. She will feel that everything possible has been done for her. Her agony will be diminished for a few minutes by the thought of duty done. Through the thickening mist of decomposing personality and heavy sedation her last thoughts will be, "What will happen to the children?"

The old man whose stony gaze has obliterated his features sits alone with his dog at the edge of a down so bleak that it reflects the perpetual winter in his heart. He is less frozen in this arctic redoubt than in his home where his wife has received him for decades with a glacial stare.

At right angles to the same road another dog, its eyes, its whole body, every sentient molecule in its tissues dedicated to expressing agony, is chasing fruitlessly a car which accelerates steadily and draws away from it. The car is driven by a man, featureless as the other but for the different reason that he has never needed to display any emotion other than self-satisfaction. Once he needed a big dog to prove that he was a big man, that is to say that he had been accepted as middle middle class. Now, with the price of meat what it is, one has to cut down a little. It is sad that the dog will not die of a physical broken heart when the car touches eighty. Remember he is chasing with despair what he still loves. Come to that, don't we all do this a little? I understand that the killing of unwanted dogs is sudden and humane. As Pangloss said, all is for the best, in the best of all possible worlds.

I cannot believe in Pangloss. The truth is absolutely to the contrary. This is the worst of all possible worlds. Look hard at this statement and do not commit the crime of calling it pessimistic, because in this lies our greatest hope. This is the worst of all worlds. There are weeks and months when we walk in hell and it is better to recognize it as such but to remember also its dazzling consolations. There is no fire and brimstone but sunshine slanting over my shoulder and the aspens soon will shed their golden coinage. And always there are better worlds to come. They will not be designed according to the vicarage lawn Christianity where the dead heads have been removed from the roses and the deity is not like God at all, but obviously a gentleman. In the meantime we are in hell.

We are in hell because the tragedies I saw in one day are so small compared with the total of human misery that they are hardly worth quoting. How many died in Buchenwald and Auschwitz? Can you enter the minds and relive the feelings of Jewish women who threw their babies out of cattle trucks to prevent their falling into the hands of the Gestapo? Leaving aside these delectable dramas, spiced with incident, provided for us not entirely by monsters, but by devotees of the tribal instinct and practitioners of the team spirit, is there not tragedy enough in passing from youth to the decrepitude of age when arms which once circled a lover, their joints knitted with arthritis, claw mutely at closed doors in the blank darkness of the hours after midnight? Surely the very transitory nature of things is evil? Surely it is tragic that daffodils which, in the winds of March, anticipate the stillness of the sun of summer, should end in wrinkled petals and the sprawl of desiccated down-trodden leaves? What is transitory is itself evil because it expresses imprisonment in form. In our beginnings in this world we were all returned to matter because it was only by so doing that we could achieve the refinement of a psyche, independent of matter, which is necessary for the emancipation of the individualised spirit.

This, then, is my first message, that we are in hell and that the function of the prophets is to teach us to endure its tortures with dignity and in peace. When we speak of Christ descending into hell we should mean that he came to this earth. Do not let us be misled by the false prophets who tell us otherwise. To see clearly from the beginning this message, that here and now we are in hell, is of all the most cheering we have ever heard. We have in fact reached the lowest point of our development and we endure it somehow. Let us count also the blessings with which we are surrounded in our passage through the shades. We can still in this world encounter disinterested impersonal love. We can still by passion light a candle for ourselves in what seems like night.

If this is hell it is not the contrived and punishing hell of the theologians. It is the darkest episode in the story of the Cosmos. Consider the inevitable consolations of the seasons and how, with earliest spring, the snowdrops whiten the drenched grass and how later the cherry blossom sends white, pyramidal tapers towards the pale spring sky. Consider in my garden the cascade of roses descending from the branches of the fruit trees, wracked and distorted with age; the first wave of the country breaking on the shore of the city. Remember, too, the lisp of willows lighter than ever by the stream in autumn and, in winter, the flowing curves of the woman earth, whom we have glimpsed before through a veil of leaves and now see naked before us.

What kind of God presides over this hell of suffering and this surfeit of beauty? From my youth I asked of myself, of .ny elders, of priests and their bedraggled intellectual fledglings being educated in theology, what kind of a deity, all merciful and at the same time all powerful, could preside over a planet where a boy of fourteen died in two days of a finger prick and thousands died in two hours in a flood in China? There were two main answers I received. These things, I was told, were sent to try us. It seemed that what I found horrible was, in fact, an exercise in character building. I could not but notice that the great mass horrors were reserved for the inhabitants of other countries. God seemed to have the same predeliction for Anglo-Saxons he had once had for the Jews. This appeared to me, to say the least, capricious. Throughout the last war, with all the intricate sadism men reserved for others in the concentration camps, there were still thousands of believers, with more faith than enlightenment, who believed that we were sent into this world to temper the steel of our character. This did not explain how *I* became better when a prisoner was flogged to death by the Gestapo.

It seemed to me that, in such circumstances, the non-intervention of God was not only a horror but a blasphemy. What right had man to credit God with his own worst attributes and decorate his own bestiality with a title of divinity? Voltaire said that God created man in his own image and that man immediately returned the compliment. This etched in my brain the deep-cut inscription that God is a man-made product. He, the God of our choice, does not create us. He is something fabricated to suit our convenience and drug our own perplexity.

The alternative answer to my inability to reconcile an all powerful, all merciful deity, with the horrors of this world was based on the doctrine of free will. In this I was instructed more by priests and intending priests. My college at Oxford had a strong theological basis. The less than a handful of medical students, unusually innocuous by nature, were outposts of Anti-Christ to the more eccentric dons, vague to the verge of dementia in their personal lives but rigid to the point of rigor mortis in their furtive life of fervent belief. I was touched by the mixture of fervour, pity and contempt with which the implications of free will were explained by these stars and their spluttering satellites. God had certainly given man free will to choose between good and evil. If he opted for the latter God simply could not interfere. Surely I could see that clearly. It was like a game, a kind of celestial football, which needed rules if it were to avoid chaos. If God, the supreme referee, impeded the machinations of evil it was all against the rules. God, to my friends, had to be a gentleman and *comme il faut* as well as a deity. The Second World War provided problems for my Oxford contemporaries, by this time clinging to the magic of the sacraments while civilisation disintegrated. One had vivid pictures of the Jews going of their own free will into gas chambers while, equally freely, the Germans turned on the gas. Perhaps my trouble was that I saw too many pictures and that my clerical friends did not visualise enough but mapped out, with mathematical conscientiousness, the only way to God.

What my clerical friends and those who reverenced them — I noticed that many unstable individuals worshipped the priest rather than the religion — never said and perhaps never saw, was that to say that God gave man the choice between good and evil was to assume the existence of these two powers in the universe before the creation of man. Apart from this being a howler in terms of logic, it implied the existence of a God who either connived at the creation of evil in the universe or was powerless to stop it. I say the universe rather than this world because, if man is given the choice between good and evil at his creation on this planet, the two powers concerned are more widely disseminated through the Cosmos than on this earth alone.

What is the nature of the God who presides over this world and the destiny of the people in it? What is His or our purpose? What other worlds succeed this? What are the higher zones of consciousness which we attain after our residence in hell? My book is my answer to these questions. We must first consider the nature of God.

It must be admitted that when we turn for guidance to what is called the Holy Scriptures the evidence is confused and borders on obscenity. In certain books of the Old Testament we are left in no doubt that the God of the Jews was a nationalist idol. He smote the Gods of neighbouring peoples, being particularly careful, in his more belligerent tantrums, to leave not a woman or a child alive. Perhaps he was opposed to the association of gods or goddesses with fertility. He disposed of rewards and punishments to his own people according to the degree of their belief in him. For failing to accept his suzerainty over the gods of other peoples he had nothing to offer but destruction. I was told one day that I would find information as to the true meaning of the word abomination if I searched Leviticus and Deuteronomy. My aim in so doing was to see if the word could in any way be interpreted as implying homosexuality or some of what used to be called sexual perversions. It was quite clear that the word abomination had no sexual connotation. It meant believing in any gods other than those of the divine imperialist of Judaism.

One of the assumptions of one's education was that the Jewish concept of monotheism was an enormous advantage in the spiritual and cultural development of man. In the naiveté of my early years I assumed that monotheism was the installation of a sinless, stainless and disinterested deity in place of a pantheon of all too human gods and goddesses, who sinned as we did but on a bigger scale and were no doubt maintaining the principle of quantity before quality. But the world lost heavily by the cult of monotheism as revealed in the Old Testament. Reverence for the nationalist God of Judea was extended to include dominion over all the known nations. It was spelt out in the words "Thou shalt have no other Gods but me." The warlike implication of this maxim was applied imperialistically to this world. The benefits of the world to come were stressed less than the glories of earthly imperialism imposed by God. This idea of a God with territorial ambitions and tortured always by the question of *Lebensraum*, spilt over into the New Testament. It is clear that on several occasions his disciples thought of Jesus as a Messiah come to restore the earthly fortunes of Israel and to impart to them, if they were lucky, key positions in the new administration.

All religions founded on concrete rewards and punishments are debased. They are among the harsher cries of the world's infancy. They are systems of magic generated by priesthoods with a special insight into man's infinite capacity for illusion. Either by edict or sacrament the priest indicates that by the provoked intervention of God or the gift of grace, he who offers prayers and sacrifices will be suitably rewarded. Magic has no place in religion. Even white magic designed to protect against evil is suspect. Magic is always black or grey. Its infiltration into religion is inseparable from systems of rewards and punishments. This or that ritual act is associated with this or that benefit. The God of the Old Testament was not satisfied with the ritual sacrifice of animals. He demanded also Jeptha's daughter. Other examples of ritual murder can be found by study of the sacred writings found in the world's best seller.

There is a kind of Christian who finds this variety of criticism unbelievably crude and who asks, with strenuous hope, "But who nowadays pays any attention to the Old Testament? Was not Christ come among us to interpret the spirit of the law of which the Old Testament was the letter." We may ask immediately of this God, however and in whatever form he exists, to preserve us from the application of the letter of the law as abominable as that enunciated in the Old Testament. Leaving aside such incursions into logic, the whole system of rewards and punishment is to this day so impregnated in official Christianity, which is best called Judeo-Christianity, as to be archetypal. The belief in spatial heaven and hell may be eroded. Modern man may be little impressed by deities who inflict the tortures of hell on the sinful. After all, we have caught up with this punishing deity in producing such scientifically manipulated hells as Dachau. Nevertheless, it is possible that we exaggerate the degree of contemporary man's sophistication in religious matters. To the Jehovah's Witnesses only a few can be saved, presumably from hell, and this sect is increasing rapidly. The idea of a hell of punishment, not necessarily spatial but described speciously as a state of mind, is still an article of faith among the Protestant sects founded on the teachings of Calvin. The Catholic Church, as represented by its cultivated English converts, skirts gracefully round the question of hell, but what is the absolution which follows confession if it is not a protection against punishment for misdoing?

Leaving aside these sociological observations of the Christian scene, I would say, from my personal knowledge and judgment of many practising Christians, that the element of reward, and to a less extent of punishment, still operates in the vast majority of cases. Certainly we have tended to diminish the fact of punishment. Modern man prefers to be rewarded all the time. God is, for him, the Beveridge of the supreme welfare state.

The Old Testament God of rewards and punishments was still near and dear to the heart of the well dressed, well mannered, highly articulate and seemingly sophisticated husband who interviewed me about his wife who was in hospital with a depressive attack. He was less concerned with her symptoms than with the question of why she and he should have been afflicted in this way. He himself was not depressed but utterly bewildered. "Why," he asked, "should this happen to us?" My explanation that it could happen to anybody did not recommend itself to my questioner. It appeared that he and his wife never failed to attend Church every Sunday. That she should have become ill in any way after such prophylactic measures was unthinkable. It was clear that he regarded the ritual of the Church as an insurance against disaster in this world and the next. A high-ranking professional soldier and a good and practising Catholic slightly addicted to proselytisation told me with utter sincerity that he was a Catholic because he feared hell. A more picturesque punishment, designed to operate on this earth, was planned for a Catholic girl by her devoted mother. The latter induced truthfulness in her offspring by indicating that if, after her own demise, the girl told a lie, the mother's hand would rise accusingly and break the surface of the earth where she was buried.

The God of the Old Testament, who is far from dead and

lives on in the unconscious of the majority in the West was, in his slaughter of his enemies and the punishments he inflicted on the unfaithful, frankly diabolical. It is more logical to regard him as the devil than God. Yet he is credited with the creation of this earth. Could such a being be entrusted with the creation of anything? All he could possibly create was hell.

But before we confuse God too much with the devil let us see first how much the Old Testament version of God has been amended by the sacrifice Christ made for us and through the doctrine of grace and redemption. My thesis is that little of what he taught, which was singularly sparse — it was what he was that mattered — has infiltrated the barnacle-encrusted rigid structure of official Christianity. Nietzsche was largely right in saying that every Christian is a kind of Protestant Jew. The ban on cards and piano playing, which was the rule two or three decades ago in the Free Church of Scotland and other extreme Protestant cults, stems directly from the hawk-eyed inquisitorial God of the Old Testament and owes nothing to Christ's dictum that the Sabbath was made for man and not man for the Sabbath.

The New Testament God with whom we are presented in these days is an infinitely more gentlemanly fellow. Here again he shows signs that we have created him rather than he us. If we are to go by the propaganda of the theologians he resembles the God of the Old Testament in being all powerful. We have been told too often of his strength by too many weak men that we can be forgiven if we believe it. Unlike the angry Jehovah of the Old Testament he is fashionably part-time. He differs also from the totally dedicated early God of the Jews who required for his enemies full scale massacres or nothing. He has preferred to leave us to our own devices. He has a distressing habit of being elsewhere when he is most wanted. Where was he when the Nazis were administering Dachau and Auschwitz or the Russians Katyn and the massacre of the Kulaks? It is perhaps significant that the Pope, God's most influential earthly emmisary, did little and failed to offer any adequate protest when the Nazis invaded Catholic Poland. We can endeavour to explain these horrors by calling in the flabbily illogical doctrine of free will because those I have mentioned are vile actions perpetrated by man on man. But how does one account for the earthquakes, typhoons and tidal waves which engulf a diversity of people who cannot all be accused of making their own hells? Is it perhaps significant that the insurance companies refer to such disasters as 'acts of God'? In using such a phrase are we still accepting that God is all powerful but have we, with unusual logic, given up hope that He is also all merciful?

The advent of Christ and the teaching of the New Testament do not invalidate in any way our previous contention that the world was created by a lower and demonic entity. The same logical arguments apply to the world before and after the Crucifixion. If God is all powerful and at the same time all merciful, why did He permit His only begotten son to be crucified? This was, on God's part, neither an exhibition of power or mercy. To use such arguments as these is to place ourselves voluntarily in the outer darkness as far as Christian theologians are concerned. That this is where one would be happy to be is perhaps irrelevant. The defence of the Church is that, in raising such questions, one is a lost soul who fails altogether to understand that this was the very purpose of the incarnation of Christ, that the son of God should die for us to show how power could manifest itself in the form of love and redeem our sins. But the Christian doctrine of Christ's incarnation, of our redemption by grace, is a continuation of paganism in its worst aspects. We are not here using the word paganism in the sense in which it is implied by the orthodox to include, among other things, the great philosophers who preceded Christ. This doctrine of the incarnation and our redemption through grace is paganism at its most debased, a pretentious refinement of the ancient idea that the king or his son should die to redeem his people. The Eucharist is the frail, faintly conscious reverberation of the barbaric idea that we gain strength if we eat of the flesh of the royal sacrifice and drink his blood.

Certainly different practising Anglicans interpret the Eucharist in many different ways, following the tradition of the Anglican Church that it has room for everybody, that we can hold divergent views provided we do not express them with clarity in public or, worst of all, commit them to paper. Nevertheless, however one interprets it, the Eucharist remains a magical rite, its magic diluted in the Protestant sects but, to my knowledge, never purely commemorative.

Though for two centuries after Christ primitive Christianity retained much of its earlier truth and simplicity because the emanation of Christ's psyche still persisted among those who

had known and loved him, in actual fact the devil entered
Christianity very soon after the Crucifixion. The message of
Christ was polluted with magic. He never intended an organized
Church because such was incompatible with his teaching. That
he should be credited with the doctrine of grace by redemption
is nauseating. This terrible creed, which insists that a man's
private virtues and efforts count for less than a prophet's death
on the cross two thousand years ago, horrifies any ethical sense
we may possess. Its fundamental immorality is hidden from us
by the pollution of magic prescribed by the priesthood and kept
reverberating in us at the celebration of the Eucharist, in virtue
of which, after two thousand years, many are still, at different
levels of consciousness, eating and drinking the martyr's blood
and making this the heart of their religious life.

Have we, then, made a case for a lower entity being
responsible for the creation of the world and, if we look fairly at
the horrors which have happened in this century, as responsible
at all times for active dominion over it? It is dangerous to quote
from the New Testament, not only because protagonists of this
and that theory quote out of context but because errors of
scholarship have obliterated the true meanings of words attributable to Christ and others. If one takes the view that the Bible is
divinely inspired one ends in an ethical morass. But surely the
Gospels contain the most positive allusion to the dominion of
the devil on this earth. What could be more unequivocal than
the description of how Christ went into the desert to pray and
how the devil tempted him with power over all the kingdoms of
the world? Does not this clearly imply that such power was in the
devil's gift?

Are we asked, then, to face the fact that we are in a world ruled
over by the devil and that, the world being what it is at the
moment, the cards are stacked in his favour? Certainly we have
to reject on this earth God as all powerful and all merciful. Must
we therefore turn against God and regard Him, if not as the
Jehovah of the Old Testament and synonymous with the devil, as
a heartless experimenter in human emotions, seemingly merciful
among a plethora of roses in the high-noon of summer, but
seemingly indifferent to children dying of leukaemia? "As flies
to wanton boys are we to the gods, they kill us for their sport".
Must we opt for some fatalistic doctrine as this, which has all the
vices of a bad narcotic in that it acts partially for a time and fails
us in the end? Must we rage against this man-made God, whether

he appears wholly committed in the Old Testament or a little off-hand in the New? Must we, turning on his emissaries on this earth, indulge in anticlerical resentments or hatreds? Emphatically not, because by so doing, by accepting naively that religion is an opium of the people, we blind ourselves to the truth as much as the theologians have done in the past.

The fanatical theologian and the ferocious anticlerical are both of similar psychological make-up. Both are exclusively devoted to intellectual systems and are fanatical opponents of those who deviate from them. What we must recognize from the beginning is our own culpability in misconceiving God as a power. For God to be all powerful on this earth would be to deny His nature. A God who subjugated the devil by power would be utilising the devil's weapons. So far as most of us here on this earth are concerned God is love or nothing. This does not mean that He is a helpless, personalised being gently deploring the sins of man and inviting the victims of the barbarisms of this world to rest, temporarily or permanently, on his bosom. Such a God is a kind of pensive negative of a positive devil.

When one speaks of God, seen from this earth, as love or nothing, one is not speaking of love as a sentiment but as a living energy like evil. It is a vibrating energy which is inexhaustible because it is manifested from the beginning which never was to the end that will never be. Beginnings and endings, as we shall see later, are artificial terms we use in a time-ridden world. Love is merely the ultimate engulfing energy of goodness. It triumphs wholly in the end, but not in this world. The word love is preferable to goodness because it conveys more the communication between psyche and psyche, and ultimately between spirit and spirit, which marks the ultimate Oneness we lost at the Fall and to which we inevitably return. Love acts as a solvent of evil. Love, like water, is the gentlest thing in the world and can wash away mountains. At the present time its capacity is limited, because we are living a veritable Armageddon of evil, on which the fate of man ultimately depends.

It is our primary error that we think too positively of God and too negatively of the devil. This is one of the terrible weaknesses of European thought, allied to and inevitably connected with, the untenable idea that evil is merely the negative aspect of good. We have created, in our minds, throughout the aeons, the concept of a personalised God endowed with power. In so doing we have projected from our mass unconscious a great and fabricated evil which it is justifiable to call the devil. We can do this for the very reason that what we have created is personalised. What we fabricate from our worst attributes is necessarily diabolic. It is a sound instinct of some semitic creeds, other than the Judeo-Christianity we still practice, that pictorial representations of God should be avoided. This is because what is given form reflects both the Fall, which involves the assumption of matter, and therefore form, by what was originally a spirit, and because to depict God by the same lines and contours as humanity is to suggest a transitory being. As we shall see later truth is what is changeless in the midst of constant change.

Seen with the limited vision of this world one can make out a better case for the existence of the devil than for that of God. Belief in a devil, reflecting our own shape but with transcendental powers is, if we have the wisdom of the heart which is all that matters, more infinitely reasonable than belief in a personalised God. Certainly God exists but to claim that we know His nature and can communicate directly with Him from this time-dominated world is an absurdity. The Buddhists are wiser than the Christians in saying little or nothing of the nature of God and eternity. They recognize that we do not possess the instrumentation for so doing. There is a complex hierarchy between ourselves and God. From its members, from those who have died and acquired wisdom in so doing, we learn not only of the nature of God but of the supreme creative force behind him. In the meantime we see the beliefs of the theologians as efforts to jump the gun, and the different Christian creeds with which the world is beset as ideational systems, originally devised by dominating intellectuals without insight into their own motives but determined to appoint themselves as the representatives of God on earth. This is not to say that the different Churches have not contributed their quota of saintly and good men. In every community there are sheep as well as goats. How would the goats endure without a supply of sheep to corrupt?

It may seem that the force on the side of light is of small weight compared to the power of darkness, and that the half-committed so-called God of our own fabrication is having little effect in a world where, apart from the international tensions which could lead to an atomic war, each separate community in Western civilisation appears to be disintegrating from the rise of violence and vandalism within its frontiers. One can only respond, but surely adequately, by Christ's words that his kingdom is not of this world. In all he said on this subject he utterly rejected any idea of achieving earthly dominion over the principalities and powers of evil. Even those nearest to him, his disciples, except perhaps John, were too crude to perceive his abnegation of all power, of all Messiahdom, even of all hope of success in this world. After all, one has to remember that Christ was crucified. Was not Christ describable, in a term beloved of the insightless professional optimists as an apostle of doom? Did he not foretell the destruction of Capernaum, of Jerusalem itself and of the whole Judaic community? Did any other prophet of world stature ever utter such a catalogue of doom? His God was emphatically not a certain winner on this earth. It was left to the priests to bribe us by erasing the unpleasant fact that all of us are born to suffer and that the good God himself is powerless to deflect the impact of our suffering, though he may send us comforters of different descriptions.

Our idea of a personalised God is tied up with our concept of a kingdom of heaven. No such spatial or time-bound dominion exists. We have rejected it in favour of what desperately intellectual Christians call a 'state of mind', and which can better be described as a higher zone of consciousness. As for God, no truly supreme being can be thought of as a transcendental version of the form of man. One discovers, in the pantheon of classical antiquity, a multiplicity of gods and goddesses representing human qualities and often human errors on a bigger scale. In monotheistic Judeo-Christianity we are limited to one God whose qualities we have discussed already and who is as riddled with human failings as the gods and goddesses of antiquity with, perhaps, an added coldness. But essentially the supreme creative principle is not personalised. Anything we see from this earth, and conceive of as God, is bound to be fallacious. We have not the requisite instrumentation to perceive to the full his or her substance. In Europe men of genius have seen beyond what we personalise and visualise as God to a more ultimate creative principle. Goethe's eternal feminine outlined in Faust is an example of such a conception. One stresses the attitudes of Western man simply because Hinduism and Buddhism, however much the former is cluttered up with gods and goddesses, prefer not to define the ultimate creative principle but to establish as close as possible contact with it through the world of feeling rather than a course of theology.

The idea that God is not omnipotent on this earth destroys for many the basis of religious experience. They cannot endure the thought of a God incapable of defeating his enemies. If he is powerless on earth what is his power in the universe? Surely his relative impotence here implies that his role in the Cosmos has been exaggerated. Are we, then, on this earth and beyond it, playthings in the war between the forces of good and evil and left to our own devices by God? We are not playthings but targets both of the energies of good and evil in this world and those nearest to it. What matters is that in the end good should triumph and consciousness, including that of the individual, should be preserved. In this world we are, over the aeons, as much exposed to the forces of good as those of evil. It is our misfortune that in the age in which we live the power of evil is at its height. Nevertheless we are still bathed in the emanations of good from places and people. The natural healer, whose numbers are increasing in our day, is able to do so because he acts as an instrument for the ultimate vibrationless harmony which existed before the great chasm between good and evil which accompanied the Fall. We have to count also the blessings we take for granted, the glitter of starlight over snow, the piercing chastity of mountain streams in winter, the first uncertain indrawn breath of spring, the opulence of summer and the lingering lament of autumn. Where nature lays her finger gently on our arms she is telling us that the things we call beautiful are outposts of God in a bitter world, and that the lower entity who created it is still part angel and that the light shone within him as he descended to the darkness of matter. Beauty is a harmony between good and evil. Its influence is immense because it is more primordial, and its origins nearer to the unflawed Oneness from which all things came. Beauty *on this earth* is the projected image of a reality which existed before the Creation and which will always exist. Beauty is the permeating translucence of what is good. Ugliness is the expression of evil. This is why in these days we see so much that is ugly in architecture, poetry and painting as well as in common deportment.

2.

Hell and Happiness

The obvious contemporary and popular response to the suggestion that this world is hell is the idea that we make our own hells. This is the kind of statement which in these days will always be received with an approving nod. To say we make our own hells implies that we are not doomed to make them and that, with a little care and consultation of the right authorities, all will be well. If we cannot obtain a heaven on earth we can at least live luxuriously in the cocoon of our own non-hell.

Did the open-natured, generous, radiant girl who died of a malignant tumour which consumed her in a few weeks in her twenties initiate this hell for herself? Did the eight thousand Polish officers murdered at Katyn because they were Poles and officers bring on themselves this degrading end? Was it due to flaws in her own character that this woman, married to a sadistic husband, endured the tortures and obscenities he inflicted on her? Many have suffered the worst hells because they have been engulfed by the cloud of circumstance. There are individuals and families prone to disaster in the form of death, disease or tragedy of some kind. It is significant that, in particular, persons prone to disaster are often exceptionally good people who least of all merit the tortures they endure. Does a person contrive his own hell because his capacity to emanate goodness attracts towards him the forces and agents of darkness as a magnet attracts iron filings? Or one's hell may originate in past incarnations. If you are aware of several you can remember and relive so many tortures and tragedies that for months the year is darkened and a cloud obliterates the summer and the weather of your heart is always winter. Fortunately such intense recall does not endure more than two or three years. Is it being responsible for your own hell that you remember what you suffered at the hands of your persecutors sixteen centuries ago? Are we to be held responsible for what was done to us not in this life but centuries and millennia ago? In one of the darkest hells, that of possession, of the benign individual by the dark entity, how can the victim be said to initiate or facilitate his own hell? How can this be if he is taken over by another entity which dictates his actions and feelings, plunges him into the dark night of the soul and encourages him to destroy himself? It so happens that among those I have known who have suffered from possession, were some of the most tender, gentle and best intentioned people I have ever encountered. In what way did those who suffered because they were good crave for admission to hell?

We can make a superficial case for the hating and envious creating their own hells. If they hated and envied less they would suffer less from the desolate sense of separation which marks them off from their fellows. But how many, thus demarcated from their kind, feel no desolation and are compensated by the exhilaration of the power they achieve over others? What has to be remembered about those who *do*, by hate and envy, create their own hells is that so many are born with the potentiality for so doing. How many are genetically doomed, by inherited and inerasable flaws of character, to create hell for themselves and disseminate misery to others? It is important to recognize how they affect the innocent who surround them. One may argue that one is preaching a kind of beneficent nihilism in which nobody is responsible for anything. That this is not so will be obvious later. Even among those whose intolerance and wish to dominate create hells for themselves as well as others, no man consciously wills his own inferno. If the latter is determined for him by conflicts in his unconscious or by errors in his upbringing or genetic equipment, here again he is not asking for hell.

Going beyond the naturally vicious to the minority of living individuals capable of possessing others to their detriment, here again these psychic transmitters of evil are, for the most part, not asking of God or the devil to create the hell they bestow on others. They are born and shaped to be the natural agents of evil. True, there are those who definitely will evil to others and have the emanatory capacity to achieve it, but such people are found only in significant concentration in dark ages such as our own. The evil discarnate entities who, after death, possess others to their detriment or destruction are common enough, but here again the hell inflicted on the innocent victim or on the helpless tool of the evil entity is not something of his own choosing.

The idea that we bring on ourselves our own hells is an undesirable western adaptation of oriental philosophy. Life is suffering; suffering stems from attachment, and the latter from desire. We therefore eliminate the latter and, whatever the circumstances with which we are surrounded, we diminish and finally obliterate an inferno which was of our own making. In the concentration camp we do not distinguish between ourselves and our captors .One is not criticising Buddhism or Hinduism which are, in many ways, more reasonable and soundly based than the religions of Middle Eastern origin and have, over the centuries, a better record of tolerance and non-violence. But, dealing as they do with states of feeling and attitudes to life rather than to precise beliefs and dogmas, they are ill-adapted to the needs of the obsessional West. When a civilisation dies, and that in the West is almost extinct, it reaches desperately in all directions for consolation and salvation. It endeavours to satisfy its own needs by attitudes and projects to which it is ill adapted. A proportion of those attracted by oriental philosophies are seeking to escape from their immediate occidental predicament. The huge majority of mankind, certainly those of European derivation, are incapable of what, at its worst or best, is a withdrawal from the world's agonies.

When the Westerner believes in the doctrine that we create our own hells he is seeking for detachment. He finds not only his own egoism but his own sufferings a burden and seeks to escape from them. It becomes convenient, even though it does not accord with the facts, for us to believe that we make our own hells if acceptance of the latter concept enables us to be rid at one go of all our troubles. But European man is, by his psychic tradition and inheritance, wholly ill-suited to such an attitude. For better or worse we are involved in mankind and cannot detach ourselves from the agonies of the world. Our attempts to do so involve us in a considerable casualty rate. For several decades there have been groups in Britain and elsewhere who have sought to achieve detachment. These included those directed by Gurdjieff, Ouspensky, Nichol and their derivatives. It was expected of their adherents that they worked on themselves to perfect the instrumentation with which they were endowed, that, in contemporary language, they raised their level of awareness. Certainly some results were achieved. A number so sterilised their thinking and feeling life that they lost all spontanuity. They were literally dead to the world. Others conducted on themselves self-analysis so disintegrating that they were incapable of boiling an egg without looking for the moral. Others became spiritual athletes who checked their own evolution, as a runner studies his times for the mile, and were totally unaware that they were sinking beyond redemption into the most dangerous form of self-consciousness.

The doctrine that the avoidance of self-created hells necessitates the cultivation of detachment is in some cases dedicated to the achievement of absolute invulnerability in this life. This, for me, reached its peak in my encounter with a self-appointed guru, educated at an exclusive public school, who had acquired, after considerable absence of thought, the fascinating belief that truly to achieve awareness and detachment had a prophylactic effect against all the ills that flesh is heir to. This applied not only to individuals but groups. The prophet quoted the case of a heretical sect, not named, which, in the seventeenth century, managed to escape persecution from both Catholics and Protestants. My informant regarded this as redounding enormously to their credit and developed the interesting theme that Cathars, Huguenots and other ill-instructed non-members of the British intelligentsia, were gravely at fault in having attracted persecution towards themselves. The martyr, it seemed, was inevitably at fault. The idea that those who were bundled into gas chambers were as much to blame as the persecutors is nauseating as well as ridiculous. The thought that inoffensive and often humble victims of religious persecution who have died for the truth are as indictable as their own murderers, that human suffering, even in great causes, is a sign of spiritual immaturity, is an extreme example of what absence from clear thinking can do to someone incapable of suffering anything. That the individual concerned was regarded as making a significant contribution to modern enlightenment is interesting. His views are an extreme example of the apotheosis of fatuousness which can be achieved by those who believe that we create our own hells. Surely to believe that in this world we can override all pain suffered by ourselves and others, is an insidious and more dangerous assertion of man's right to dominate nature. It also reveals clearly that so many aspects of the new thought are as much based, as the old religions, on the desire for protection and rewards.

These respectable, if turgid, forms of escaping from the so-called hell of one's own making have now deteriorated into short cuts which includes six week courses of transcendental meditation three times a week at ten guineas a time, with the distinct promise of eternal bliss in lieu of a diploma. They involve being 'opened up' by holy men, often lodged in conditions of considerable luxury, so that, with love in our hearts, we can transcend our own pains and push back in a fortnight the threat of atomic warfare by the force of goodness released by ourselves and people like us. Others use psychedelic drugs like LSD to atone for creating their own hells by taking a tablet to make them unaware of the hells which happen to others.

The idea of a self-fabricated hell is a potentially ethical but evil catchword. It was foisted on us first by a priesthood seeking to wield power over us by dogma of their own construction. The sinner made his hell on earth and the presiding deity prepared for him a more centralised and presumably more efficient hell. To the ecclesiastic we make our own infernos by our sins. In actual fact it is often only through love that we undergo the tortures of hell. It is only those who love us who can hurt us deeply. Our anguish for them when they are ill or in danger is inescapable. Nor is this seemingly intensely personal agony of our own making. Were we responsible for falling in love? Is the latter process a willed operation?

The contemporary version of the idea that we create our own hells is little conditioned by priestly domination. It is an expression of a peculiarly facile and superficial optimism which chooses ironically to express itself at one of the darkest phases in the world's history. It is based on the idea that if we know, or effect to know a cause, we can do something about it. The whole idea that we create our own purgatories is a vast lie. Hell was created for us by our birth on this planet. Our private hells are a reflection in miniature of the evil intentions in the world about us and in the nearest zones of consciousness subjected to its influence. No human being is of himself a generator of evil. He is always merely a transmitter even though there are those so evil that we may use the word generator in a relative sense. It is insanity to believe that the power of evil can originate in a single individual of its own volition and by the co-operation of his will. Evil is a universal power. Even those who seem most destined to create a hell for themselves and others are not persisting entities in themselves but passing instruments of a power of evil abroad in the universe. In their next incarnation they may equally be transmitters of the force of goodness.

Man is a part of nature and not its lord. In a discussion like this, to consider only the species to which we belong is vain and savage. We must think, too, of the animal kingdom. Can it be said that animals create their own hells? Is it due to some psychological or moral flaw in the make-up of the deer that it becomes a target of the stag hunt? Is it a consequence of their sins that calves are tortured to produce veal, that lambs and pigs are dragged protesting to the slaughterhouse? Is it an adequate defence to say that the animal due to be butchered has no knowledge of where it is being taken? These seemingly humane but sickeningly egotistical arguments are a rationalisation of man's sense of guilt. If a dog, taken across Paris for the first time and boarded at a vet's for observation for sickness, is able to escape and finds its way back to its mistress's flat on the other side of the city, who are we, with our god-like assurance, to say that an old horse does not know when it is being led to the slaughterhouse?

All life is indivisible. The same impulse which leads men to resist death in the intricate mechanised hell of the concentration camp governs the unfolding of the chestnut buds in April and the wakening from the earth's sleep visible in the first snowdrop. All that feels has a psyche. It is ridiculous to assume that the flowers trodden down by careless feet, that animals hunted by men for meat, for game, for delight in killing, implore to fates to confer on them the distinction of hell. The personality of even the domestic dog and cat is not sufficiently developed to create its own purgatory. The latter idea is an intellectual's concept. Intellectualism at its most intense is halfway to diabolism because, to explain the universe in terms of human reasoning, is a vicious form of blindness, the cold, uncholeric resentment of man because of his own incapacity to see. Those who say we create our own hells have never seen into hell or felt in any depth the agonies of others. They are cold-blooded animals who take their spiritual temperature from the environment and only happen to be classified as human beings. The priest dying of Hodgkin's disease and frantic with thirst, who sucked a sponge by his bed because there was no water on his table, did not summon up, of his own volition, this brief reality of hell. Hell was about him, external to him, imposed on him by the granite-faced sister who raged at the medical student who gave him water because he was interfering with the nurses' duties.

Have we, then, to think of man as helplessly manipulated in the hell of this world? If the vast majority of the sorrows he endures and the evils which befall him are not of his own choosing but are reflected shadows from the darkest corners of the Cosmos, is he not utterly helpless and are not all attempts, on his own part or that of others, to extricate him from his predicament, vain and pathetic? The answer is emphatically no. It depends to a large extent what we mean when we say, what can he do? There is a great deal he can do. He can above all see life as it is. It is only by so doing, by looking directly into the very craters of hell, that we can achieve any peace and happiness on this earth. This is not to court suffering but to see life as it is. The aim of life is not to transcend it but to see through it.

One of the infallible truths of psychiatry is that our most insidious and obstinate pains arise from our evasion of reality. My method with those in the horrors of agitated depression or who have suffered some grievous loss is to say, "You know yourself you are going through hell. You know that those who offer you specious comfort at these moments — in a month you will feel better — are human featherbeds who never really permit you to rest on them. There is nothing to be gained by not realising that you are in hell. I, sitting with you, know it. You know that, as far as I can, I am together with you in hell. These states of hell are to be regarded as seasons. They are, in the climate of the heart, either the torment of autumn with its wind-tossed leaves or the ironbound earth of winter. Like the seasons they pass but I do not expect you to believe it at the moment." The degree to which words such as these lighten the burden of the victim varies with the latter's nature. I notice that the psychic who, for me, mean those more directed by the psyche than the personality, are more responsive than others. This is because they are more accessible to the truth. This is inevitable because their capacity to disperse themselves through time and space enables them, in the higher zones of consciousness, to tap the sources of truth close to us because most of us are looking at a landscape from a dugout rather than a star.

The more we blind ourselves to the realities of pain for which we are not responsible, the more our eyes are blurred to the compensating beauties which nature lavishes upon us. It is those who endure the greatest agonies who appreciate most the subtler beauties, provided one does not practice the mechanised imbecility which expects beauty to work like a mood-elevating drug at the apotheosis of human suffering. We have to wait for the agony to pass in order to appreciate the beauty.

It is a toxic lie in the soul, poisoning our deepest tissues, to believe we make our own hells. This is a lie engendered by priestly and secular pundits to hide the fact that, through no fault of our own, we are involved in a pattern we cannot alter; that in our darkest moments this pattern appears to us a trap and a predicament, but that nevertheless it is the destiny of each one of us to make our way through it. We are fated to do so because this is the whole point of reincarnation, the reality of which cannot be doubted and the evidence for which I have more than adequately provided elsewhere. In the process of reincarnation we learn, not by sin and atonement, by systems of concentration and awareness, but by sheer experience. What we learn is that we can only know the refinements of truth by being emancipated from matter. Whatever our aptitudes we go on reincarnating until we have learnt finally, by the multiplicity of our pains and the subtlety of our joys, that we would be better off elsewhere.

While the majority of psychiatrists are materialistic and deny the existence of a psyche, there are some that admit that man has a soul which the therapist too often finds impossible to incorporate in his psychiatric system. Some of these croyant psychiatrists are prepared and even happy to co-operate with the priesthood. When psychoanalysis first penetrated deeply the foundations of European civilisation, it was anathematised by the Pope as anti-religious. Now both priests and religiously inclined psychiatrists with the tendency to pontificate see that power can be gained and retained by a self-appointed elite by preaching that man creates his own hell, not by the flaws in his psychiatric make-up but by his response to what are usually regarded as adverse circumstances. This is one of the reasons why it is regarded as cosy, and above all, progressive, that priests and psychiatrists should co-operate. The reasons given for so doing are crudely expressed and do not approximate to practical truth. The psychiatrist is the last person to stand in the way of his patient receiving the comforts of religion. The priest ripostes gracefully by saying how ardently he wishes for the patient to receive the benefit of what he mistakenly calls science. The human personality and the psyche are apportioned to the psychiatrist and the priest respectively. Both tend to get lost in the process.

This matter of self-created hells is determined by the fact that in terms of religion man, earlier in history, was judged by what he did rather than what he was. The salvation of his soul depended on his subservience to Church dogma and ritual. Then, with greater sophistication, or growing ecclesiastical subtlety, being rather than doing became the vogue. Mary replaced Martha to such a degree that nowadays to be a do-gooder is an opprobrious epithet. The idea that we make our own purgatory sounds more reasonable and sophisticated than that we are saved by religious observance and ritual. This approach reveals the influence of psychiatry. We quieten the heart by resolving the conflicts and in the ensuing silence we may hear God. It sounds well enough but in actual practice it is one more expression of the insurance policy to religion. The evil we do to ourselves we can undo by going to the right priest, psychiatrist or guru. We automatically put ourselves in the power of others when we say we create our own hells. They, in utilising this power, engage themselves in the practice of evil because religious experience is indefineable and anonymous, and cannot be perverted by conversion into dogma.

We attain truth and with it peace by neither doing nor being. Both these factors are important, but a third is necessary. What we need is to *know* in such a way as endows us with a perceptive attitude to life and the verities. This may seem insanely dogmatic, but when I speak of knowledge I am not doing so in the theological or pedagogic sense of the word. I am referring to the unaggressive, built-in knowing which comes from a profound and deeper experience of this and anterior lives, and which enables us to see that, far from creating our own hells, we are the result of our destiny to date and that what we have acquired of truth or wisdom is the result not of thinking, or self-analysis, of raising levels of consciousness, but of sheer experience. We acquire wisdom by the same process as, in this life, a child learns to avoid a hot bar on which it has burnt itself previously.

We can never attain perfect peace and continuing serenity in this world. To expect to do so is ludicrous. Before we became terrified because the psychiatrist said that protection was domination, we preserved our children as long as we could from the injustices of the world. The sooner the child realises that there is no justice on this planet the better. The sun shines alike on the just and the unjust. The attitude that we are in hell, that perfection in ourselves or others is unattainable, is more likely to reduce tension and even induce peace that the strenuous disability of too much hope. The idea that by our efforts we can create heaven on earth is imbecile, though those who hold it cannot be described as such because their seeming amentia is induced by the process of mass illusion. This frenzy of optimism, still indulged in by earnest but insightless Christians, necessitates the belief that it is possible that every being on this earth can achieve the same degree of civilisation at the identical moment. This is so fatuous that it is a waste of time to refute it. It is one's plain duty to one's fellows, above all to the weaker and more flatulently optimistic bretheren, to emphasize that the barbarian is always at the gate, and now, as never before, and that the margin between civilisation and barbarism is minute.

We must see things as no better and no worse than they are. This woman, of whom we hoped so much has proved herself a shallow egoist floating gracefully on the tideless waters of near schizophrenia. Contrarywise, the first leaf buds opening as the traffic storms the boulevards of Paris are far more lovely than we deserve. One needs also to take a seasonal view of the hell we live in. It has, when we fall in love, what resembles the delirium of blossom in April. When we are in pain it is the night of winter. This seasonal approach to the world, this metereological assessment of the hell around us, can occur at several levels. It is least efficacious when it is determined solely by intellect and reason. It is more effective when it is conducted by the psyche. It is most effective of all when the psyche is wakened to the degree that it recognizes that our black depressions derive from tragedies in past lives, that our apprehension of impending horror, called acute anxiety states by the psychiatrists, recall often our subjugation, centuries ago, to intolerable tortures, and that our illnesses themselves are repeated in this life at the season in which we suffered from them or their like in past incarnations.

It is this attitude of knowing the nature of ourselves, of the world we live in, of the being who created it, which will help us more than any religious or ethical system derived from being or doing. On the face of it, this would seem to be an unnaturally passive attitude but to take this view is to misunderstand altogether the nature of the psychic process involved. In psychiatry, where psychic contact is truly established with the patient, when we are not standing aloof from him and assessing his symptoms with our personalities but fusing our psyche with his in those instants when cure is taking place, diagnosis and treatment are inseparable from each other. We cure the patient by recognizing him and ourselves for what we are at our deepest levels. We form with him a continuum of awareness in which we are no longer separate beings. We are the beginnings of the endless chain of indivisible consciousness. In the same way, in looking at the world passively but from the psychic level, in ceasing altogether to try to remake it according to the heart's desire, our passage through hell is achieved with less pain.

What it boils down to is this. We cannot expect to be continuously happy in hell. We have our compensations in the form of beautiful things and above all, beautiful moments. To expect continuous serenity in this world is the supreme egoism. Those who achieve it are either hebephrenic or monsters. True serenity consists not in excluding the pains of the world but in sharing that of others without protest. We are not here to transcend life. To aim at so doing is all too pretentious. Flaubert offered a prescription for happiness in this world. One needed, he said, to be healthy, stupid and selfish. He added that the first two qualities were immense but that even they could not succeed without selfishness. It requires supreme selfishness to be happy in a world created by a lower entity, where the undeserving suffer the afflictions of Job and the young and beautiful are mutilated and destroyed by war and pestilence. The saints transcend life. The more humble would be happy to see through it. So many of the saints are so insupportable that it is best to be content with being a sage.

I have known a number of people who, to outward appearances, seem to have exuberantly happy natures. They had one thing in common; all had learnt early the tragedy of life. There was the girl engulfed but untainted by an alcoholic heredity and otherwise alone in this world except for her brother. In her late teens she was diagnosed, not by myself only but by the best neurologist in Europe, as suffering from a cerebral tumour for which the consequences were blindness, death or both. After admission to hospital I was informed that her brother had been killed in the Fleet Air Arm. I rang the hospital and insisted that she should not be told the news until the investigations necessary to confirm the diagnosis and determine the treatment. the investigations were themselves in part surgical. As she was wheeled into the operating theatre her temperature chart was propped up against her feet enabling her to read, written in red ink and heavily underlined, "This girl must not be told that her brother has been killed in action". This was the last thing she perceived before going under the anaesthetic.

That she recovered by psychic intervention without major surgery from an undoubted cerebellar tumour is another story. Thirty years later, fascinated by the constant cheerfulness she showed to the world under all conditions, recalling the horrors she had endured as a girl, I touched for the first time, almost accidentally and not at her or my instigation, on the meaning and purpose of life. This happened because she wished to know something about the Cathars of whom she knew I was writing. Because she had neither the wish nor the capacity for philo-sophical discussion I hastily implied that Catharism would be of little interest to her because it stressed the power of evil and the sadness inevitable in this world. She replied by speaking with fervour and conviction, for the first time and only time in her life, of what she believed. With her eyes aflame with sincerity she said, "Of course life is a tragedy" and returned immediately to her unbroken and cheerful assessment of things as they are. Of course this woman had her worries like the rest of us, but she confronted the world always cheerfully and without a shadow of psychiatric depression. I found constantly that the unselfish, unsensual minority who maintain an effervescent cheerfulness have always accepted early the limitations and horrors of the world we live in.

3.

The Pursuit of Truth

This book, expressing my philosophy of life, is based exclusively on personal experience. I have been inordinately busy all my life and have never had time for the laborious and antlike construction of truth by ratiocination. Of course the truth as I see it is to some extent determined by inborn temperament because the latter moulds for each of us the nature of his experience. One may find comfort and even reality in painting, another in perambulating the slums and insisting that good works are the sole form of evolution. These inborn tendencies determine our basic attitudes and therefore our particular contact with circumstances. As a doctor I have learnt from the suffering of others. In no sense am I expressing what I have thought, or needed to have thought, to explain the agonies I have seen and felt in the course of my life.

I reject altogether any philosophy, religion or so-called truth founded on what is called reasoning. The latter is a useful equipment for the office or the committee room. It unfits one for life. Yet it has been argued by Aristotle for the laity and Thomas Aquinas for the Church that secular and religious truths are founded on reason. That there should be two truths is a contradiction in terms. Truth, like God, like the supreme creation behind any god we can know on this earth, is an absolute. The idea that the truths of eternity can be split into clerical and lay fragments is puerile, sickening and an echo of the Fall. Plato himself smacks of the Oxford senior common room. There is too much point scoring, too much intellectual cornering of the opposition, too much metaphysical infighting. Whatever is true in Plato was what he remembered of the ancient mysteries. We are safer with Luther who said that reason was the devil's whore.

In this book I reject everything which I have not felt with my hands, my heart and above all with the psychic antennae whose touch is more subtle than the highest refinements of palpation and vision. I refuse to wander in the no-man's land of other mens' ideas. I deal only with what I not only feel myself but which was directed towards me from other worlds.

I am entitled to say what I know rather than what I think or feel because, God knows, I have thought, reasoned and verified enough in my life. This will be clear to anybody who has read my books *The Cathars and Reincarnation* and *We Are One Another*. My B.Sc thesis at Oxford was so mathematical that William Browne, the Reader in Psychology — Oxford was justifiably terrified to erect a fellowship on the subject — advised me to study differential calculus. I have learnt that not peace only but truth ensues from the abandonment of reasoning and verification. Yet the two latter are necessary because those who have never lived the life of reason and proof, intellectualism and verification will never know its limitations and their ignorance of these is a form of immaturity.

I have said that I am perhaps less interested than I should be in other men's ideas, but an obsession with ideas is not the truth. An idea is not an absolute. It is not life but an interpretation of it and is always wrong. The saints and sages of the Church who interpreted the Bible are neither saints nor sages and the value of what they produced has been over estimated. Call them Catholic or Protestant, the results are the same. They in their works are so toxic with ideas that they have induced in men the supreme illusion that belief is important and an inevitable step to salvation. From the third century A.D. official Christianity first poisoned the world with intricate systems of ideas revealing its reverence for the act of belief. It seems that without belief, which is an intellectual act of homage for something itself produced by the intellect, man cannot be saved. This means that our intellects are the weapons of our human personalities, separating us from each other, but also the means by which we establish contact with God through theoretical systems produced by these same intellects. The very belief in belief is a gross philosophical error. We learn through our psyche and our individualised spirit. Beliefs are the pins with which we seek to transfix the wings of our souls and spirits. We establish contact with truth, reality, God and what is beyond him, through those parts of our nature, the psyche and spirit, which are beyond the time-bound limitations of the personality. Intellectual systems are the effervescent protest of a human personality which knows its own transitory nature.

What does the soul or spirit of man gain by accepting the doctrine of the Holy Trinity and of Transubstantiation? Is it better or worse for a purely intellectual exercise? It always amazed me that people have to be instructed before they can enter the Catholic and other Churches. How can you teach God to the aspirant? You can only offer him slick answers to refute the arguments of more intelligent opponents. These specific beliefs such as those I have mentioned serve only to divide man. It is almost a comfort that millions have killed each other on these issues and so disposed of a few believers in belief. What is important for us, and enables us to see how much we have been misled by malice or stupidity, is that most of these systems of belief were established long after the death of Christ the prophet. Search the scriptures for clean-cut references to the Holy Trinity and such subjects and you will find none.

The ecclesiastics, essentially the reasoners, however much their reasoning is from false premises, established early in modern European history a closed shop dedicated to an imprisonment of man in systems of belief. In what way is it evolutionary and creative to believe anything set to the seductive music of the Anglican creeds? Is the individual produced necessarily better than that species of modern robot, whose mechanised emotions are dictated by hate and envy and who believes in the principles of Marx and Engels? All belief, clerical or lay, is intellectual homage. As such it is a profitless exercise conducted in the brains of isolated men conditioned or enchained by their familial or cultural environment. That men have risen to great eminence by the erection of systems which have attracted millions of adherents need not concern us here. The tribal instinct of man is his lowest acquisition. It reinforces any current system of ideas by which he is inflamed. Under its impetus he commits his worst errors and wallows in his most absurd beliefs. Bismark was right when he said that the majority is always wrong. This is inevitable because the action on the majority of the tribal instinct is always at its strongest when its exhibition arouses the hate and envy of the mob, who need the cohesive forces imposed by systems of belief to gain what they desire. Truth is unattainable under such circumstances and at such times.

4.

Psychic Development

I belong to no religion and no philosophical society. I am concerned only with the difference between truth and illusion. This is not discoverable through organized religion. One is conditioned by the latter to think in terms of specific dogma, an obliterating fog which conceals the truth because the latter is not intellectual but a total experience.

Any attempt to organize the truth to ensure its propagation is the work of the devil. To organize the truth it is necessary to express it in intellectual terms. When *the* truth becomes *a* truth it has already ceased to exist because the truth is absolute or nothing. To attempt to codify the truth is not only to deface it but to destroy it. To tell the message, that the man blind from birth sees again, that another sick of the palsy can walk once more and that Christ was seen on the road to Emmaus is one thing. These are manifestations of perception based on fact. To organize and manipulate Christ's teaching is another. He himself avoided intellectual instruction. He preferred to speak in parables, to create an atmosphere, above all to avoid a theology. Another of his vehicles of communication was poetry. "Consider the lilies of the field, they toil not, neither do they spin." It is the function of poetry such as this to touch a chord vibrating at a deeper level than the coarser rhythms of intellect. Keats communicated at the same level by his "beauty is truth, truth beauty." The difference between Christ and the great poets is that he could exist and communicate perpetually at this level whereas Keats and Wordsworth could only achieve the equivalent once or twice in a lifetime.

When Christ seems to be speaking more directly he is still not proving his statements intellectually. He avoids altogether systems of ideas. The Sermon on the Mount is not theology. It is a series of exhortations. The most mystical of the gospels, that of St. John, is more concerned with the nature of Christ and what he did than with His teaching. The most mystical part of the gospel is the first chapter. Nobody could call it an intellectual exposition of a system of ideas for the simple reason that so many millions of people have spent so much time trying to discover what it means. "In the beginning was the word" sounds like a straightforward statement of fact. Certainly no explanation is offered. This is what we must acclimatize ourselves to in dealing with revealed truth. We have to ask ourselves whether these seemingly dogmatic statements hang together as a whole. More than this, we have to have achieved a certain level of evolution, because the words we read in the first chapter of the gospel of St. John are not designed to convince us by argument but to set in vibration new chords which transform us as a whole.

There is not the slightest evidence that Christ ever set out to establish a religion. Isolated quotations such as his statement to Peter that the latter was the rock upon which he would build his Church need only be accepted in theology, surely a pseudo-science unique in that it manufactures its own raw material. Perhaps Christ was saying that Peter's lack of comprehension in comparison to that of John, only fitted him to deface the message by seeking to express it in the form of an earthly organization. In chemistry one has to find the basic elements such as calcium and magnesium before discussing the construction of the compounds. In theology one assumed the existence of the equivalents of the basic elements and, until the secular authority intervened, its practitioners burnt those wise enough to see through these assumptions but not sufficiently discreet to refrain from questioning them in public.

Those who translated the gospels were prone to error. How can we accept that all the statements attributed to Christ were made by him? Most of all, how can one be sure after two thousand years that they have been described in their right context? The only statements of Christ we can cling to are those compatible with the emanation of the total being perceived from the story of His life and His more reverberating messages.

There is not one theological doctrine of contemporary Christianity which was not produced long after Christ was dead. Where in any gospel is there any reference to the Holy Trinity or to the doctrine of Transubstantiation? There are isolated sentences which might be used in the same way as haphazard and dishonest builders seek to make bricks without straw, but it is neither scientific nor reasonable to erect such items into the pretentious substance of an international theocracy which, with the connivance of kings and princes, ruled Europe for centuries.

What is truth? One should ask, like Pilate, but wait for an answer. Let us begin with truth in its most accessible form. In these days, when the world is biased in favour of scientific method and when even its administration and destiny are technological rather than political, we think of truth in terms of what we call science. There are the laws concerning gravity and the transmission of light. We are faced immediately with the fact that we have passed from the singular to the plural, that we are dealing not with truth but truths. But truth by nature and definition is something absolute and indivisible. Can we say therefore that the laws of science, like those concerned with the transmission of light and the movement of the heavenly bodies, are ephemeral and inaccurate? Certainly in some cases what the scientists until recently insisted were as immovable as the laws of the Medes and Persians have proved fallacious. Einstein's iconoclastic contributions have shown that some of these laws of science have a shorter life than their discoverers insisted. Nevertheless Newton's Law of Gravity has had a long innings and may well defy the erosion of time.

That Newton's contentions have not been challenged is of particular significance to us. His background was truly religious and he wrote voluminously on the subject. His approach was cosmic. The laws which govern the course of falling objects were to him the echo of a single chord which made part of the total harmony of the universe. Herein lies the heart of the matter. The truths of science are no more than explanations, often fallacious, often ephemeral, of reactions occurring at the periphery of the universe, that is to say in and around our own planet. It is no part of my intention to deny that Koch's bacillus is the cause of tuberculosis or to insist that Boyle's law is a protracted illusion. What we must understand is that these so-called truths explain only what occurs at the outer fringe of existence which is our life in this world. It is only natural that we should seek to account for what is accessible to us. What a few find in this life, which more may discover in the zones of higher consciousness which succeed death, is that these particulate and fragmented truths perceptible in this world are minor wheels in the internally circulating mechanism of the Cosmos. Boyle's Law and Newton's Law of Gravity hug the frontiers of what Sir Thomas Browne called the mystical mathematic of the city of heaven.

With regard to the question of "scientific" truth as the far reflected shadow of ultimate truth, it is significant that great physicists like Eddington are in part mystics in seeing what they comprehend as part of a whole, inexplicable from the foggy redoubt we inhabit in a world situated at the periphery of the universe. What is literally blinding and, in its ultimate application terrifying, is the modern insistence that only truth which is accessible and above all measurable is valid. This means that only what can be seen down a microscope, measured with a slide rule, or recorded electro-magnetically, can be regarded as truth. The latter has become the private requisite of the laboratory assistant. The less dogmatic scientists may part reluctantly the eyelids of vision to the degree that they say they cannot accept this or that phenomenon as true without further evidence, but those more dedicated to the construction of the new society, which is death in life, insist categorically that what cannot be seen and measured is non-existent. These men are more dogmatic and limited than the Inquisition. Their basic mental equipment is the same. Anything which deviates from their own rigid and unspiritual conception of the universe is to be utterly rejected. Like the Inquisitors the dictators of the laboratory do not apply persecution themselves. Like their spiritual ancestors they arrange a society in which persecution becomes inevitable. In past centuries thousands died condemned by the Inquisition for heresy. In our own day millions have died in totalitarian states based on scientific dogma. The 'truth is measurement' edict is the inevitable religion for those who desire to infect us with the toxic lie that man is a mere behaviourist product of his wordly environment, a soulless, biochemical and glandular accretion whose whole history and destiny can be adequately represented by a distended dossier in a pathological laboratory.

We have arrived at this science-orientated concept of truth because of the unfounded supposition that what is true is arrived at by knowledge manipulated by reason. The defect of such an attitude is that it is concerned only with partial truths uncoordinated in total truth and applicable to this world only. Worse still it leads to the numbing fallacy that truth is directly accessible to anyone of adequate education and with sufficient application to benefit from it. Such an attitude is inevitable in a society where every man has the right to know everything except the secrets of state. The latter phrase can be translated as meaning the machinations of those in whom the obsessive love of power over others reflects the death of the soul.

Though I did not know it at the time my contacts with truth began in early childhood. Some of these encounters were more concrete than others. I was transported at the age of four in what I have elsewhere called a dream but which I now know to have been a conscious flight of the psyche to a world more beautiful but less painless than this. I have described elsewhere the afterdeath, palpitating reality of the colours of this other world and how I knew I had quitted my body and how I tried to explain to my mother the bliss of my experience. In dreams I felt my psyche descending to this earth and felt, alone in the darkness of my bedroom, the fall through space which was somehow immeasureable and divorced from time. I was, as I have described in *Obsession**, invaded from a world of dark entities in which I felt the power of evil but was too young to know that what I saw and felt was an emissary from a darker dominion and that, even then, as a young child, I was involved in Armageddon between good and evil which was to flair up in my late middle years and in age.

What have my early experiences to do with the nature of truth? They indicate that the latter, in its absolute form, is changeless. Truth, in being timeless, is essentially the opposite of all that is transitory. My vision of another world at the age of four was a psychic experience. So was my recollection in dreams of the descent of my psyche into matter. So also was my encounter with a satanic entity that night of childhood when the air was taut with the vibrations of evil. What is a psychic experience but a manifestation of the psyche in action? Such phenomena are timeless because the psyche, reincarnating as it does on this earth and being more intensely alive between one's different incarnations, is essentially immortal. It is divorced from chronology just as the egocentric human personality is rivetted in it. The discarnates with whom I have spoken of my previous incarnations stress their emancipation, and that of the psyche, from time. Their independence of chronology is obvious from their conversation because, while they are aware that our earthly commitments are dependent on time, they themselves have little sense of duration.

Psychic or, to use more modern and less accurate phraseology,

extrasensory experiences are independent of time except in the
case of earth-bound psyches which, after death, are still drawn
towards this planet and as such remain subject to the operations
of time. This is the crucial difference between the human
personality and the psyche. We build the former ourselves
through a compromise between what we wish of life and what
society will allow us. Our personality grows from infancy to
senility and is therefore expressed in time. Our psyche, on the
contrary, is mature at conception and carries with it the memory
of past lives. It therefore follows that it operates in a timeless
medium as clearly as it is obvious that the movements and
impulses of our personality are determined by time. We wish to
achieve some set ambition in the future. In our regrets we keep
reverting to some frustrated desire in the past. In psychic activity
the emancipation from time is obvious. This is particularly so in
clairvoyance and precognition. The individual sees and feels
what will happen in the future. It is not difficult to check
whether or no his prognostications are correct. In far memory of
past incarnations the emancipation from chronology is equally
obvious. Telepathy, too, occurs in a timeless medium. If
someone three thousand miles away knows instantly that you
have had an accident, the obliteration of space basic to this
phenomenon involves also the annihilation of time, if we
consider that our common thoughts and feelings have crossed
the ocean instantaneously and therefore immeasureably faster
than any plane or ship. These are striking and undeniable
evidences of the psyche's capacity to operate out of time. They
are natural gifts in a small minority of adults. Such gifts are
largely inborn but here we must ask ourselves whether the adult
psychic, with his independence of time and, through it, his
access to direct truth, is relying solely on a rare innate capacity
or whether his psychic gifts are due to a special tenacity which
has enabled him to retain more than others capacities far
commoner in childhood than people generally imagine.

We are all born with a fully developed psyche. Our future
depends on how quickly we close our ears to the prompting of
our most valuable asset. Certainly young children are aware in
early childhood of the actions of their psyche. Many experience
levitation in dreams, feel the memory of it by day and are
laughed at or reproved as liars by their parents and others if they
risk describing their experiences and sensations. At a later age,
say, from eight to puberty, precognition and clairvoyance in

particular are far commoner than is imagined. I know this to be true because I encountered it often in the children's clinic where I worked for thirty-six years. I have described elsewhere these clean-cut clinical manifestations of psychic activity in childhood. I have been concerned mostly in the past with children who have clung, in spite of opposition, education and repression on the part of others or by themselves, to their psychic endowment. What I am concerned with here is the question of to what degree many children live in their psyches without producing verifiable phenomena such as precognition and telepathy. To what extent are we born psychic and why is our natural inheritance stolen so early from us?

It is not merely a question of being actually born psychic, seeing that at conception the psyche has already entered matter. This is not only the basis of much philosophy from Pythagoras onwards. It was realised also by those unknown to us who were responsible for the Eleusinian Mysteries. It is clinically manifested by women who have retained the capacity for psychic perception, and who know by indefineable sensations and by being pierced by waves of light the moment at which they have conceived. Apart from the more dramatic signs of psychic perception manifested in childhood are there not many children who are living easily and undramatically in their psyches? Do not most of us possess in our first years something precious which we lose later and never regain? Is not the faculty of wonder, the love of the object we see, be it never so dilapidated, for its own sake, a sign that the psyche predominates over the personality? When a child discovers with joy and examines with wonder an old cocoa tin forgotten in the shrubbery, is not this a manifestation of the activity of the psyche rather than the personality? Were it the latter would not the child's capacity for wonder be vitiated and dispersed by such questions as to what practical use could be made of the tin?

This faculty of wonder, of being transported by what is immediate, of identifying oneself completely with the object contemplated, played an enormous role not only in my childhood but well into boyhood. I must have been little more than an infant when I was first aware of the fluttering patterns of leaves against the sky. I do not merely remember a whitebeam in the shadow of a wall, the white under-surface of its leaves more pallid still in the lightless autumn but lit by the embers of its dark red berries. It returns to me not in memory only but with the same stab in the solar plexus I felt when I made psychic contact with patients and knew they would recover. It was amusing and pathetic to see the tree alive after sixty years, a wind-shrivelled relic stunted by the sea wind, but to me the talisman of something unchanging for more than sixty years and indeed unalterable for all eternity because it represented for me the last, far extended antenna of a power of beauty I knew to be unchangeable, originating in a vibrationless calm beyond even the eternal energies of good and evil.

Such experiences of these are truth in indefineable form. They merit the description because they are changeless in a shifting world. The whitebeam may die or be cut down but what it evoked was the full power of truth not because I remember it always but because when I first saw it I recognized it for what it was, a trailing tentacle of beauty seen by me, not through the eyes of personality but through the psyche, as projected from a changeless harmony, from an inviolable truth which existed before the fragmentation of the Cosmos into good and evil and before the creation of form.

This conviction of another world coming to me through beauty continued throughout my boyhood. The sun on the bramble leaves stained crimson in autumn, bent in taut curves by the spiders' webs, were whispered intimations of a beauty which was absolute, all pervading, most of all undying. The leaves, the morning, the suspense of autumn made for me a mysterious and continuous reality. It was as if I were part of an unending process, deeper than sensation, in which there was neither subject nor object but a feeling of oneness and that time was dead.

There were evenings in late winter when the light came in from the sea at sunset. It flooded the trunks of the leafless trees. When I walked home from school by a detour which, in those days, was through lanes deserted and eerie in the twilight, it was as though the light around me was the glow of a world beyond the desolation of the fated trees. This was the truth inside me. It was not of the brain and not only of the heart. It was buried in the darkness of my deeper tissues. It was irresistible and beyond definition.

I know that in those moments I was suspended in the air of a kind of suprareality because, for years afterwards and well into manhood, I could recall what I had thought at such instants when I turned this corner, what I felt in my heart in descending that hill. Nor was I at that time thinking of anything especially dramatic or moving. Memory such as this, for individual and undramatic thoughts recalled after decades, is surely a function of the psyche. Only the psyche could record seeming trivia with such intensity that one recalled it after decades. Surely such a process is analogous to that manifested by the psychic child who has proved himself by precognition and telepathy and can remember back to infancy.

Sometimes I was meeting another aspect of truth, something more specific than my general cosmic awareness that the hills and lakes of West Cumberland were faint reflections in a mirror of a burning reality unattainable in this life. Turning round the corner by the white house with the wine stain of japonica thrown over its walls, going down the hill to the bridge with the curtain of honeysuckle blown out from the hedgerows by the high west wind, what passed through my mind was retained for years because, centuries before, I had walked these roads. What I had thought and felt at certain points on the road in this life was what I had pondered at the same place thirteen centuries before. It is a paradox and an irony that what we remember most acutely comes to us in these moments when we escape from time. Memory, which we regard as looking back through time, is actually at its sharpest when time is eliminated. In the moments I have described I was reliving simultaneously what I had thought and felt across a gap of what in terms of chronology was thirteen centuries. Thoughts I had had in my head on crossing a road in this life, the flowers in a hedge and the outward curve of the shadows of the hedgerow, were retained in my mind for years because centuries ago, when the land was scrub and forest, this or that misfortune had happened or my mind had been troubled by some painful thought.

I was in my mid-teens when, going down the road where the billowing folds of honeysuckle blown out by the seawind smelt sweetly after rain, I relived, unknown to myself at the time but recalled years later and confirmed by the discarnates, an obsessive boyhood problem in seventh century Cumberland when the Roman missionaries were smoothing out the innocent irregularities of Celtic belief. The problem was posed to me in this life in the simplest form. If salvation depends on people hearing and accepting the word of God, and if it is inevitable that many in the darkness of barbarism are doomed to be deprived, where is the justice in this world and, more important, how can this be permitted by a god described as being at one and the same time all powerful and all merciful? This was not an original thought. It is hard to believe that it does not occur to every thinking person, but it was of enormous importance to me. Out of it arose my incapacity to believe in belief and my conviction that, far from evolving, men deteriorated by homage to systems of ideas.

For years I was at a loss to understand why I, who was to spend my life wholly available to others, should have been in my boyhood and youth at such pains to avoid their company. I was not afraid of my fellows and was never persecuted by them. So far as I can estimate I was popular with my schoolmates and any revolt I displayed to my teachers was not from resentment of authority but originated in high spirits and sheer mischievous-ness. I had a chameleon-like capacity to adapt to my surroundings. The crucial point was that, given choice as in the holidays, I opted for solitude in ten hour stretches alone in the country. I had the good fortune to grow up near landscapes of great beauty. To me the road over Fangs Brow to Loweswater is still perfection.

Alone, confronted with such beauty, I was living in my psyche. The contemplation of what is totally absorbing in its beauty is the simplest form of psychic activity. We are unaware of the passage of time and feel as though we had been in another world. This is literally true because such timeless experiences are determined by the suspension of personality and its partial subjugation by the psyche. The latter takes over from the human ego because the psyche is always concerned with total experience and the personality with only its fragmentary expression.

During my hours of solitude I was nourishing my psyche. I was unaware that this was a necessary and logical proceeding related to my future as a doctor. I was to become one of those who diagnosed, aided and healed, albeit all too little, through their psyches. Those who, in their psyches, are able to disperse themselves through time, as in far memory and precognition have, if these faculties are sufficiently developed, the capacity to heal. This is achieved by their ability to operate in a limitless medium. It is only by living predominantly in the time-bound personality that we suffer from the state of disharmony we rightly call dis-ease.

What was released in me in spring mornings by Loweswater, with the daffodils golden and the lake flat calm in the hollow of the hills, speaking to no one in that silent world, was to be my main equipment twenty years later in dealing with patients in a claustrophobic out-patients department towards which I made my way so many wintry Fridays with the dark sky low. Because I was not working at the level of personality, what I said to these patients was often of secondary importance. I know this to be true because so often patients dated their improvement to statements I could never have said but which were uttered when the psyche was erupting through the layers of the unconscious and fusing with that of the patient.

I was as little addicted to systems of medicine as I was to sectarian religions. It seemed to me that to practice the systems of Freud, Jung and Adler was to see patients with other peoples' eyes, a ludicrous and impossible concept which erects a barrier of insulating intellectualism between doctor and patient.

There was another way in which my solitary hours in Loweswater, Crummock, Bassenthwaite and Wythop contributed directly to my usefulness as a psychiatrist. These passive, creative periods in my life were spent in places in which I had lived and suffered in another life. I was feeling, for the most part, below the conscious level though at times very near it, what I had experienced thirteen centuries before. One day I stampeded in a state of panic down a fell path leading down the road to Loweswater. It was here in the seventh century I had saved women on two separate occasions from a mob inflamed by superstition and a vicious priest. Under such circumstances, my psyche was not only being given air to breathe but was directing my personality and in so doing was preparing me for the exercise many years later of that therapeutic psychic contact through which I became an agent in removing patients' symptoms. It is unfortunate that my conscious remembrance of past lives only came so late in my life. Had it done so earlier my therapeutic value would have been considerably greater.

In my boyhood and youth I was aware of a truth that was inexpressible and implicit in nature. I had no more need to define my conviction than a young man needs to explain that he is in love. This was because what I felt was not merely a conviction. It was something perceived, a self-evident reality as natural and inevitable as the leaf buds opening. I felt this because in the depths of my being, in the profounder reaches of my unconscious and in the still less accessible dark recesses of my tissues, I knew that consciousness in men, plants and animals is indivisible and continuous. This, if you like, was my idea of God.

It is ridiculous to dismiss such an attitude as pantheism. To do so is to give a name to a belief rather than a process. Words like pantheism used to describe my state at this time are theological diabolisms. I do not believe that what I experienced was unique or even uncommon. Was I not reliving what Wordsworth, who was born nine miles from my home, had felt, thought and described, with so much regret. I came, as we all did, not in utter nakedness but trailing clouds of glory, not from my past incarnations but from the intervals between them when one lives closer to God. Baudelaire said that art consists in being able to capture one's childhood at will. How is this done? Baudelaire was in error in attributing this to any act of will. The artist is he who is able with ease to return to what in his childhood is his most precious acquisition, his capacity to live more than his fellows in his psyche, from whence his inspiration derives if he is to be any more than a pretentious hack re-echoing the more seductive platitudes of the age he lives in.

Wordsworth described how the shadow of the prisonhouse closed over the growing boy and meditated how, in later life, he had lost the capacity to feel the vibrating living vitality he had shared with stones and streams. In me, what I had in boyhood never wholly died. What is regrettable is that I ceased to be guided by it. I was never separated from nature because always the beauty of landscapes and flowers were my main solace when I was fatigued by the demands of my profession. What I *knew* was overlaid, but not heavily or for long, by belief in the pretentious and myopic infallibility of the kind of science which believes truth to be a prerequisite of its own speciality. I had already shed this in my twenties when I heard of Freud's doctrine of the unconscious. I did not realise then how much he was in error and that his system was not merely rigidly materialistic but mechanistic. It was enough for me that, even in medicine, there were more universalised factors than symptoms of disease. What I had still to learn was that, however genuinely I had glimpsed the truth in my boyhood and youth, I was following only local rivulets and all too far from the main source.

5.

Everyday Miracles

What I failed to realise until the later years of my life was that there are living sources of revealed truth. I have spoken with people with psychic gifts enabling them to see with verifiable accuracy events happening to individuals or communities in the future. One morning a woman sees another more than a hundred miles distant, last heard of as healthy, lying unconscious on a bed with all the signs of a severe stroke. This is an accurate observation and as such an aspect of truth. The same applies to another I have known who foretold in detail such disasters as aeroplane crashes. Where these faculties are acutely developed they are often accompanied by far memory of past lives. Such individuals know what they felt and thought in previous incarnations. They are able to trace those constantly repeating facets of wisdom which have stood up to the test of time. They are nearer, in fact, to the eternal verities. There is nothing new under the sun, and if we find this or that motif constantly repeated in several lives we are surely drawing nearer to ultimate truth, that is to say, to the sole, unalterable factors which remain constant in a world of change.

Where these faculties are sufficiently developed the individual may see not only into the near future of his life on earth, as in clairvoyance and precognition, but into the distant future concerned with the fate of our planet and the destiny of man. I have known one such person in my life, who, in dreams, in trancelike states and in waking consciousness, saw backwards to an incarnation around or beyond 2000 B.C. and forwards to the destruction of this planet. Those who would question her capacity to do so would surely have to bear in mind her unerring accuracy in foretelling events happening to others, and to feel disasters occurring at a distance of thousands of miles. To reproduce in her own body the injuries originating in past incarnations is surely evidence of her emancipation from time and of being an instrument of direct truth. The doubters would also have to consider cases of cancer she has irrefutably cured, the pains of serious accidents she has removed in an instant. One should note in passing her infinite compassion and her constant availability to all who suffer.

If we are able to achieve the near impossible and throw off the conditioning in which we have been reared, if we can consider the matter without prejudice, and freed from set forms of belief, we have to admit that these are Christlike qualities. Whatever historians say the gospels tell us more that is striking and unique about the man and his actions than about his beliefs. If we are fair minded we should admit that there is nothing original about the idea that we should love one another and our neighbour as ourselves, or about any of the prescriptions for good living recorded in the Sermon on the Mount and elsewhere. These are merely the decencies of life as practiced by the civilised at any place and at any time. They were recognized as desirable and practiced by the minority in the civilisations of Greece and Rome which preceded Christ. In our day they are to be found among those practising religions other than Christianity. Incidentally it has been my experience that I have found more fundamentally good natured people outside Christianity than in it. I have been struck by the almost unfailing good nature of Tibetan Buddhists. In my experience the majority of those who have truly loved and helped their neighbours have either ceased to practice Christianity or to manifest towards it no more than a perfunctory respect founded on habit.

In considering Christ as described in the Gospels we are dealing with the man, the Son of God if you will, rather than with any stunning and revolutionary, or evolutionary, message he had to offer. Have the words he himself uttered, according to the Evangelists, transformed life to the same degree as those say, of Rousseau, that man is born free and is yet everywhere in chains, that he is born naturally good — be it said a ridiculous supposition — and needs only a propitious environment to render him perfect? Christian Churches of all complexions may protest vehemently, most of them have lost even their vehemence, at such a blasphemous assumption, but surely the immense Christian transformation of the world was achieved not by Christ but by what man added to his gospel, if it merits the name, rather than what he said himself. Christianity swept the world by means of the doctrine of grace and redemption, that Christ was God incarnate and came to die for us on the Cross to redeem our sins, to save us the effort of improving ourselves a little. There is no evidence for this in the words of Christ himself. Contemporary accounts describe him as a man who performed so-called miraculous cures. Miraculous is an unfortunate word. Natural healing without the aid of medicine or surgery is, even in this world, a recognized reality with classical accompanying signs and occuring through people with special but easily recognizeable qualities.

Christ healed by his presence, by touch and, in the case of the centurion's servant, by what we would now call absent healing. He was precognitive in that he foretold the destruction of Capernaum and Jerusalem. He saw into the past in that he told the woman of Samaria that she had had three and not one husband. The fame he achieved in His own time was not widespread. He is scarcely mentioned in the records of con- temporary Roman historians. Certainly he achieved a very considerable local reputation, otherwise he would not have attracted the attention of the Jewish authorities which resulted in his death on the Cross. What acquired for him this reputation was emphatically nothing originally or specially characteristic in the words he spoke. They could have issued equally well from the mouths of Buddha or from some of the Greek and Roman philosophers. What was responsible for such fame he acquired was, firstly, what he achieved, which was regarded as miraculous and, secondly, the emanation of the man himself. "What manner of man is this that even the winds and the sea obey him?" It is inconceivable that His reputation could have been established among simple people by the nature of his message. Its very simplicity is evidence of its non-unique nature.

There are periods in history when the climate is spiritually favourable to the advent of such beings. These eras are often characterised on the surface by gross materialism which stimulates in a minority an emanatory goodness associated with all manner of psychic and spiritual gifts. Among these latter is the power to ignite others so that they are enabled to live on the same plane as these powerful transmitters of goodness. When Matthew left the seat of custom it was not because he was convinced by any arguments of Christ that he should abandon his profession but because psychic and spiritual contact was established immediately between them. At such periods the vibrations of earth, air and water are especially beneficent at any rate in certain places. The stars are auspiciously disposed. In the Gospels we are not only referred to the star in the East but to the fact that the Magi were directed to Bethlehem by such means. Another period in history when such influences were at work, in producing philosophers and healers who had shed the impediment of materialism, was round about the sixth century BC, which so far as we can estimate, produced the work of Pythagoras and Heraclitus in Greece, of Buddha in India and of Lao-tse and Confucius in China. The twelfth and thirteenth centuries in Europe were similar epochs when the Catholic Church, dominant in terms of temporal power, was in a state of spiritual decomposition and stimulated the phenomenon of Catharism, a non-materialistic philosophy the practitioners of which were liberally endowed with psychic and spiritual gifts.

We live in another such age which shows the two main characteristics required of such eras. Firstly, we have a world wide and dominant materialism, represented in hundred per cent concentration in the Communist blocks, which are resisted by the free world devoted to the same principles, but to a less degree partly because of their prevailing inertia. Secondly, we have revolts against materialism in a proliferation of semi-mystical cults. This resembles the state of affairs which preceded the final disintegration of the Roman Empire.

At such times the earth produces, by a process of psychic ignition between man and man, a number of healers and prophets whose words are listened to with special attention precisely because they are accompanied by clear manifestations of healing and prophecy. It is certain that in the first two or three centuries after Christ there were others with such Christlike gifts. It seems almost fortuitous but was inevitably part of a pattern that Christ was chosen to be the Saviour of the world rather than Appolonius of Tyre and others who had many of the same qualities. One should always remember that the selection of Christ as the Saviour of the world was not the work of God the Father but of a posse of ecclesiastics who saw to what extent the doctrine of grace from on high, in the death of the Son of God, could be turned into an instrument of power, temporal and otherwise, with themselves as its wielders.

It is my serious contention that in every generation there are a handful of people with Christlike gifts and capable of doing all, or most, of what he achieved. The number of such people is impossible to estimate. There are times when those with such qualities must necessarily remain anonymous. It is both dangerous and mistaken to reveal themselves too much. What, for example, would be the use of a person revealing, in the rationalist eighteenth century England, that they could heal disease by out of the body visitations to the sick or by acquiring their symptoms, or that they could see not only future events in individual lives but the end of the world and look back to past incarnations over millennia? To have done so would have been to have ended in Bedlam. Towards the end of the said century Blake and Swedenborg were held by many to be mad because of their visionary experiences even though the latter foretold with accuracy the great fire at Stockholm. People with such gifts are, at the present moment, able to reveal themselves more openly, though the best of them prefer to remain anonymous, recognizing that what gifts they possess are not self-generated but arise because they are acting as passive instruments of the power of good.

I know for certain, from personal experiences, that there are people able to cure cancers, even when the latter are generalised and where secondary deposits have been discovered in various organs of the body. They have been able to do this by touching or by out-of-the-body visitations to the sick. I know there are others from whom nothing can be hidden, who see into the past and future of the individual. Telepathy in my experience is utterly commonplace and includes not only the reading of thoughts and feelings at a distance but the somatic manifestation in which the individual takes the pains and physical signs and symptoms of those ill or severely damaged in accidents at distances of hundreds or thousands of miles. I have known individuals so precognitive and clairvoyant that they could truly be called prophets. As they have been so unfailingly accurate in picking up what was happening to people thousands of miles away, and as what they said was subsequently confirmed to the tiniest detail, I can but accept what they say of the final cataclysm and how civilisation will finally disintegrate. In such people intuitions so merge with frank psychic capacities that one sees that intuition at its highest is an extrasensory process. When it is asked of them they advise on any matter their questioner cares to pose with a piercing intelligence divorced altogether from intellectualism. Their intelligence is essentially practical and wholly uncontaminated by theory. They are able in a second to see to the heart of the matter, to distinguish the vital broad issues from the irrelevant details and to see both the wood and the trees.

I submit, with becoming deference to the views of the orthodox, that such people have many of the same capacities as Christ exhibited on earth and are of the same substance. So far as precognition and clairvoyance are concerned I have encountered many examples equalling and even transcending anything I have read of in the Gospels. When we deal with healing it is surely pointless to argue whether it is a more portentious feat to cure one sick of the palsy than those riddled with cancer. To enable a man blind from birth to see is perhaps on a higher plane of therapy; but is it much higher than that of the girl, congenitally blind in one eye and reduced in her twenties to grossly blurred vision in the other during an operation, who is now able to see by a mysterious process of psychic healing? Certainly one can say Christ went farther in raising Lazarus from the dead. We can argue that the latter was not dead but in a deep state of coma, possibly diabetic, epileptic or cardiovascular in origin, but to do so is to repeat the sins of the theologians in picking out those titbits which fit one's own arguments. Even here I have known a close parallel. Certainly the woman in question was not, in utterly material terms, raised from the dead but this is to what all intents and purposes happened to her. She was in a coma following widespread virulent peritonitis from a ruptured appendix. While in coma and partially because of it she suffered the grave complication of pulmonary embolus, a clot in the pulmonary artery with, as a consequence, a collapsed lung. She was described by the doctors as sinking. One asked for instructions as to whether she was to be cremated and where her ashes were to be scattered. To the amazement of everybody concerned with her case she recovered. She appears in the records of the clinic in America as a miraculous cure. This tribute, offered in a civilisation described as materialistic, is worth recording as a pathway to the raising of Lazarus from the dead. It was later revealed that the girl had been healed by a combination of out-of-the-body visits from the living, combined with healing by a discarnate entity.

So far as we are concerned with the miracles of healing performed by Christ I have evidence that in this generation there are one or two capable of at least parallel procedures. So far as feeding the five thousand is concerned I know of no modern or contemporary parallel. I cannot avail myself of the argument that the whole phenomenon was based on mass illusion, an umbrella term used to account for what we cannot explain and to me, as a psychiatrist, a non-existent phenomenon. Individuals and those in their vicinity may be affected by hallucination but not five thousand. So far as walking on the water is concerned, is it any more remarkable than out-of-the-body experiences such as those I have described in *The Lake and The Castle*, *The Psyche in Medicine* and other works? In such experiences, the healer is seen, certainly not in the flesh, but otherwise in his or her full reality, often thousands of miles from his or her actual domicile. Certainly, we do not see the healer's actual movement through space. It is profitless to argue that this is less remarkable than the fact that the disciples saw Christ walk on the water. The point is that the two phenomena are allied in nature and indicate a capacity to live and move in something other than the physical body. That Christ was seen to move, and the movements of out-of-the-body healers are invisible, is less important than the fact that the two phenomena are different aspects of the same process.

To compare the miracles — a sloppy and fallacious term — performed by Christ as similar to those attributable to a handful of people in every generation may appear blasphemous to the Church; but we should remember that, since the 1920s, the latter, certainly in the Anglican persuasion, has produced an impressive number of priests in whom non-understanding is blended with a kind of false and sickly tolerance. An impressive number of bishops and lesser luminaries have pointed out that it is possible, even probable, that Christ's miracles were performed not on the physically sick but on suggestible neurotic subjects who were merely aping physical symptoms. In other words, the man sick of the palsy had a hysterical paralysis. The man blind from birth was similarly hysterical. (He did well to show signs of hysteria at birth and to keep it up so long). All this is nonsense. If in our contemporary and largely unbelieving materialistic world lay persons without medical training, but with intense psychic gifts can cure cancer, delete scars from faces doomed to distortion in the opinion of plastic surgeons, and restore unrestricted vision to those condemned to impaired sight after accidents, it seems to me folly to deny Christ credit for the acts of healing he performed.

Most of Christ's feats of healing were of the same nature as the most dramatic of those which have come my way. This means that they occurred at the level of the psyche. Either the healer travels through space in his psyche or, in virtue of somatic telepathy, takes to himself the patient's symptoms. He may also heal by touch. Different healers vary in the type of healing they favour. Christ seems to have specialised in touch and in what one would nowadays call absent healing, vide the centurion's servant. Apart from psychic healing there is also a form of true spiritual healing. By the latter, I do not mean healing by faith or prayer or anything organised by the contemporary Church, or accompanied by invocations to God on high. I mean simply healing conducted at the level of the spirit, convinced as I am that man consists of personality, psyche and individualised spirit, though the latter is tangibly developed in this life in only a tiny minority. The Gospels are not very informative in distinguishing psychic from spiritual healing. We are reduced to the statement that in one case Christ, when the woman with the issue of blood touched the hem of his garment, felt that virtue had gone out of him. The evidence is insufficient for one to say with certainty that this was a case of healing at the level of the spirit. The point at issue is that he felt himself drained by the procedure. Those capable of psychic healing, especially out-of-the-body experiences, are not necessarily exhausted by them. In many cases they are unaware that these visits have taken place. Most natural healers do not give themselves totally to the patient in the process of healing. For those with great experience of the psychic contact resulting in healing, it is not a wearying process unless continued too long. In terms of vital energy the healer very often gets back what he gives. This is inevitably implied if we accept that healing of this nature involves effortless fusion of the psyches of healer and healed.

Healing at the level of the spirit is less common than psychic healing. As I have indicated in *The Psyche in Medicine* those healed in this way are convinced that something of the healer has been built into them and has altered them permanently for their benefit. It is obvious that healing of this nature is more likely to occur in beings with an emanatory capacity resembling that of Christ than in psychic healers, but this is not to deny the existence in each generation of a handful of healers operating at times at the level of the spirit. In this they resemble Christ but with the difference that what spirit healing they achieve is rare and spasmodic, whereas Christ's emanatory healing capacity was maintained continuously at the level of the spirit.

While healing at the level of the spirit is rare in any generation there was, in European history, an era in which it was more common than at any time since the primitive Christianity of the first two centuries after Christ. This capacity to heal at the highest levels of the spirit was canalised in the sacrament known as the Consolamentum. I had always regarded the claims on behalf of this sacrament as exaggerated until, as I have described in *The Lake and The Castle*, and *The Psyche in Medicine*, I encountered two examples of people who relived their experience of this sacrament which they had received seven centuries ago. Until the incidents referred to, I had discounted completely the frequently expressed idea that Cathar priests had the power, through having received the Consolamentum themselves, of transmitting to others, through the bestowal on them of the sacrament, of their own capacity to transcend pain by being unaware of it. From my experience, I have no doubt that for the Cathar priests there were two initiations. By the first they became priests. Through the second those thought suitable were trained specially either for meditation, healing or the like. A few had, and developed through the second initiation, this capacity to remove by spirit healing the pain of others.

It is perhaps for this reason that those of esoteric persuasion have regarded the Consolamentum as of immense significance and Catharism as one of the high peaks of European development. So it was, because a proportion of the Cathar parfaits revealed again the galaxy of gifts manifested by Christ himself and by his adherents in the first two centuries after his death. This is indeed why the Cathars were so ruthlessly persecuted. They represented and revealed a return to an age when a sizeable number of men and women had the psychic and spiritual gifts denied to an unevolved priesthood sterilised by dogma and intellectualism.

In spite of my previous scepticism, I have no doubt now that the Consolamentum, as administered by the Parfaits the night before the *bucher* at Monségur, enabled those of the victims who received it to die without agony. One should note carefully that it is precisely this capacity totally to abolish pain which distinguishes the few, who in this life, have the Christ-like capacity to heal, be it only spasmodically, at the level of the spirit. I have recalled in previous books how a healer took the pains of a woman doctor so completely that the latter felt no pain after the trauma which caused a severe fracture of the tibia. The same healer enabled a surgeon to feel no pain whatever when his face and hands were badly burnt by an explosion of gas, and, on another occasion, in a motor accident when his face was cut to the degree that he required twenty-seven stitches and his eyes were almost closed by fragments of glass. The same healer totally absorbed the pain of a woman, living in another country, who, trying to avoid a fall through a window, cut the tendon of her wrist so badly that it needed one repair operation and was threatened with two. The latter turned out to be completely unnecessary. The same absence of pain applied also in the case of the woman who lost both breasts with cancer, whose liver was riddled with secondary deposits and who was given two months to live by the doctors. She completely refuted their prognosis in recovering and felt no pain throughout the proceedings.

One has surely to admit that this capacity, on the part of the living being to heal so that others feel no pain and that an inexhaustible spiritual energy has permeated their being, approaches, at these periods, the Christ level. One is not suggesting that these healers remain permanently at this level or that they are without flaw. How could they be seeing that they are living in the flesh in this world? Had they been without fault they would not have been required to reincarnate. At the same time, I repeat that in each generation, as the discarnates have confirmed, there is a miniscule minority which chooses to reincarnate because of their compassion for suffering humanity. Also, can we say that Christ, as recorded in the Gospels, was without flaw? I can see no point in cursing the barren fig tree. The adherents of non-violence should note that he attacked physically the money-lenders in the Temple.

Certainly Christ was a superior and special kind of being. Even those in the West who reject that he was the Son of God tend generally to allow that he was supreme among the prophets. Are there any special features which lift him above the category of the tiny minority which, in each generation, have special psychic and spiritual gifts and who are noticed or remain unnoticed according to the climate of opinion? He appeared after death several times to his disciples. This, to certain churchmen, both ordained and lay, is a unique experience. This is why such churchmen have been almost universally hostile in the past to those claiming to have seen or to have spoken with the dead. This attitude still lingers. It accounts for the distrust and often horror of spiritualism manifested by the clergy. I have listened myself to an envenomed reply by a senior member of the Anglican Church to a young spiritualist asking modestly a perfectly reasonable question. It seems an article, perhaps the fortieth, of the Anglican Church that, while it was perfectly *comme il faut* for the disciples to see Christ on the road to Emmaus it is simply not done if the deceased Mr. Jones appears to his widow while she is working with a washing machine. This attitude is a sign of the generalised addiction of the clergy of all Christian sects to look with disfavour at anything they crudely call supernatural. Direct communication with the dead, and with those beings in the discarnate hierarchy accessible to us, is frowned on because the Churches have always insisted that direct revelation is suspect and that the truth can only be filtered through minds trained at theological colleges. Judging from my experience at Oxford I would say that what the priesthood learnt at the said colleges was a series of stock answers to difficult questions, a kind of semi-celestial version of Lady Trowbridge's book on etiquette. This over-emphasis on the unique nature of Christ appearing to his disciples after death is ridiculous. I myself have spoken directly to five of the so-called dead, hearing their voices as plainly and distinctly as though they had been alive. My experience is obviously far from unique.

In considering in what way Christ differs from those who share his gifts on this earth there remains the question of the Transfiguration on the Mount. This to me was the supreme gesture through which he demonstrated his special nature. Others before and since his time have shared his gift of healing and his psychic and spiritual power. In showing himself as revealed in light he was demonstrating the relatively immaterial nature of his being. In modern jargon he lived more in his etheric and astral substance. In the Transfiguration he revealed to what extent he could stay in his astral body. Whether or no we are justified in using these terms it is clear that, at the Transfiguration, Christ showed himself more readily and completely escaping from matter than the rest of mankind.

Nevertheless are we justified in saying with such authority that he differed absolutely from the rest of men? In the out-of-the-body manifestation phenomena, which are common enough in my experience, the healer has shed matter to the degree of being visible thousands of miles away. People such as these have also been seen enveloped in light. I am not here talking of auras of different colours but of figures seen in light and, in spite of their own radiance, being outlined against the background of a golden glow. This visionary experience has happened several times to a girl in the New World, herself very psychic, who has seen the greatest out-of-the-body healer I have known and, more rarely one or two others, revealed and enveloped in light to the degree I have mentioned above. Here again the sceptic can say that an unstable person in a state of heightened suggestibility can see whole battalions arrayed in light and moving through it, but such contentions do not apply when the woman in question has shown herself to be deadly accurate in her precognitive and clairvoyant capacities as I have described adequately enough in *The Lake and The Castle*. She was also gifted with piercing intuition which enabled her not only to know how this or that person would react but how they had reacted in the past before she met them.

The point I am making is that, while Christ was a particular kind of being, he was not completely unique. He was, possibly, more gifted in certain ways than those who preceded or followed him, but he was not so outstandingly blessed as to be called the Son of God, unless we use this title of those so obviously inspired as Leonardo da Vinci and Beethoven. In every generation, scattered over the surface of the globe, there are a few like him. This has always been so and always will be. There are periods when a number of those resembling him are higher than at other times. They appeared in thirteenth century Europe and at the present day because it is only in periods of horror that such beings appear. This is because they are most needed to instruct the minority to carry the world through dark ages which persist and intensify.

Here we approach the crux of the question in our search for reality and the nature of truth. It is through such beings as Christ that absolute truth is maintained living in this world at however low an intensity. This is his supreme importance and that of those like him. Let the credulous derive tenuous happiness from calling him the Son of God, but it is more important to regard him and others like him as torch bearers carrying the light, not only to the dark corners of the earth, but through the periods of midnight when the whole world seems to pass into the shadow of evil. It is vital that in a materialistic age there should exist a handful of people with knowledge of what we can rightly call revealed truth because it is disclosed to them through their particular qualities which involve the capacity to function independently of time and space and thus to discover what is changeless. In addition to what such people reveal to us, they are instructed in still deeper truths by the discarnates who reveal to them at times what they have learnt from the higher members of the hierarchy who have outlived the need to reincarnate.

Before the advent of Christ truth was, at certain periods, revealed more clearly. One can indeed say that he spoke too often in parables and thereby offered too much opportunity for theorising to the theologians and to the schismatic of esoteric persuasion who are often as intellectualised and dogmatic as the priesthood. There is nothing in Christ's message as clean-cut, as offering itself so clearly to the test of experience, as the basic principles of Buddhism as expressed by the founder and his immediate disciples. The oracles of classical antiquity, as for example, those of Greece at its best, revealed truth more directly but only to those fit to receive it. Possibly Christ acted in the same way to His inner circle, but even this is doubtful because the degree of comprehension exhibited by those closest to him was not necessarily superlative. The extent to which his disciples regarded him as a Messiah sent to rule the kingdoms of this world shows a disquieting lack of insight. In speaking to the multitudes he scattered by the wayside seed only a small proportion of which could ever fructify. In this he differed completely from the practitioners of the ancient Mysteries before the latter had become contaminated. The oracles, during the heroic periods, were prepared to divulge and demonstrate absolute truth but only to a perceptive minority. They instructed others less perceptive to a degree which enabled those who consulted them to live a little more wisely. The time came when they revealed what could happen in the future to the living regardless of the latter's degree of development. This of course was a step downwards. In its decline Rome was rotten with professional soothsayers.

We come to an issue which may startle and wound orthodox Christians. For better or worse the Christian message is for the whole world. This applies both to the fabricated non-Christlike Christianity originating in the third century AD and to the teachings of Christ himself. He was essentially a man for the multitude but confined himself, in His public utterances, to exhortations to love one another and simple ethical maxims. He did not directly confront his mass audiences with deeper realities of existence. This is perhaps because in him the healer was predominant. What he was, what he emanated, what he could do were more important than what he said. The methods of the oracles of classical antiquity were different. They only imparted truth in any concentrated form to those capable of benefiting by it. Truth was, in fact, given like medicine, in adjustable doses suited to the requirements of the individual. In the Mysteries, many of the initiation ceremonies were designed to estimate to what degree the individual was able to benefit by the truth. It was recognized that premature confrontation with reality, about oneself or about life as a whole, could result in harm. I am referring to the Greek and Egyptian Mysteries before they were degraded in the latter phases of Greek and Roman civilisation.

Not only the philosophical but the general spiritual attitude such as prevailed in Greece and Crete round about 2000 BC is unthinkable to modern man. He has lost the capacity to confront reality as did the founding fathers of what civilisation he has retained. The theologians have told him that there was no real religion, at any rate in Europe or the Middle East, before Christ. Here, they say, are the clear-cut principles of religion. What was the Greek or Cretan truth equivalent to the doctrine of the Holy Trinity, to that of Transubstantiation and of grace by redemption? This is, in fact, the crucial point. The orthodox Christians destroy their own case by raising it. There was in Greece and Crete no such fixed doctrine because there was no theology. There was no religion but the perception of fact. The contemplative faculties were used to connect and interpret the facts. This was the basis of a philosophy of a very high and, to some, unparalleled order. This philosophy began from the basis of revealed truth, and it is for this reason that philosophy of a transcendental nature has stood European man in better stead, and inflicted less agony on him, than the vapid though nevertheless menacing fabrications of Christianity.

What the Greeks and Cretans of classical antiquity were concerned with was not theological doctrine derived from ideas about truth but with something more basic, with, in fact, truth itself and the difference between truth and illusion. This Greek attitude spilled over to some degree in the life and work of Christ himself. He could well have functioned as a greek oracle of the highest order.

The idea that a culture like that of Greece, which produced so much that was exquisite in sculpture, poetry, philosophy and drama, was incapable of feeling or recording religious experience in the fullest oceanic sense of the word is rubbish. We must always remember that, in deploring the deficiencies of classical antiquity, orthodox Christians are comparing classical culture not to the teachings of Christ and the primitive Christianity of the first two centuries, but to the intellectually synthesized international theocracy which stands in no relation to life and the teachings of Christ.

What we are faced with, in speaking of the Greek, Cretan and Egyptian oracles who preceded Christ, is that they were chosen not because of their devotion to any theological system because none existed. They were concerned with the facts of life and the ordering of the universe and these were communicated to them directly. They were what we call sensitives, that is to say they were capable of hearing the voices and seeing the forms of discarnate entities as others hear and see living beings. They did this in virtue of a capacity of inner perception which transcended the use of the five senses and which was revealed in their capacity to see forms invisible to others and to hear voices inaudible to the multitude. They were not mad because their capacity to foretell the future accurately and to see the march of events before others indicates suprareality rather than confusion. Some of the truths of the universe they saw in virtue of their own innate powers of precognition, clairvoyance and the like. Other information was imparted to them by the discarnate entities, the messengers of the gods with whom they conversed. The acolytes who were permitted to consult them fully and regularly were themselves people of special constitution capable in their turn of becoming themselves oracles. Such people, both oracles and their acolytes, are still among us. We prefer to call them sensitives. Their value is enhanced or restricted according to the sophistication of the civilisation in which they live. Until recently, in the last two centuries, their use to mankind has not been considerable. Scientific man has seen to that.

Among the qualities of these people with special constitution a taste for theology is not included. Revealed truth disposes of the need for theology. That is why most Christian priesthoods are so suspicious of it. Ecclesiasticism is based on theologies rather than revelation. Love of the former very often impedes any aptitude for the latter. The Christian priest can argue that his faith is formed on supreme revelation. No supreme revelation is possible to us here on earth. The idea is ludicrous. In this world we have not the instrumentation to see the absolute and ultimate truths. To claim that we can do so is to lack humility.

The oracles who preceded Christianity were of essentially the same nature as the highly psychic in our own generation but their opportunities were greater. Like modern sensitives they were precognitive, clairvoyant, telepathic, with a heightened perception of atmospheres enabling them to assess quickly those who consulted them. They saw into the past and were in communication with discarnate entities. In the civilisations of Greece and Crete it is clear that some discarnates were regarded as gods and goddesses but it was more common for the oracles to speak, not with the so-called divinities in the Pantheon, but with their messengers who were of exactly the same nature as those discarnates of lower grade who talk to us in contemporary civilisation. The oracles had mediumistic qualities but did not permit themselves, except during periods of decadence, to be used for giving advice to the individual about his future and particularly for personal gain. By the time the emperors had been reduced to consulting the oracles as to the result of battles in which they were to be engaged the Mysteries had become decadent.

The trancelike states the mediumistic oracles were forced to assume were often accompanied by epileptic convulsions. It was for this reason that epilepsy was regarded as the sacred disease. In full trance, our contemporary psychics with the highest range of mediumistic gifts show epileptic signs but these do not proceed to the level of full convulsions in the creative sensitive. Long after the decline of Greece, epilepsy was still regarded, in Eastern Europe and the Middle East, as the sacred disease.

The capacity to communicate with discarnate entities is an absolute essential in the acquisition of truth. This must seem a whole world away from the Aristotelian conception and a whole universe away from the satanic, computerised concept of truth in virtue of which we have nailed ourselves to the cross of materialism. Nevertheless what I have said in this connection is fundamental. This is because it is only those who have undergone the educational process of death, that is to say the evolution of rebirth free from matter, who are able to communicate to us truths which we simply cannot absorb in our life on this planet because we have not the necessary equipment of heart and mind to do so.

Death is the supreme teacher. The aim of life is to prepare for death. Those who, in this life, hear the discarnates are already potentially dead to themselves and to the world otherwise they would not have acquired the capacity to communicate. It is against this undeniable concept that the Church, in all its multitudinous guises, has so resolutely set its face. It seems to me lacking in humility that it should not accept that those entities who have crossed the threshold of life and death and whom we recognise as good, are enabled to enlarge our vision and present us with aspects of the truth which we cannot see for ourselves.

This leads us to the crucial difference between contemporary Christianity and, not the religion, but the Mystery cults of Greece and Rome. Remember that the word signifies a secret hidden from the majority. To us the practice of Mysteries sounds like an elite talking to an elite, which is a shock to Christians, and above all to our evangelical and Protestant ideas that salvation is available to all who are prepared to receive it, independent of the observance of Church ritual. After all, for what did our Protestant ancestors die if it was not for direct access to the teachings of Christ in the vernacular? The Roman Church has never really claimed to dispense to all the teachings of Christ. It has preferred to offer to the people the messages interpreted by the saints and scholars of the Church. But, whether Catholic, Anglican or Protestant, the Christian approach to the truth is seen through a web of theology. The negation or watering down of such Catholic doctrines as Transubstantiation is just as much an intellectual veil obscuring us from the truth as is a full acceptance.

It is repugnant to our modern ideas, particularly in an age of democracy, either free or enforced, to envisage inequalities of opportunities in the search for truth. But such injustices are the lot of man and inexorably woven in the fabric of life. We should remember also that the statement that the sun shines on the just and the unjust alike applies only to this world and those nearest to it. In dwelling on the injustice of truth being communicated only to a few we are subscribing to the one man, one life, one chance of salvation idea which is wholly untenable. All I am saying at this stage is that those capable of appreciating revealed truth are necessarily in a minority. In this life they serve as a leaven for others until, in a succession of incarnations, they themselves have absorbed sufficiently the substance of truth to obviate the necessity of reincarnation and to enable them to exist in higher zones of consciousness where truth at its most absolute becomes accessible to them.

In this life the essence of truth is mostly revealed to us by discarnate entities. These are recruited from those who, while alive in this world, had attained something of the degree of insight possessed by those most accessible discarnates who, after death, remain in communication with us. This necessarily means that the number of people in this world at any time with direct access to the truth must, in our age at any rate, be necessarily small.

Before writing more of revealed truth it is necessary to study more fully the opposition exhibited towards it in the last two millennia. This involves a consideration of the nature and origins of the ecclesiastics who have directed us in these matters. This will be dealt with in the next chapter.

6.

Christ and the Feminine

The history of Christianity is that of its exploitation for profit by the ecclesiastical organisers of religion. One is tempted to say that this applied to all religions but we cannot be sure that this is true in the case of Hinduism, the origins of which are veiled in remotest antiquity. Certainly it can be said of Buddhism. The multiplication of Buddhist sub-deities in some areas is directly contrary to the teaching of the master. So is the ornamental ritual which often obscures the fact that from some points of view Buddhism is a philosophy, or even a psychological system, rather than a religion. Islam has never indulged in priests but the elders of the Church have exhibited, in the course of centuries, many of the worse attributes of the clergy. It is still possible for a princess to be killed because she wishes to marry according to the dictates of her heart. The leader of a forward-looking Arab state with Marxist leanings is still so pleasingly old fashioned as to wish to restore the penalty of stoning to death for women taken in adultery. One understands, with fatal ease, that this gentleman is a devout moralist.

In these matters it is better to avoid too universalised generalisations and to stick to Christianity which still influences us whether or no we have reacted against it. I am convinced that, in the subtler reaches of psychology, it is an easy, sloppy and inefficient safety valve to say that men are the same all the world over. This simply cannot be so. The contents of the unconscious of man must vary enormously according to the part of the world and the particular culture in which he is reared.

The Old Testament was composed in those centuries, or even millennia, before Christ which saw the flowering of

Cretan and Greek culture. As we have indicated in the last chapter, the religious experience of Greece and Crete was not organised in terms of doctrine, as it was in the Old and New Testaments. The Mysteries were direct communication to those capable of benefiting by them, plus simpler instruction to less perceptive subjects. The Greek and Cretan Mysteries were only transmitted orally. One Greek dramatist was tried for having profaned the Mysteries by revealing their nature. Plato himself has been accused of committing to writing what he remembered, or had gathered, of the Mysteries but by this time the latter had been corrupted and lost significance.

It is absolutely fundamental to realise that there is no Greek literature which directly brings us the actual nature of the Mysteries.

The Old Testament is quite another matter. Here a great deal of space is taken up by the history of the Jewish people and a considerable amount of attention devoted to the practice of the Jewish faith. Note that one says practice rather than religious experience or even belief. Without indulging in esoteric speculation we have to admit that it is difficult, from scrutiny of the Old Testament to discover what the Jews of those days actually believed. What they had to *do* was clear enough. What was required of them was that they accepted only their own God, their most significant and dubious contribution to theology. A good deal of attention is devoted to the externals of practice; indeed there are parts of the Old Testament which resemble remarkably the manuals of hygiene written by committed Victorians who washed their souls clean with soap and water.

Monotheism, as revealed in the Old Testament, does not lead us to believe that it was, in its beginnings, the great forward step it came to be regarded by the Christians. First it was merely an extension of the insistence that the Jewish god was superior, that is to say more efficient, than that of other nations. He established his claim to dominion over others by his greater skill in the exercise of power and in the conscientiousness he displayed in the wholesale slaughter of his enemies. One cannot take seriously the counting of the foreskins of the Philistines as a religious ritual. The Old Testament God exhibits indeed all that is most aggressive in the male nature. This leads us to a still more cardinal point.

The Old Testament covers, in its vast scope and across deserts of unutterable tedium, references to the Gods of other nations. Sometimes it lets itself go and refers to female gods. These are all, without exception, unspeakable. To worship anything other than the God of Israel was an abomination. To replace a male by a female deity was unthinkable. Names like Ashtaroth implied vice at its most profligate, dedicated to the service of evil.

It is clearly implied throughout the Old Testament that woman is the temptress, potentially evil and a snare to mankind. The Bible always begins with this assumption. Evil is introduced into the world by Adam and Eve eating the forbidden fruit. The nature of the latter is not specified, but the male Adam, and whoever wrote the book of Genesis have no doubt where the blame lies. "The woman tempted me." This bleating alibi has never ceased to echo down the clerical and secular corridors of society. There can be no doubt that the truly original sin was regarded as sexual. Arguments based on allegory are not necessarily illuminating. They may intensify the shadows of ignorance. Certainly the erring couple became aware of their nakedness and covered their sexual organs with fig leaves. The latter were acting clearly as a cloak for sin and the location of the latter was specifically indicated. True, enlightened religion begins in sexuality. It cannot do otherwise because the creation of men, animals and plants were the first miracles with which primitive man was confronted. The sin of the Old Testament was, from the very beginning, to mingle guilt and religion. Worse still the blame for the second fall of man was not equally shared. Holy Scripture leaves us no doubt that the woman was the chief transgressor.

Scattered through the Bible are numerous references to women as the natural polluters, both physical and moral, of man. Some of these references read like manuals of hygiene. Woman is a physical contaminant and to be treated as such. A moral inferiority is often taken for granted. Worse that this she is regarded almost as a spiritual impediment, something which has fallen across man's path to enable him to have children and to be conveniently forgotten once this has been achieved. Adultery in a woman is punishable by death. At the same time Solomon and David are free to pursue their female chattels and the latter arranged a

convenient posting for Bathsheba's husband. Though the Old
Testament is saturated with this anti-feminine attitude a little
common humanity seeps in through the crevices. The Song
of Songs, a seemingly erotic hymn, has been described as a
mystical invocation of Sophia, the heavenly wisdom, the
latter conceived of as woman, but the arguments adduced are
not impressive. One should also remember that, possibly as
an act of sanitation, the Song of Songs was relegated to the
Apocrypha.

We learn in Holy Scripture that in heaven there is not only
no marriage and no giving in marriage but there is only one
sex. It is argued, rightly, in defence of the writer that he is
trying to convey that in heaven the souls of the departed
have shed the hazards of sex. But why the statement that all
the souls will be male? This is unmistakeable evidence of
belief in masculine superiority. Heaven is, after all,
conceived of as a reward. The Koran is even more specific
than the Bible. It states with legalistic finality that woman is
an inferior being.

It would be comforting to say that all this changed with
the New Testament but this is not so. Certainly it can be said
of Christ that he was in revolt against the doctrine of male
superiority. To me his exhortation of what I have in former
days called the woman principle is his most significant
exoteric contribution. Respect for women is a pretty good
yardstick by which to measure the level attained by a
civilisation or culture. Christ's attitude to Mary Magdalene is
highly significant. He treats her as an equal. He goes further
than this in his statement that her sins will be forgiven
because she has loved much. He implies that the physical
love she bestowed on many was itself worthwhile. It is not
necessary to infer from this that he himself had availed
himself of her services. Such ideas as these are an example
of the desire to shock which is the best contemporary culture
can do in the way of inspiration. Such statements do,
however, at least hint that Christ excluded sexualilty from his
assessment of human beings and of the moral systems of his
day. His compassionate attitude to the woman taken in
adultery is astonishing seen against the punitive background
of his times. Christ's intervention on behalf of the woman
was altogether revolutionary. We must also consider his
attitude to the woman of Samaria at the well. To the world

she had one husband. Christ revealed to her that he knew that she had had three men. There does not appear to have been anything condemnatory in His attitude. Among the number of persons specifically named in the Gospels as belonging to the entourage of Christ the proportion of women is remarkably high. It should, had they been able to think logically, have given the more ascetic desert fathers of the first and second centuries food for thought. No other world prophet has been recorded to have included so many women in His circle. Remember the women stayed with Him up to and including his Crucifixion. No such feminine associations are attributed to Buddha, after he received enlightenment, to Lao-tse, Confucius, Plato and the rest.

Christ is not only concerned with the emancipation of women for the sake of emancipation and common justice. He recognises, as do all prophets worth their salt, that the female virtues of intuition and compassion are not merely more praiseworthy but nearer to God and reality than the aggressive attributes of the male. It is a tragedy that some of the immortal figures in the Christian story had little or no idea that woman can act as a catalyst transforming man into a creature of God. St. Augustine lived with a woman and described himself as loving her. He makes it quite clear, however, that the battle is on between his love of the woman and the salvation of his soul. The idea that the former can contribute to the latter is not considered. This repellent character who excluded from the city of God the woman he had loved is one of the major saints of Christianity. Mere human nature can be forgiven for seeing him as a sententious cad.

Abelard is another father of the Church who merits a little closer inspection. He packs Heloise off to a nunnery having developed, since his castration, a greater concern for his soul. His love for Heloise is not in doubt. What is clear for all the world to see is that he regards it as an incidental beauty come into his life and cannot see that she could, more than anyone else, have acted as his way to God. I have watched the face of an earnest English convert to Catholicism regarding me with dumb wonder, and saying that he could not understand how I could put the love of the woman to whom I was married before the love of God. The idea that the one is not only supplementary but a guide to the other was beyond his comprehension. One might, in these particular matters, amend the word of Christ to say that if you cannot love the woman you can see, how can you love the God you can't see. In any case the claim of any human being, Christian or otherwise, to know the nature of God is totally blasphemous. We in this world are so low in the hierarchy that we cannot see God at all from our present point of disadvantage, and if we glimpse a little of his nature, it is most often through the intervention of those discarnates higher than the hierarchy who wish to instruct us a little.

The true prophet has a markedly female psyche. The passive, receptive nature of the latter facilitates the timeless experience. Without the latter there would be no precognition and clairvoyance and therefore no prophecy. Equally there can be no truth because the latter, in its absolute and concrete form, is mostly relayed from the higher echelons of the hierarchy, with God at the pinnacle and behind him the eternal feminine. It is passed on to us from these elevated strata through the discarnates still in contact with the living. It is, however, the fate of the prophet with the female psyche, that what is felt and transmitted orally to those in his immediate circle becomes organised into an intellectualised dogma which is a form of male aggression. Men have the impulse to dominate others. Where they are incapable of doing so by physical force, or where the circumstances are unpropitious for its exercise, they use as their weapons systems of ideas. This is what Paul is already doing in the Epistles. Certainly his virtues are more than have been allowed him by would-be mystical Christians with a genuine, if sentimental, attraction to St. John. But there can be no doubt that in his writing women are put firmly in their place, and it is stated clearly that to make themselves attractive to men is infinitely to their discredit. The excuse that Paul was talking to Greek women, against a background of loose morals in a decadent period, and that he had therefore to treat them like Girl Guides, is naive. Perhaps in writing his Epistles to the Corinthians he was influenced by the idea that every nice girl loves a sailor.

In describing the prophets and others as having female psyches one is not referring in any way to homosexuality. Many males have virile, active and strongly masculine personalities, but at the psychic level, are strongly feminine.

To say that because a man is gentle, compassionate and intuitive rather than a reasoning animal he is necessarily inclined to homosexuality is rubbish. In that case all the best doctors must be homosexual, a fact which has certainly escaped my notice. Incidentally, I have only met one with the slightest tendency that way. One should note that many homosexuals are prone to ascribe such virtues to themselves, and, in addition, to claim that a ridiculously disproportionate fraction of the world's culture is attributable to their efforts. Contemporary attempts have been made to show that Christ was a homosexual. These are said to be based on psychology and are imperceptive to the point of dementia. Another such foetid but contagious idea is that art is not art unless it is super-saturated with sex in its less common forms. People who produce works of this nature are only thinking on one plane. They cannot escape from that of personality. The latter is always classified in terms of gender. Those prophets with female psyches are beyond gender and are expressions of an ultimate creative cosmic principle which Goethe called the Eternal Feminine. The latter is totally beyond the world of gender. When one talks of the Eternal Feminine or the Mother Goddess one is referring not to sex qua sex but to an eternally passive attitude best called feminine but no more sexual, in the human sense of the word, than the earth waiting to be fertilised in Spring.

It can be argued that what we have said of the subjugation of women in Old Testament times, and even after Christ's death and the establishment of Islam, is merely an example of the low grade of civilisation to be expected at those times, something we have in fact grown out of. This is a poor argument. We cannot pinpoint accurately the dates of the early books in the Old Testament but we know that in the Cretan and Greek civilisations which preceded or coincided with them the status of women was infinitely higher than in the Middle East. We can go farther than this and say that woman, far from being the temptress and the whore, was in those early days in the Aegean the purveyor of truth. In the Mystery cults the prophetesses were at first dominant. Males were not placed in positions of authority, neither were they given the status of priests. The replacement of priestesses by priests was the beginning of the decadence at Eleusis.

The farther we go back in antiquity the more the

purveying of truth and healing is the prerogative of woman.
It is no good dwelling on the little notice given in Plato and
Socrates to women. These men have been almost deified by
repressed English homosexuals, happy to know that the
passion for a choirboy with acne is amongst the highest
human achievements. In any case in Plato's day the rot had
already set in. Men had begun to define what once they felt
and this is always a downward step. Even in the days of
Socrates and Plato, the female courtesan was often a woman
of culture capable of bestowing consolation, a kind of
tarnished descendant of the early priestesses. Perhaps they
acted as an antidote to the over-intellectualised, point
scoring attitude to truth adopted by these two masters we
reverence so much. We may be stirred, by their intellectual
subtlety, to believe in the existence of an immortal psyche
but such an idea is a pale shadow beside the word spoken to
the oracles by the discarnates because the latter acquire
greater wisdom by the transfiguring experience of death.
What we hear from those nearer the ultimate reality, or, if
you like, the hub of the universe, is superior to anything
organised by synthesized and intellectual truth. In all
fairness this element does appear in Plato's writing. He
acknowledged inspiration from discarnate sources, and said
that all that was good in his work came from God through
the intervention of his daemon.

To understand more fully the dominant and healthy role
of the priestesses we have to go back further in history and
study the connection of religion with sex and fertility but, in
the meantime, it is necessary to point out that the
ecclesiastical attitude to woman as an inferior being is very
much alive among us, at least in Europe. The Catholic
Church took the simple and logical measure of preaching the
celibacy of the priesthood. That in the twelfth and thirteenth
centuries priests lived in open concubinage is hardly likely
to be accidental. The poetry of the troubadours, extending
from twelfth century Provence and the Languedoc to its
successors in Italy in the fourteenth century, was an
attempt to return to the evaluation of woman as conceived of
not only in primitive Christianity but in remotest antiquity.
Many of the unnamed ladies to whom the Provencal
troubadours addressed their poems, along with Dante's
Beatrice, Petrach's Laure and Boccaccio's Fiametta,

represented a kind of concentrated divine wisdom, a female holy spirit or a return to the Eternal Feminine, a conception which was a light in the darkness in a priest-dominated community. This died away with the passing of the Renaissance. It is noteworthy that, in Michaelangelo's Last Judgement in the Sistine Chapel, all the male figures including Christ appear ill-tempered. The Virgin Mary is a shade better but the most beautiful and reposeful face is that of the oracle of Delphi.

When the Catholic Church was replaced by Calvinism the status of women was not enhanced. There were Catholics sufficiently pagan to be sensuous and to know on which side their bread was buttered. The teachings of Calvinism in certain countries produced such open revelations of the psychopathology of the ecclesiastic mentality as John Knox's fulminations against the monstrous regiment of women. Not twenty years ago a number of his fellow countrymen, presumably endowed with a modicum of insight, good Presbyterians and Free Church of Scotland men, refused to attend the annual dinner of the local clinical society because their wives, not common law but blessed in matrimony by the Church, were to be allowed to eat with their husbands for the first time in the club's history. The pure had a rival dinner in another place on the same night. Perhaps some of these men must have noticed that their own mothers and those of their children were women. Perhaps they resented the fact.

Relics of woman conceived of as the polluter of man remain in the Anglican literature. The churching of women is described as a thanksgiving for the birth of the infant but surely the element of purifying the woman creeps in, otherwise why is the father not Churched? This is a polite survival of practices in primitive tribes who insist on the segregation of women during menstruation and during and after childbirth.

I have often thought that I would have been better employed writing a natural history of the British people with the woman as slave as a cardinal theme. It is well enough to argue that woman has gained equal entry to the professions — is it all that equal? — but do the intelligentsia know what, after two thousand years of Christian civilisation, was the lot of the working class woman up to the advent of the affluent society twenty years ago? I was very reluctant to put leading questions to women about their symptoms. It was more profitable to allow them to do the work for me. At the same time I questioned them about their social background to a degree which they had obviously never experienced before, and which they obviously thought bordered on the indecent. I learnt that it was almost the rule for a girl who, while courting, had been taken to the cinema or the pubs every night of the week, to go for ten years after marriage without a single such cultural divertissement. Well over eighty per cent of the women did not know how much their husbands earned a week and regarded my question as blasphemous. When a little more information was forthcoming it was common to discover that the husband spent as much on beer and cigarettes in a week as he allowed his wife for her maintenance and that of the house and two or three children. These men were not monsters. They were merely living on the assumption that they and their wives were receiving just portions to which they were entitled. The women accepted this view. The working class mother in my early days of practice spoilt her sons abominably at the expense of her daughters. Not all this was the Judeo-Christian inheritance but at least it goes to show that the female virtues has had little effect in two millennia of so-called female virtues has little effect in two millennia of so-called Christian civilisation. The persistence of Judeo-Christianity, that is to say Christianity still heavily impregnated with the teachings of the old Testament, is still shown in the Sabbatarianism of countries where extreme Calvinism prevailed. In my young manhood it was still taboo in Scotland to play cards or even the piano, except for hymns, on a Sunday. On the Sabbath there was not a single cafe or tea shop open in Edinburgh's main street. How this ties up with Christ's statement that the Sabbath was made for man and not man for the Sabbath I do not know, any more than I can explain what is the relation of such restrictions to religious experience.

In all religions we encounter restrictions and taboos which have little relation to religious experience and are of no deep esoteric significance. The symbolism of washing before entering the mosque and of bathing in the Ganges is obvious and need not be laboured. The cleansing of the body is preparatory to and facilitates the cleansing of the soul. It is all absolutely without foundation but as long as there are men on earth there will be those who derive great benefit from the fact that many share their illusions. From whence arises the obsessional ritual of so many religions, the insistence on strict dogma, in itself of no religious significance, the idea of woman as inferior and the temptress, and the erecting by males of theological systems which dominate by the threat of the withdrawal of grace if the ideas expressed in these systems are not accepted by the faithful? It must always be remembered that the system of ideas, whether clerical or lay, is a means of coercion. To some degree such systems are necessary. One has no patience with the intelligentsia who have no use for those concepts for law and order without which their inapplicable minority ideas would be engulfed in chaos or brutally eliminated. But is what is necessary to maintain some sort of order in a secular community required to confirm in verbal systems the inexpressible phenomena of religious experience? What, in fact, are the origins of priesthood and why, within its rigid establishments, have its governing members become almost exclusively male? To answer these questions we have to go back to the primordial sources of religious experience. In doing so we will do well to limit ourselves to the European and Middle Eastern origins of the Christianity in which my generation was reared. What one says could apply largely to some aspects of far Eastern religions.

7.

Women and Religion

There can be no doubt that the beginnings of religious experience were in sexuality and its consequences. It must be understood from the start that one is not preaching, rehashing or justifying in any way the doctrines of Freud which have had so potent an effect on Western civilisation. Freud is simply not primordial enough. Religion began when the consciousness of man began to ponder his origins. This surely takes us millions of years back. It is difficult to conceive of any sentient being failing to wonder how or why he got here.

In the beginning man's first religious or philosophic attitude must have been to distinguish between light and darkness. We use these phrases nowadays to symbolise good and evil but to our distant ancestors the light and darkness *were* good and evil. The light enabled man to go hunting while he still lived a nomadic existence. It permitted him later to dig his earth and plant corn. With the coming of night he could do nothing for the maintenance of his own existence. This was also the time when his enemies and hostile animals lay in wait for him in the forest. Amid the fears and hazards of his stressful existence man needed a comforter. He discovered the sedative value of certain herbs but this was pitifully impotent and and acted so slowly in moments of crisis compared with sexual contact with a woman. Here we see the beginnings of the woman as comforter, as the supreme, combined excitant and sedative whose calming effects were felt all the more because of the excitement she first aroused in the male. Sex, to our first ancestors, was the prime consolation. In a huge proportion of cases it is to this day.

Note well that one stresses the consoling element in sex. It is generally accepted that sexual desire in the male is a kind of generous overflow of high spirits and that his desire for a woman is highest when he is feeling good. This is favoured by poets in whom optimism is a substitute for talent. "In the Spring a young man's fancy, lightly turns to thoughts of love". Is the word "lightly" justified? Is there not in much sexuality in the male a note, if not of desperation, of some inevitable fate? In my experience, the desires of the male are often at their maximum when he is most tense, anxious and so tired that sex, logically speaking, would seem out of the question. It is assumed by many psychiatrists that depression reduces the sex urge. This is true in some cases where depression is intense but to make it a rule reveals that the therapist's powers of observation are limited. There are many anxiety-depressions in which sexuality reaches its maximum with the intensification of the attacks. In an agony in which men feel their own isolation and total apartness, they crave for the Oneness which, though given to them all too fleetingly by a woman, is nevertheless a symbolisation of the cosmic harmony from which we are derived and to which we will all ultimately return.

It was inevitable that when man lived close to nature, he learnt truth at first hand because he had to do so in order to live. Against such a background he must have credited woman with gifts he thought magical. She had, in her body, the power to console him, to remove his fears, to provide sensations of delight and to induce the frenzied forgetfulness of the orgasm. Was there not therefore something magical in her composition, something of the goddess insofar as they were able to conceive of such beings? This feeling was reinforced by the observation that what was also a delight conferred other benefits. She was able to produce children who later would work for him and serve him in his old age. This attitude, together with the worship of the sun, which brought light and goodness by day, was the beginnings of the worship of the Mother Goddess, who, in her sexuality, was the supreme personal consoler and, in her fertility, the assurance of the continuance of the species. The understandable reverence of the sun merged with the cult of the Mother Goddess. In remotest antiquity the sun was regarded as feminine. How can anything so cold, disdainful and withdrawn as the moon be feminine? Was not femininity expressed by the warmth, ardour and quickening growth produced by the sun? We retain this old belief in the sun's femininity when we talk, with reason, of the man in the moon.

The woman, as the extension on earth of the Mother Goddess,

was also not only responsible, through her own innate fertility, for the continuance of the species but for the fertility of the crops. Women and the light were thought of in unison with each other. The light and warmth of the sun was necessary for the growth of the corn and other edible plants. Sex, fertility of human beings and crops, the light, the sun and religion were all incorporated together in a single system. The origins of religious experience in sex, fertility and the sun is something which has to be accepted. This is not to denigrate religious experience. Far from it. What one has said gives to the whole substance of what is called religion a greater reality. The word religion is itself an obstacle to reality. One uses it because it has become the custom and without so doing one's own meaning might be less plain. I myself would prefer to stick to such simple phrases as truth seen in contradiction to illusion. Religion is essentially in its organised form a secondary process. It is a reaching back to lost realities. Among what we have lost is the connecting thread between the primitive and justifiable belief in the connection between religion, sex and fertility and such ultimate revelations as those provided by the teachings of Lao-tse and the life of Christ.

In view of what one has said it was only natural that, when man moved up from the biological level and became a more feeling and thinking being, when, on the evidence presented, he opted for a deity, he chose something between the woman with whom he lived and the goddess, and a priestess or female oracle rather than a male priest. As we have mentioned, in the first Mystery cults women were dominant. They supplied the priesthood and the men served in an inferior capacity. One of their earlier concerns was healing. This was natural. They had in their bodies what was regarded as a semi-divine capacity to soothe the anguish of men by sexuality. This led inevitably to healing. If woman could sooth one pain, she could well heal others. Of course healing by sexuality still continued. It persisted until the Eleusinian Mysteries in Greece. The Greek tradition of the sexual woman consoler continued for a long time. The hetaira or Greek courtesan, persisting until Plato's day, was a cultured woman qualified to advise and to comfort mentally as well as physically. The temple women in the Hindu faith and the exponents of Tantric Buddhism still practice sexuality on the grounds that it is only by such means that some kinds of men are enabled to obtain a glimpse of that Oneness which leads ultimately to Nirvana. I have heard it said in our day that prostitution begins in pity. This is a convenient and stimulating phrase that needs amplifying. There is a kind of woman who realises that she can only comfort with her body. She therefore does so but without asking the recompense we associate with prostitution. Such women are usually basically respectable and are to be found in greater numbers in periods of national calamities such as war. The stimulating motive is that the doomed warrior should be consoled on his way to the shades.

Death on a large scale also stimulates what is called promiscuousness. This was noticeable during the earthquake at Messina in the early years of the century. In such calamities as these the Mother Goddess impulse is operating on a wide scale to console the bereaved. The mother impulse is also in action. Nature is replacing by widespread sexual activity what has been suddenly lost. This happens not only in mass disasters. There are women who have suffered bereavement who are instigated immediately to create another life and replace what has been lost. These people are far from being monsters. They are literally repressed by systems of morality. They are the secret heretical emissaries of the Mother Goddess.

Gradually, inevitably, except for a diminishing minority, the priestesses of classical antiquity abandoned the woman's power to heal and console by sexual activity.[1] The next supremely logical step was for women to become healers but with the process of healing extending over a larger period than the brief paroxysms of sexuality and designed to deal with more diverse conditions. This was often achieved by the laying on of hands, to be regarded as a direct continuation of sexuality in being another form of physical contact. Later, the imposition of hands became an art which utilised for its purpose a knowledge of the physiology of the body. Now no true healer has healing as her sole psychic capacity. She is also precognitive, clairvoyant and telepathic. The priestesses of Crete, Greece and to a less degree Roman antiquity became therefore in virtue of their gifts of clairvoyance and precognition, oracles as well as healers. Those who were richly endowed with a particular capacity practiced more exclusively their own speciality. The precognitive and clairvoyant became prophets. The healers functioned principally as such and combined their healing with their other activities.

The most outstanding characteristic of the psychic is that detailed far memory for several past incarnations is always accompanied by the intense development of precognition,

clairvoyance, telepathy and healing. This is because the annihilation of time involved in far memory is accompanied by the
above mentioned capacities which operate out of time. Far
memory for several past lives is also inevitably accompanied by
the capacity to communicate with discarnate entities. It has
been said that one must distinguish completely between true
cases of reincarnation and what is said to us by discarnate
entities and can be misinterpreted as evidence of reincarnation.
This is a very misleading half truth. What those who argue in this
way fail to realise is that, at a certain stage in the psychic's
personal evolution, it is from discarnate sources that his
knowledge of reincarnation is added to and confirmed. He is
also supplied directly with other truths, the most important of
which is what happens to us after death. Truth of this nature is
the most positive we are likely to achieve with true and
disinterested discarnates because, after all, they are, in our
terms, described as dead and can report directly, telling sensitives
what happens in worlds beyond our own. One says true and
disinterested discarnates. This means those who seek us out
rather than we them and who announce in doing so their
credentials to us. They often require of us that we work hard to
verify their credentials. I myself had to toil hard at an epic of
historical verification before I satisfied myself that one of my
chief discarnate mentors was Braida de Montserver. I had to do
the same historical checking to know that my most intimate
guide was Helise de Mazerolles, or Camillia as she was known in
the Roman incarnation, but here I had also to undergo months
during which this was revealed to me through a series of
synchronizations described in *The Lake And The Castle*.

We are always sought out for a special purpose, to transmit
the truth. Whether we choose to do so is left to us. I would have
been glad to escape from the pain of some of my re-echoes of the
past but it is impossible for me to contemplate that I could ever
have failed to relay the truths imparted to me. It was after all for
this reason that they were shared with me. There is a huge
distinction between those chosen by the discarnates who
instruct us creatively, and those who seek positively to establish
communion with the dead, to learn a little more of their destiny
or to acquire an effortless summary of our past incarnations
which can have no positive use if we are not ready for it. No
properly evolved discarnate entity, occupying a place in the
cosmic hierarchy, will act as a gypsy on a fairground and tell the

future to us because we ask to know it. To attempt to use this kind of discarnate to seek contact with the dead may lead to distortion and error. We should only be happy in making contact with the discarnates when it is their wish and not ours.

What I have said above applies to the highly psychic in all ages and in ancient Greece and Crete as it does now. In a word we do not ask to be told the truth. To me there are strict limits to the degree to which we should seek it. The highest truth we can achieve is what we acquire from such discarnates as I have described through the agency of those human sensitives whose precognitive and clairvoyant capacities have been observed for years and never found wanting. We must of course be aware that we live in an age of false prophets. When a minority are raised to a higher state of awareness, usually at the end of a civilisation, the sheep are confused with the goats, and unassertive and often anonymous transmitters of truth are engulfed by those who, under the cloak of pretentious nomenclature, sell half truths and lies in the market place for personal profit. This state of affairs prevails at the moment in Western Europe and resembles greatly that of Rome in the decadence, when the incorruptible instruments of truth were outnumbered by hordes of soothsayers consulted by the credulous and frightened to learn the future in the vain hope of avoiding its horrors or reaping its benefits. Many oracles with genuine gifts who lent themselves to such procedures were themselves contaminated. The same is true today.

It is in this exploitation of the highly psychic oracles of antiquity that we see the beginnings of organised religion as we know it. Who first transformed the Mysteries so that Eleusis became a congested Mecca of the ancient world? We can be sure it was the work of man as distinct from women. Slowly, inexorably, the Mysteries became contaminated by the male impulse to dominate. In them we saw the first seeds of the diabolism which contrived alliances between Church and State. The Christs of different epochs may say clearly that their kingdom is not of this world, but men will see to it that the prophet's kingdom is established on earth with, of course, suitable rationalisations to the effect that it is only by suitable organization and the formulation of doctrine that the work of the prophet can be preserved.

One can see clearly how such a state of affairs came about. A woman had the gift of healing or prophecy. This could be turned to profit. One is not speaking of profit in coarse terms involving monetary gain. The transmutation is more subtle than that. Woman has powers, in the plural. Improperly utilised she can become the agent for giving man the horrifying gift of power. Man is inevitably the organizer. Woman gives naturally and anonymously. This is part of her essential nature. To this day the women I have met with the greatest gifts shun publicity and have a passion for anonymity. This has become heightened in the passage of years because they have been heretics. So many were burnt as witches and heretics once male domination was established.

With the replacement of scattered female oracles, unorganized into Mystery cults with a name, the step downward began. This woman was able to heal, another to prophecy and a third to see into past lives. But why should such pearls be scattered before swine? Did she not need an organizer and keeper to see that she was not exploited or, the most subtle argument of all, to ensure that her gifts were used in the interests of humanity as a whole? This is the most diabolical insinuation of all and is used by those who care, or affect to care, for an amorphous entity they call suffering humanity rather than for suffering people.

Gradually the supply dries up. In the course of time the gifted and genuine psychic woman refuses to be further exploited. Those who offer themselves are inferior material. Those who go on alone are regarded by the male organizers with hate and designated as witches. With the attempt to organize truth, which includes true gifts, into religions and sects the role of the woman is finished. This is something that the gifted female oracles not only see themselves. It is demanded of them by their male organizers who have now become their aggressors and persecutors.

The male priesthood is at this stage faced with a problem. It can no longer utilise genuine gifts of healing and precognition, natural to a minority and falsely defined as supernatural, and is faced with the necessity of replacing what was thought miraculous but sinful by something more dramatic, and if possible magical, of its own devising.

The situation did not become critical for the budding male ecclesiastic until the birth of Christ. This was because, to the male priesthood, psychic gifts were conferred on female oracles by some god or goddess in the classical pantheon. In the beginning there was nothing interposed between the woman expressing the truth and the sources of truth. She practised her precognition and clairvoyance in virtue of her own gifts but the truths of life, death and reincarnation which she imparted were given to her directly from the messengers of the so-called gods whom, as we have seen, were themselves discarnates, exceptional in this world and endowed with the power still to communicate with it. One of the first efforts of the organising male ecclesiastic was to assert himself between the oracle and the discarnate sources of her wisdom. In this he degraded her function. What she had previously dispensed was the whole truth about life, death and the zones of higher consciousness succeeding it, reincarnation and the psyche's ultimate destiny. The function of the priest was to ensure a partial fragmentation of truth. She was forced to submit to the male attitude that you cannot dispense too much truth at a time and conserve a reputation for possessing powers. The latter word ultimately became translated into the more sinister description of power alone.

This seizing of prestige and power by the male priesthood is shown in their manipulation of the Mysteries. In the earlier manifestations of the latter, the acolyte, already psychic and on the verge of far memory, was enabled, by the gentle co-operation of the oracle, to see past lives for himself with a little prompting and redirection from his mentor. (This natural healthy process is what happens today where those with a knowledge of past lives never inject into others information calculated to make them obsessed with their previous incarnation). These old, wise, gradual initiation ceremonies were degraded into something like such modern short-cuts as regression by hypnosis or drugs. The infiltrating male priesthood, in the decadence of the Mysteries, offered sudden increase of insight, in itself an impossibility, to the leaders of the world. The latter acquired prestige and with it increments of earthly power from having received the Mysteries.[2] In addition, they received information as to the outcome of future battles, sometimes reliable and sometimes fraudulent. To sum up, the direction of the Mystery cults by male priesthoods resulted in their degradation because by this time their practice was contaminated with the desire for personal gain.

The shifting of the balance of power in the Mysteries from the woman to the male priest resulted in the steady depletion of the psychic potential of those presiding over them. The male priests were not endowed with the psychic powers of the female oracles who preceded them. They sought to remedy this deficiency by the employment of what cannot be called magic in the strict sense of the term, but which certainly involved mechanical accessories to stimulate perception and aid recollection of past lives. The use of mirrors reflecting light and darkness is an example of this tendency. This half-hearted, symbolic, almost innocent magic, was to be replaced later by the immense and potent magic the raw material of which was provided by the crucifixion of Christ.

At the time of the birth of Christ the known world swarmed with the wreckage of the Mysteries, with self-appointed priests of bogus cults offering salvation and psychic powers at a set fee. The situation approximated to what is advertised about the current gurus on the posters of the London Underground today. In Rome the vestal virgins were still venerated as sacred to the state, as the House of Lords is still a holy of holies to certain clubmen. But the vestal virgins in no sense resemble the female oracles of Greek antiquity. Nothing was expected of them in the way of healing, and little in the way of prophecy. They were to a large extent a state investment in the supposed power of virginity. It is significant that in their later history they were allowed to return to what one might call lay existence at the age of eighteen. Perhaps the Roman belief in the power of virginity was not deep rooted. New organisations claiming to be continuations of the ancient Mysteries were founded and flourished, with sex as the predominant note in the harmony with a little religion mixed with the other ingredients as an aperitif. The women involved were the pathetic and debased descendants of the cultivated hetaira. They were more degenerate than the women of Corinth who so upset Paul. (Nobody has recorded how these unfortunate women reacted to him).

It is vital to realise that, while the European scene pullulated with mystery cults, either decadent or orgiastic, with psychics, semi-psychics and pretentious frauds wrapped up in esoteric garments, in Judea a rigid, long-established, austere and powerful priesthood was still preaching, as it had for centuries, the letter of the law and implying that woman was an inferior and polluted being. In the Greek civilisation which prepared the ground for Christianity, the woman, as consoler, healer and prophetess, working within the confines of the Mysteries, had largely disappeared from the scene. (Individuals continued the anonymous practice of these basic, creative feminine arts as they have always done and will continue to do in isolation no matter what civilisation we are condemned to undergo in the future). In spite of the decay of the Mysteries as a living force, no male ecclesiastical system analogous to Judaism had established itself on the shores of the Aegean by the time of the coming of Christ. By male ecclesiasticism one means the tendency of a masculine group to dominate by systems of ideas based on metaphysical abstractions such as we still encounter when the Church gives itself too feverishly to subjects such as the doctrine of Transubstantiation and the concept of the Holy Trinity. The ecclesiastical mentality existed in excelsis in Judea. An appropriate raw material was available in the Aegean countries where budding ecclesiastics could be recruited from the wreckage of the Mysteries and from the probing metaphysicians in which these regions abounded.

Both Judaic and Hellenic elements were provided with, and seized, a great opportunity with the coming of Christ. Here was a male worker of such wonders of healing and prophecy as had been, in centuries previously in Greece and Crete, to a large extent the prerogative of women. While his life was an opportunity, his Crucifixion was a godsend. He had not only died on the cross but had been seen many times after death by his disciples and had spoken with them. Here was a worker of miracles whose powers did not cease after death. Here was the oracle to end all oracles, who had died a dramatic and ignoble death. While those who had loved Christ continued to work, motivated by the emanation of his presence, the special circumstances of his death gave to an incipient Christian priesthood an opportunity he himself would have spurned as another temptation of the devil. By the energies of Paul and other mistaken Evangelists the magical as distinct from the psychic was introduced into Christianity. The miracles of Christ were not magical or supernatural. They were the inevitable by-products of the emanation of his personality. Magic was introduced with the idea that Christ was the Son of God who had died on the Cross to save us from our sins, in itself a resurrection of the pagan idea of the blood sacrifice, that the king must die for his people. Magic is the cement on which the fabric of Churches is built. The stones are the works of the healers and prophets but the foundations are laid by those eager to make coherent, from the divine nebulae of religious experience, the unremitting dogma of religious practice.

For the first decades after Christ there were still those who, stimulated by his emanation and transmitting it to others, were able to reproduce his healing feats and his prophetic utterances. As early as Paul, who never knew Christ and qualified for writing about him by having persecuted his adherents, the perversion had begun. This, as near as we can say, was round about 80 AD. In saying this one is well aware that the modern denigration of Paul is excessive. He did at least grasp that Christianity was a spiritist movement. It was later, in the numerous councils which began in the third century, that Christianity became what it was and still would like to be, a dogmatic, rigid theocracy based on magic and recruited not from people with special gifts like those concerned with the expression of truth in the ancient Mysteries, but from people who acquired power by manufacturing their own weapons, the dicta of theology. It is absolutely indisputable that nothing of the basic dogma of Christianity is represented in the contemporary or near contemporary gospels. There is no reference to Transubstantiation, the Holy Trinity or to the gospel of Redemption by grace. The historical basis of Christianity is there, that Christ was born the son of a virgin in Bethlehem. While it is certainly implied that he was not born by natural means, an event which has been attributed to other prophets before him, it is certainly not said specifically that he was conceived by the Holy Ghost. The latter was also a product of the theologians.

How did the fathers of the Church persuade people to accept these theological abstractions in which there is no truth but which have nevertheless persisted for almost two millennia? The answer is that such a gigantic confidence trick could not have been contrived except on a basis of magic. Those who, in his own lifetime, had, or would have been, inimical to Christ and what he taught accepted, and possibly added to, the miracles which had so influenced simpler and less contaminated minds. They absorbed lock, stock and barrel not only the healing miracles, but the walking on the sea and the feeding of the five thousand. What they would have spurned as contemporaries of Jesus they seized upon avidly after his death. With ecclesiastical lack of insight they were unable to see that Christ's so-called miracles were cases of healing by emanation and essential to His nature. To them it was always magic. And with his resurrection, the drama of the empty tomb, Christ appearing not once but many times to his disciples, the element of magic, capable of being turned to good purpose, was intensified. Christ as the wonder worker, the being who could do what others could not, was ideal for the foundation of the new faith. What he had taught was largely irrelevant in the third century beginnings of Christianity as an international theocracy. The memory of Jesus, the wonder worker, was enough. His theology, if any, could be left to others.

The Crucifixion was a little more difficult to account for. If Christ was the Son of God why had not the latter intervened to save his progeny? But Christ's death on the Cross was no ordinary death in that he could be raised from it and appear in genuine living form to his disciples and others. This was admittedly an obstacle but easily surmounted. God had let Christ die for a special purpose. It was still a manifestation of God's power to let him die and to raise him again. The theme of death and rebirth had been the basis of much pagan belief and ritual before the birth of Christ. The idea that at times a king, or a deputy chosen by him, must die for his people, was a refinement and intensification of the theme of animal sacrifice. The bigger the sacrifice, the better the result. The sacrifice of the bull, a king among beasts, in the cult of Mithras, was infinitely more compelling than that of a lamb or goat. Here, with the Crucifixion of Christ was the supreme opportunity. Here was the sacrifice to end sacrifices. God had sent His son to die, permitted him to do so but had raised him again. What was the price to be exacted? First of all it was necessary that as close a substitute as possible to the sacrifice of Christ should be enacted. This involved the drinking of Christ's blood and the eating of his flesh. By the third century, which saw the cohesion of so much utilisation of magic to suit the needs of theology, (itself a welding of ideas to serve the purposes described above), it was necessary to fabricate the doctrine of Transubstantiation, to encourage the credulous to believe that the wine drunk at the Eucharist was truly the blood of Christ and the Host equally truly his flesh. This was not enough. The eating of flesh and the drinking of blood would do for any blood sacrifice, even for the supreme effort made by God Himself in giving His son, possibly to atone for his own shortcomings. The right of communion was therefore combined with an idolatrous worship of the crucifix. A political murder, contrived by a combination of Jewish ecclesiasticism and a remarkable and rather atypical obtuseness on the part of the Roman authorities, was turned into an act of God based on the abnegation of Himself.

What is astonishing is that the ecclesiastics who founded Christianity as an international theocracy should have clung to the baser beliefs of paganism. At the time of the birth of Christ the sacrifice of the Mithraic bull was merely an exoteric manifestation for the imperceptive and untutored. The more evolved adherents did not indulge in such practices. They saw that the slaughter of the bull symbolised the control within themselves of male aggressive impulses. By the time Christianity had become the official religion of the Roman Empire, animal sacrifices and the cult of Mithras had dwindled to the occasional cutting off of chickens' heads. The fact that the animal kept on walking after it had been decapitated was taken to indicate that the soul was separate from the body.

No one can say what political genius among the not so early Christians first conceived of the idea of the doctrine of redemption by grace and added to the Eucharist and veneration of the Cross the idea that Christ died for our sins and that, in doing so he endowed us with grace without which we could not be saved. What was even more subtle was the idea that this enormous benefit should not be broadcast too haphazardly. What is given too freely is not appreciated enough. A time came when to receive the Mass was virtually a prerogative of the priests themselves. Rood screens were erected to prevent the laity from observing the priests receiving the sacred rite. It was only reasonable that those who had been to the trouble to fabricate so intricate a theology should especially benefit from the magic sent from on high. This was a time when the laity were only required to go to Mass a few times in the year at the special festivals. We talk of the decadence of the times we live in, of our predilections for short cuts to salvation, of the necessity of being 'opened up' by this or that guru, so much preferable to the old fashioned conception of personal effort. Surely the founding fathers of Christianity were masters of such techniques. Surely the Eucharist was the supreme short-cut. I myself am appalled that my contemporaries believe in so many of the "salvation at one go" techniques which proliferate around us. I am no more bewildered and horrified than the Emperor Julian the Apostate when he first heard of the doctrine of grace by redemption which, to him, was the height of immorality. Why, he asked, should partaking in such a rite as the Eucharist confer spiritual benefits and salvation denied to people who have lived soberly, honestly and helpfully for years without the benefit of the Christian clergy?

The aim of the priest-craft was to constitute a body of middle men dispensing grace by redemption at a price. This is not to say that all practising priests up to and including the Middle Ages were instigated by such motives. For the majority it was easy to pass from the belief in magic, always, be it understood, of their particular variety, to a belief that magic itself was holy. There were, however, goats among the sheep for whom the temporal power of the Church was the presiding motive. By the time the Church was indulging, in the early Middle Ages, in its injust tithes, in its gross extortions, in its bestial persecution of the superior minds who opposed it, the sheep and the goats had hybridized unnaturally.

It is pointless to argue what is obvious. It is incredible that an organization calling itself Christian should ally itself with the secular authority of kings and princes to oppress the people in the name of a man who never sought to found any church whatever and who said that his kingdom was not of this world. It is still more incredible that there were centuries in European history when the kings and princes of the world cowered before the threat of excommunication and when the papacy was stronger than the secular authority. How was this power achieved? Was it merely that a majority opted freely for such metaphysical abstractions as the doctrine of transubstantiation or the intricate composition of the Holy Trinity? The idea is absurd, except that in the Byzantine empire theology at times, particularly in the ruling classes, seems to have been a kind of contagious epidemic.

What kept people subservient to these ecclesiastical systems was not intellectual homage but stark fear. When a religion is based on magic there is always the threat of the magic being withdrawn or being diverted against the dissident. In the Middle Ages, man lived constantly under the threat of hell. The Church aided him wholeheartedly in his submissive attitude by the mass manufacture of sin. The latter manifested itself at its most deadly in heresy and sex and the greatest of these was heresy. Goodness of heart and natural charity counted for nothing compared with orthodoxy and submission to the priesthood. This is clear to anybody who takes the trouble to read the depositions made to the Inquisition in the Middle Ages and afterwards. The inquisitors indeed pay often grudging tribute to the chastity and goodness of the lives of their victims and make it quite clear, in ensuring that they were tortured or burnt, that natural goodness counts for nothing compared with subservience and conformation.

As to the sins of sex the Church anticipated Kraft-Ebbing by centuries in indicating, with obsessional absurdity and prurience, what was permitted and what wasn't. This preoccupation with sex was not instigated by disgust with sex per se. The lives of the clergy in the Middle Ages, particularly before St. Dominic, indicates their willingness to use women as a pleasing sedative. But the monument to sexual sin, which was one of the most imposing in the massive museum of Christianity, centres, as we shall see in the next chapter, rather round hatred of woman qua woman than round the act of sex.

NOTES

1. In due course sex disappeared from the true Mysteries. This is not to say that in the decadence of Rome, in the third or fourth centuries AD, there was not a proliferation of sects calling themselves Mysteries but acting largely as covers for full-blooded orgies.

2. Some paid for what they received with insanity, the latter due to the effect of sudden precipitate revelations on the immature and unstable.

8.

The Male Priesthood

In studying the birth and ascendance of male priesthoods one has to bear in mind two main factors. Firstly, women as oracles and later priestesses were first in the fields of religion and transcendental philosophy. Secondly they did not, like the male, indulge in magic. In the earlier days of the Mysteries the males rank lower in the hierarchy and were employed chiefly as healers. They had enough insight to recognize that the healing gifts manifested by the priestesses and oracles were not magic but natural to them. This attribute was radically changed with the advent of the highly discipled male ecclesiastical hierarchy which was born in the third century AD. Its members were obsessed by the need to conserve for themselves the reputation of having the control of magic in the sacraments. The number of the latter had been increased to include those of baptism and marriage. Convinced that women healers were purveyors of other kinds of magic, paradoxically regarded as dangerous because of the benefits they conferred, they set themselves against the incorporation of women into the administrative structure of the Church. In the first centuries after Christ, women as well as men were still following Christ's injunction, unique in world religions, that the faithful should heal the sick as well as preach the Word. Paul's anti-feminist fulminations helped propagandize women out of practical Christianity. Fewer and fewer undertook of their own volition to heal the sick or preach the Word. There remained for centuries remote pockets of primitive Christianity in which women still played an active role. There were women priestesses who healed and taught in the Celtic Church in Britain, the fate of which was sealed at the Synod of Whitby in 664. The Romanisation of

Britain was accomplished at the expense of the Celtic Church
on the plea that Christian worship should be regularised. In
the eyes of Rome it was apparently a prime necessity that
Easter be celebrated at the same date throughout the
Christian world. The date of Easter varied in different regions
in the Celtic Church. The correction of this enormity was, to
Rome, of primary importance. The real reason for rendering
religious practice and administration uniform throughout
Christendom was to stamp out veneration of the traditional
Celtic gods and goddesses which was still incorporated in the
Christian belief. In addition there were areas in Roman
Britain, for example Cumberland, where the gods and
goddesses in the Roman pantheon were still venerated
because of the preponderance of Romano-British subjects in
those areas where Celts had intermarried with their Roman
conquerors. What the Roman Church feared above all was a
resuscitation of the worship of the Mother Goddess of
antiquity. For these reasons the women priestesses and
healers were eradicated from the Romanised Celtic Church.
Opinion was inflamed against them and they were regarded
not only as blasphemous but as practitioners of the evil eye
and dealing in a reprehensible form of magic, the effects of
which were more than counterbalanced by the Roman Mass,
provided the latter was administered by the male priesthood.
The latter's own mechanically induced holiness served as a
natural protection for the people.

This persistence in the belief that women were at least the
equal of men as healers and purveyors of wisdom persisted
in different areas in Europe where there were Celtic pockets
to act as an adequate leaven for the enlightenment of the
whole. In the Cathar Church of the twelfth and thirteenth
centuries in the Languedoc, and Provence, up to the great
crusade against the Albigensians in 1209, the number of
women priestesses almost equalled that of the number of
men. This was at a time when the womanising tendencies of
the Catholic priesthood were such as drew down on their
heads the considerable vituperative talents of Pope Innocent
the Third who himself organized the crusade against the
Albigeois. But there is a whole world of difference between
utilising woman as the subtlest of all pleasures and crediting
her with any special significance. The inability to do the
latter is, with a few honourable exceptions in men and

movements, perhaps the greatest crime of those religions arising in the Middle East.

One does not need to dwell on the horrors of the Albigensian wars. A good Catholic like Mauriac, good in every sense of the word, said that he was unable to think of the Catholic persecutions without intense sadness and revulsion. What is necessary to point out is that 1244 saw to all intents and purposes the extermination of the woman priestess in Europe. There were many women among the Cathars burnt at Montségur on March 16th of that year. This exclusion of women from priestly office is an absolute cardinal issue. It is almost impossible to explain the conspiracy of silence which has been maintained for centuries about it. What the Christian Church has in fact said for centuries is that half the human race are, in virtue of being born with a different physiology, incapable of guiding the souls and destinies of others. We talk of primitive man but is there any more striking example of savage and uncreative folklore than this. But this was not all. Not content with setting its face against any rehabilitation of women as preachers and healers, the Church was determined to eradicate any who aimed at the private, limited and almost anonymous practice of such vocations. It must be remembered that the obsession with witchcraft and the persecution of witches dates from the Albigensian wars. Indeed, in reading some of the depositions made to the Inquisition in the thirteenth and fourteenth centuries, it is impossible to decide whether the defendant is being accused of heresy or witchcraft. The Church preferred to burn Joan of Arc as a witch because she had not revealed any of the classical tenets of the great heresy of Catharism. There can be no doubt that at this period and for a couple of centuries afterwards in the eyes of the Church witch was synonymous with heretic. The fact that so-called witches were persecuted in Protestant countries does not invalidate this contention one iota. The ecclesiastical systems for which we are indebted to Calvin were if anything worse than the Catholics in their persecution of what they called witches. One cannot fail to notice that the latter were overwhelmingly female. If many of these witches were, what their persecutors thought them, agents of the devil, it is totally impossible to accept, unless one is a Christian priest, that women are essentially more diabolic than men. The number of men who were accused of and sentenced for witchcraft is small compared with the number of women. This is not to say that practitioners of the black arts do not exist, but devotion to the cult of evil has nothing in common with the attitude of mind of inoffensive old women collecting herbs as agents of natural healing, applying what simple remedies they could and offering what consolations were at their disposal to the sick.

This last half century has given us a greater insight into the motives behind rigid, male-contrived ecclesiastical systems. When one says male-contrived surely the adjective is superfluous because does there exist anywhere in the world a religion of any consequence where women play any role at its councils? What, then, is the basic motive behind this hatred and distrust of women? One is not implying that the modern priest, be he Catholic, Anglican or Protestant, lives his life in a state of seething indignation against the temptress, punctuated by surreptitious visits to her after dark.

Few of the ecclesiastics I have met have enough insight to recognize the distrust of women which is buried deep in their composition and which motivates so many of their actions. Surely the guiding motive in the attitude of the male ecclesiastical systems is homosexuality. In arguing thus one is not falling into the recognized contemporary trap which is a legacy of Freudianism. One is not saying that because men avoid women that they are necessarily homosexuals. I have known men who have done so because they found themselves to be too flamingly hetrosexual. We are not here dealing with just a matter of attitudes maintained in a couple of lifetimes but with a tendency which is about three millennia old. Surely we cannot afford to thrust aside the attitude that, by hook or by crook, women have from time immemorial been regarded by the Church as something to tolerate, something possibly to be kind to when grace was specially abundant, but something never to be admitted to any kind of equality in affairs of the Church and never to be credited with the capacity for theological discussion. Arranging flowers on the altar and having strange feelings about the curate are one thing, but for a woman to preach the word is another matter entirely. It sticks out for all the world to see that the Roman Church has no women priests, the British Anglican Church no fully ordained women, while one or two of the nonconformist communities show a stressful enlightenment in admitting a handful of temptresses to their solemn councils.

In these matters the antics of the different Churches can be amusing as well as instructive. It will have been noted that for a decade or two women healers have been encouraged by the Non-conformist and Anglican communities. Speaking as an Anglican born and bred, I was baptised in the Church of England and I can see no way of avoiding being buried by it, I would say that the recognition of women as healers is Danegeld paid to the movement towards the liberation of women. After all, what harm can they do by the laying on of hands? It may even persuade them to desist from preaching the Word. In addition the Church is extremely careful that its women healers practice under the supervision of a priest. Much of the work they do is of little consequence, because it is based on the idea that prayer and what is called a holy life, that is to say belonging to the Christian community, are aids to healing. This is simply not so. The capacity to heal is something inborn which can grow with experience but no amount of prayer and Church attendance will turn a non-sensitive into a healer. This is not to say that there are not individuals working under the aegis of the Church who have achieved remarkable results but these are among a minority, and where this happy issue has occurred it is due to the healer's innate qualities and not to the reinforcement of any religious observance. One can say with justification that healing comes from God, but one cannot say that God Himself channels the power of goodness which healing is, towards any particular Church or sect.

We now come to one of the most crucial questions of our thesis. Whence arose this clerical distrust and hatred of woman and above all women priests? We simply cannot minimise what is of three thousand years' duration. First of all the clerical mentality is the direct opposite of that which facilitates extra-sensory perception. In the former the individual lives in his personality and all its aggressions and beligerent aspirations. In the latter the individual with natural psychic gifts escapes every so often into his or rather her psyche. To find a substitute for this clairvoyance and healing, which smack of magic to the priest because of his inability to comprehend, he has himself to resort to frank, fabricated magic. He feeds the people, who previously were guided by healers and prophets, on sacraments, god-invoking rituals and other blasphemous substitutes for the truth.

But there are deeper issues than this. Christian ecclesiasticism is strongly tinged with homosexuality. How can one translate otherwise the numerous biblical and liturgical references to women as a source of pollution? So much of what has been written by the clergy about women is expressed in terms closely analogous to what I have heard in my own lifetime so often from homosexuals either patients or otherwise. The reader should bear in mind that I have no personal antipathy to homosexuals. In my younger days I did a good deal of medico-legal work and tended to be sympathetic to homosexuals because of the ferocity of the laws directed against them. But in spite of the sympathy one felt for them as underdogs, in the years in which I was practising, I could not but wonder at the revulsion expressed by many of them at the idea of any kind of physical contact with a woman. In so doing they were condemning not only half the human race but what gave them birth.

This revulsion of homosexuals towards women is not basically sexual or even psychological. It is almost biological. A woman bearing a child is the faint continuation of the Mother Goddess. As such her wisdom comes from the earth. Her five senses are therefore sharper than those of the male. She is often also endowed with a sixth. On the other side of the fence the male is, if we are honest, separated off from the woman. No war conducted since time began has even been so fundamental and primitive as that between men and women. In terms of procreation man is almost unnecessary, a mere biological agent used for a few minutes to fertilise the ovum. Separated off, as he is, from her superabundant fecundity, and therefore belonging less to mother earth than she does, it falls to his lot to take his revenge by finding means to dominate her. In primitive civilisations, and in our own in earlier days, women could be subjugated, as could the lower classes and lesser nobility, by physical force or the sheer weight of arms. With the coming of semi-civilisation man sought to dominate by systems of ideas. In particular the cleric is the dominator par excellence. He even goes so far as to manufacture his ideas to a degree not permitted to the philosopher or the scientist.

Modern psychiatry has expended a great deal of thought and ink on environmental and genetic influences conducive to homosexuality. There may be some truth in these theories provided we see truth as operating at different levels. While environmental influence may, very rarely, tip the balance in favour of homosexuality the hereditary factor is undoubted. But whence comes the hereditary factor? Have we not to go back through the ages in order to understand that the contemporary homosexual is an individual who exhibits still his hatred of woman because her wisdom is earthy in the best sense of the word, that is to say it is founded in concrete reality whereas he has to satisfy himself with metaphysical abstractions, an impossible task, the futility of which is seen in the loneliness and frustration of the ageing homosexual male. Senile misery is his lot because he has failed to avail himself of the opportunity for recapturing that state of harmony with the indivisible consciousness which, to common man, is only achieved through women.

Homosexuality is particularly rife in the ritualistic religions. All religions are ritualistic, even the most Protestant cults because of their set repetitions. Why should there be this connection between ritualistic religion and homosexuality? Because compulsive obsessional ritual is always a response not to guilt as contemporary psychiatry has insisted but to evil or to what the practitioner of ritual thinks evil. The male ecclesiastic thinks of the woman as evil for reasons we have given before and, in addition, because he regards her preference for happiness on earth to nebulous perfections as a sign of a contaminated state. He does not realize that to be happy in the here and now is the supreme test and that without it no future spiritual evolution is possible.

As I have shown in my previous books, where man is in direct contact with the force of evil or with evil discarnate entities he responds by developing obvious obsessional tics or equally obvious compulsive rituals. Where, on the other hand, he is in contact with what he *thinks* evil but which is not evil, he erects ritualistic systems in which there is nothing reflex, because there is no real deep need to protect himself against the non-existent evil represented by the word woman. In such cases the obsessional tendency is expressed in ecclesiastical systems of ritual in which the individual escapes the obsessional tics and compulsive rituals which affect those who have fallen to the onslaught of the genuine force of evil.

I am not saying that the Christian priesthood for centuries has been riddled with practising homosexuals. It is always ridiculous to talk of proportionality in these matters. One cannot construct systems of statistics without finding the individuals concerned in *flagrant delit*.

One has to think in terms of protracted repressed homosexuality. Quite often the repression of an impulse is accompanied by a conscious ferocity towards it. The Church in its time has been brutal in its treatment of homosexuals. In other words the repressed homosexual is the worst persecutor of the active practitioner. One noticed this in one's medical career. Some of the most notoriously vindictive judges, so far as homosexuality was concerned, were themselves of homosexual make-up.

Sometimes, in the course of European history, this repressed homosexuality has reached obscene levels. At the time when the witch fever was at its height in Europe, and at its worst in Germany, in a small German town every attractive girl was liquidated. The operative word is attractive. As such she was a potential temptress and a source of defilement. This example reveals how repressed homosexuality, seeking to manifest itself closer to the conscious level, can be strongly contaminated with sadism. Note it was the pretty and attractive women who were liquidated. It was seemingly less enjoyable to dispose of the plain.

Allied to the question of clerical homosexuality is the Church's attitude to virginity. It was essential for the mother of the Son of God to be a virgin, despite the gynaecological difficulties of the proceeding. The worship of the Virgin Mary as the continuation of the concept of the Mother Goddess is one of the most precious and hopeful concepts left to us. The worship of her as a virgin for the sake of her virginity is morbid and neurotic. Virginity is a force and not a virtue. Some people cannot function at the highest level of psychic activity without remaining virgins. This is the essence of holiness if one has to use such a word. But the respect for virginity itself, when it is not conceived of as an aid to creative psychic activity, is a poor, wilting dispirited proposition. Incarcerating women in nunneries in the name of God is another expression of repressed homosexuality. Nuns were holy because they denied their womanhood. In my days as a medical student, the academic psychologists spoke fulsomely of the self-abasing instinct of woman as though it was a virtue. Such an instinct never existed. It was imposed on her by man. And of all men engaged in this repressive task the most potent were the priesthood. To me it was a source of wonder and despair that the congregation in most churches was so predominantly female. Was masochism as well as virginity a virtue, or was it merely lack of insight that prevented women from seeing that the priesthood was something not easing their path to God but an obstacle in their reaching towards Him.

One should not take too seriously the fact that many priests in the Middle Ages and afterwards broke the rules and lived with women as concubines and that some of the French Abbesses were, to say the least, rather jolly types. These misdemeanours, in view of the vows they had taken, are evidence of hypocrisy but should one be too disturbed by this? Is not hypocrisy the lip service which barbarism pays to civilisation? These male and female sexual sinners, acting spasmodically and surreptitiously within the Holy Church, caused little in the way of human misery compared with the undeviating ritualistic dogma provided by a male homosexual priesthood.

There is no doubt that in our day homosexuality is still associated with ritualistic religion. This applies more to the high Anglican community than to the Roman Church. At Oxford I noticed how a certain wincing refinement, combined with a moving tenderness towards members of their own sex, characterised those destined for the lower reaches of the high Anglican fraternity. It was notorious in the Oxford of my day that the 'Spikes', by which we meant the High Anglicans, produced a promising quota of homosexuals. How these people coped with women under stress God alone knows. Perhaps they never thought of themselves in the role of comforters but concentrated hard to learn how to swing the censer as gracefully as possible.

Not twenty years ago an Archbishop of the Church of England made a statement which aroused surprisingly little notice in a country sinking steadily into a listless dementia. This gentleman said that, from some points of view, he regretted that adultery was no longer regarded as a crime. He did not enlarge on what punishment he suggested. The reader can be reminded that at one time stoning to death was very much the vogue. At the same time the Archbishop considered that homosexuality between priests was not a matter for legal interference, that is to say it was not criminal. He regarded it as suitable material for discussion at parochial level. One can imagine that such discussion could even be enjoyable. In plain English, to the head of the Church of England, sexual relations between males which, until recently, the secular authority has regarded as an aberration and severely indictable, was passed off by this prince of the Church as a parochial triviality compared with a possible single act of unfaithfulness of a wife to her husband. This is not only lack of reason but lack of charity and humanity. To divorce a woman for one or two isolated acts of adultery, possibly stimulated by compassion or deriving from a fleeting, ungovernable physical passion, strikes me as barbarous in a community which by and large accepts that polygamy is natural to the male. In addition, it reveals sympathetic understanding and tolerance of homosexuality, which does credit to the individual concerned but places him almost in the position of a propagandist for it.

In any case the chickens have come home to roost. The existence in modern society of 'gay' priests who admit themselves to be homosexual and cater specially for the spiritual needs of those similarly addicted is, however tolerant and understanding, a frightening phenomenon. The idea that a sub-species of priest can be recruited from those sexually deviated is dangerous. The priest is still set in authority over us. Because homosexuality may be commoner among the priesthood than we care to admit is no reason for the admitted priest homosexual to exercise his authority over us. Imagine the outcry if we started an organization for brothel-haunting priests or for those whose sport was adultery. Is it surprising the Church, having so many times in its history regarded woman as a polluting influence, now permits a section of its members to rejoice openly in the triumph of homosexuality? On wholly inadequate grounds it has been argued that Christ himself was possibly a homosexual. The Saviour, as the ultimate queer surrounded by posturing acolytes, is a dramatic advance from the days when the High Church homosexual had to satisfy himself with cosy and highly sublimated feelings about chubby choirboys.

One does not wish, in a book of this nature, to litter up one's theme with too many practical examples. One or two of the more striking may be of interest to the unprejudiced. My greatest friend was instructed, in a Catholic boarding school in Poland, that women were put into the world by the devil to tempt man. He was taught this at the age of sixteen. It is no good writing this off merely as religious fanaticism. Is it really religious to hate women or indeed anybody, including animals, to that degree? By his vitriolic mindlessness the priest concerned condemned his own mother, and his father for having had her, not to mention any sisters he may have had, as well as the small item of the whole world of women. Such views can only be motivated by homosexuality in its most frenzied form. My friend, and another boy singled out for this feat of enlightenment, were sufficiently sophisticated to find it amusing and discussed going into the Church in order, in my friend's words, "To enjoy the hypocrisy".

One wonders what are the ultimate roots of such clerical attitudes as these. They must be tough and resilient to persist into the twentieth century. One can call them archetypal but does this tell us enough? I feel that some such clerics, deep down in the mass unconscious, are recalling the days when the origins of religion in sexuality were clear and obvious, and when fertility was the first step to godliness. Such men are able, by intensely repressed far memory, to look back to the days when carvings in stone and wood of the male and female generative organs were objects of worship as they are today in certain Hindu temples. The far memory involved does not extend to a conscious recollection of past incarnations. Such people are constantly tapping the underwaters of guilt induced in them by two millennia of Christianity.

Perhaps a similar explanation accounts for the fact that in Christian Churches the congregations are predominantly women. I have noticed this particularly in parts of the South-West of France where Catholicism seems as moribund as it was in the thirteenth century. I have looked in on Vespers and seen no more than half a dozen dessicated, depressed old ladies. A minority attend from long habit or from loneliness. They give to God what man does not seem to want. It is possible that some, in submitting themselves to a clergy who regarded them as inferior and dominated them for centuries, are indulging in the masochistic joy in suffering which is a feature of Christianity but I think this latter explanation can be overdone. I believe that in many cases the reason is such as would shock the clergy.

Must we not accept that, in the core of her being, woman is a more sexually impelled creature than the male? In the latter the sexual urge is more superficial, more consciously felt and more constantly available. But in the mass unconscious of woman is there not some recollection of the Dionysian and Orphic rites when they gave to man their nearest approach to Oneness, to cosmic harmony, they were likely to achieve? They did this by what was innate in their beings, the impulse to give themselves in the readily available mechanisms of sexual intercourse. May there not be among these female congregations far memory, once again repressed, for lives when sex and religion were confluent and not in conflict with each other? Let it be clearly understood that I am not preaching the Freudian doctrine that religion is sublimated sex which implies that it will disappear as man achieves more insight, as foretold in the Future of an

Illusion. I say the dead opposite. Sex is the pabulum out of which religion grew. When mankind had reached a certain degree of development it became obvious to women, whose wisdom is based more on feeling and sensation than on the secondary processes of synthesis and analysis, that the oneness achieved in sexual intercourse, transcending mere brutish *accouplement*, is analogous to religious experience. With such memories fusing with her current experience, woman sees no lack of logic in her attendance at Church and very particularly at the Eucharist. Though they accept the ritual of Church they interpret it differently. Such women are looking back to those days when the seeming magic of the phallus had not been replaced by the strenuously fabricated magic of the Eucharist.

Such women have sometimes strong religious impulses. Did not the prostitutes of Lyons agitate a few years back for a special Mass to be said for them? This relationship between the phallus and the chalice may seem blasphemous to some but it goes back to the beginning in this world of religious experience. In our present age women with strong sexual impulses who adhere to the Church are not sublimating their present sexual impulses nor necessarily atoning for past activities. If they are doing the latter it seems a pity and grossly illogical. There is surely no need to ask pardon for the basis of religious experience.

These women show no lack of logic in remaining faithful to a Church which has sometimes persecuted them and for the most part regarded them as inferior for so many centuries. In their attitude to the Eucharist they are applying their own inter- pretation. A woman's morality is always of her own making. A man's is based, or so he likes to think, on logic and he either toes the line with the herd or consciously transgresses. Many women who attend Mass regularly do not believe in Transubstantiation, yet at the same time do not regard the ceremony as merely commemorative. They have their own interpretation and their own approach. Such women are heretics who stay within the bosom of the Church because, while they have seen deeper than the opposite sex the origins of organised religion in sex and nature, they have failed to synthesize these two motives at the conscious level. Deep down they remain faithful to the Church because the ancient creative magic of the phallus is still operating within them and because it evokes the absolution offered by the fabricated magic of the Host. The man-made magic of the sacraments was designed to distract attention from what the homosexual fathers of Christianity regarded as the magical powers of the female oracles who later they designated as witches. That the holy fathers preferred to slaughter female philosophers like Hypatia, to burn virginal priestesses with the powers of prophecy and healing rather than what are called their frailer sisters, is easy to understand. The female priestess, as a representative of the Mother Goddess, was a formidable opponent to a male hierarchy impregnated with homosexuality, whereas the woman conceived of as whore, actual or potential, had a certain usefulness. She could always be exploited as a drastic purge. For the male to allow himself to be contaminated was, after all, not so bad, provided one recognised one was contaminated. There was always the absolution and the cleansing antisepsis of the Mass.

All in all we are bound to conclude that direct truth, revealed by discarnate entities to oracles and by the latter to sensitives, has been stamped on pretty successfully by the male priesthood of Christianity for almost two millennia. We can say that in this way we are damning too much the arid, essentially masculine ecclesiasticism which has dominated European religion for so long. Can't we argue that the Old Testament counters the female oracles with the books of the prophets? Certainly, but is there much prophetic utterance to be found in them? Do they enlighten us as much as to the fate of the psyche after death, the nature of God, the intricate hierarchies which intervene between Him and us and the power of good and evil loose in the universe? It is of great interest that the Cathars, as firm believers in directly revealed truth as any who ever existed, and for whom the Old Testament was perdition, should nevertheless exclude from their anathema the prophetic books and also the Apocrypha, the latter possibly because it contains more creative allegories than the historical books. Nevertheless, apart from the desert lands of arid history, the Bible contains remarkably little in the way of directly expressed truth. How otherwise can we account for the millions of words spent unravelling the meaning of this or that verse? Equally, how can we account for the fact that the Roman Church, down the ages the majority movement in Christianity, has always insisted on the people receiving not the Bible directly but its interpretation by scholars and saints? It needs a good deal more than scholarship and sainthood to comprehend with certainty long stretches of it.

9.

The Sleep of Death

I have made as best as I can the case for revealed truth. It is now time to disclose the nature of the latter. Remember that what I write is a form of message rather than an argued synthesis. This may damn it in the eyes of those scientists whose work never expands beyond the limits of the laboratory, the x-ray department or, worst of all, the institute of experimental psychology. My work will be none the worse for that. If you think of it as a form of message you have to consider the origins of the message and the nature of the messengers. The wise man accepts but sifts evidence from everywhere. Only a fool defines beforehand what kind of evidence he will accept. Too often it is that provided by other fools. A fool is a person who does not listen to others but only to some preconceived scientific system circulating like a synthesized satellite within the cramped space orbit of his brain. Such people find it difficult to accept evidence provided by the dead. One would have thought survival conferred on the latter the capacity to provide unique testimony through a wider range of vision. It is these I am prepared to call on first.

When we die it requires three days to separate the psyche from the personality. Do not ask why. For me, with my modest perceptive equipment, it would be idiotic to expect an answer. That is why death is an educational experience in that it provides us with further answers. It is justifiable to ask how I know. I was told this by the discarnates who have been my mentors. They are in a position to witness the passing of the souls of those whom they have watched over in this life. This fact is also accepted by Tibetan Buddhists and by the Cathars of the thirteenth century in the Languedoc, Provence and Northern Italy. It is for this reason that nobody should be buried or cremated for three days. To do so in less time is to simulate some of the conditions of death by violence. It can be argued that there are areas in the world in which, because of the climate, no body could be preserved unburied for three days. It is precisely in these areas that bodies are not buried but exposed to the weather and the vultures, both of which takes longer than three days to ensure the disintegration of the body.

Some highly psychic people, in their out-of-the-body healing experiences, are aware of their displacement through space. Even in life, with the strangling hold of the personality on the psyche, the latter is aware of its voyage through space. In the three days succeeding death there is no living egocentric personality to retard the flight of the psyche, but the pull of the so-called inanimate matter of which the corpse is composed may retard the unfolding of the psyche's wings.

If the manner of our descent into matter at conception remains with us in our recurrent dreams, why should not the remembrance of life remain with us for three days after death? Why should there not still be life in our tissues? Do tissues remember when brain and heart have died? There are two clinical stages of death. The first is what is officially recognised as such. It comes when the pulse and the breathing have ceased. After that is the undefined process of molecular death. Each cell has, for a limited time, a life of its own. While each cell has life and feeling the psyche is still living, because it is the final permeation of the psyche which endows the cells with the capacity to continue. Is it more extraordinary that psychic and cellular life should exist in the body after molecular death, than that many mothers are aware of the moment when the psyche enters their body at conception or that the foetus, too, has the same awareness, without which we could not in dreams, later in life, recall the descent of the psyche into matter?

After death the psyche sleeps for a time. The duration of its sleep corresponds to its development on earth. The more evolved the individual in this life the less he sleeps after death. The period necessarily varies enormously. The quickest I have known is five weeks and it was not a full awakening. These phenomena are only known to us because there are sensitives on earth with whom the discarnates make contact when the dead awaken from their sleep. It is only rarely that the dead themselves make early, and direct, contact with us. We are usually informed by the discarnates who have acted as our own special mentors. It is only later that the dead speak to sensitives.

What proportion of the dead make contact with us of their own volition? Only an infinitely small minority. A greater number have their sleep disturbed by seances arranged to allay the anguish of bereaved separated from their loved ones. This is human, pitiful, but undesirable. There is a pattern in these things and it is not for us to change it. Always the rule is that we should remain passive. If the dead call it is because they know we need them, that they have something special to communicate, that through them and us the truth of life should not be lost to others. Occasionally they call us because of their need of us. But always we should beware of disturbing their sleep. If they awaken too soon they wander lost in Hades, which is not hell but a disorientating no-man's land through which the psyche passes after death before awaking to a fuller existence in the new world of consciousness.

Those who have led self-centred, egotistical lives sleep longer after death. So do depressives who have been locked in themselves by the extent of their own misfortunes as distinct from those of others. Those who have been saddened by the horrors of the world do not necessarily sleep late. Brutal and hectoring people also sleep long, as do all those of aggressive and acquisitive nature, whose aggression and acquisition is on the plane of personality. One is talking of the ordinary human bully and of those impelled by a greed for gain. These wake in due course and take their proper place in the zones of higher consciousness succeeding death, unless their violence and lust for power was so extreme on earth as to be psychically induced, in which case, as we shall see later, they remain in all too nefarious proximity to this planet.

Those who have met violent ends, from whatever cause, tend to sleep longer and wander on waking a longer period in the shades. In some cases the converse is true. They do not really fall asleep at all soon after death. They cannot accept they are dead and their wanderings in Hades, which has nothing to do with the hell of Christian conception, continues until they fall asleep when they tend to slumber long, awaiting a happy awakening.

The stimulation of the time the psyche sleeps after death is measured from this world. When the discarnates tell us that so and so has awakened we measure the time from his or her death, but to the discarnates themselves time is of little consequence in virtue of their own almost total emancipation from it. In using the word discarnate in this connection I am talking of those who act creatively as instructors to those still living in this world.

When the psyche passes over after three days it is taken in charge by one of these discarnates in the lower echelons of the hierarchy. Those still in contact with the earth are best fitted to guide those just escaped from it. The guide watches over the psyche of the dead while it is still sleeping. To whom is this office allotted? Is it someone who has loved him in his recently terminated life and who passed over before him? The answer is usually no. He is watched over while sleeping, and guided in his first steps in the new world, by someone who has known him and loved him through several incarnations. Someone intimate with him, not necessarily physically intimate, in his dominant incarnation may be drawn towards him as his guide. By dominant incarnation I mean that in which the individual's character was formed and in which he learnt most of the purpose which was to maintain him through his subsequent lives. It would be pleasant to think that one would be cared for after death by the girl who, half a century ago, took our breath away as she swept past, in an odour of violets, on the chill morning of a certain Spring when the buds were still unburst on the horse chestnuts. It may still be her if she was our companion, lover and mentor through several incarnations, but the possibilities are not great. This is not to say that we are excluded from those who loved us in this world as we pass to the next. It is merely that those who know us best are with us on waking which is as it should be, seeing that those who know us best are surely those who have known us longest through several lives.

Those who have known us longest in our last life in this world may still provide our first mentor in the next of the worlds if they have, after several incarnations, married us or reincarnated in our family in this life but this is not common.

The most common experience reported by the newly dead to those still living in this world is the nature of the colours with which they are surrounded. All say that, on this earth, we have no idea of the colours in which they are bathed. They describe them as living and palpitating, as having in themselves a prime reality. Yet even on earth we are able at times to glimpse the nature of these colours. In illness, particularly in childhood, when the psyche is freer, we pass out of our personalities and over the border in the 'little death' we experience in our worst deliriums and in the crisis of our fevers, we see the colours with which we will be surrounded in the next world. This happened to me in early childhood, in what for years I thought of and described as a dream, but which was actually the straying of the astral body from the personality to the last limits of safety. These living colours can also be revealed to us in this life by other mechanisms. I have seen visions of an amethyst, so palpitatingly real that it defied the laws of psychology, as preached when I was a medical student, and which stated that the image is always fainter than the reality. Looking within this jewel, I saw colours so alive that they seemed to be intersecting rivers of light coiling within each other like tiny, illuminated serpents. This experience announced the presence of my mistress who employed me in my Roman incarnation. In the 'little death' in childhood my astral body was wandering from this world to another. In seeing the amethyst, the astral body of a revenant was moving in the reverse direction towards me in this world. Such experiences in this life are forecasts of what we will see in the next of the worlds.

In the next world the colours are intensified because they are the splitting off from its main source of the basic reality of light. The latter is itself impregnated with the primordial energy of goodness. The living colours seen and found exhilarating by those who have seen them after death are the bread and butter of discarnate existence. At first the newly dead discarnates live passively consorting the one with the other, in their world of colours. Those sufficiently evolved are later able to communicate with us, as well as with higher members of the hierarchy. These they see as figures outlined in light. The latter are either silver or gold. The silver outlines they see are intensifications of the silver rim they themselves exhibit when they disclose themselves to the living. The golden outlines are those of what we can call angels or Christ figures. They represent the permanently dis-carnate equivalent of those who in their life on this earth reached Christlike dimensions. Such beings are higher in the hierarchy than the discarnates who talk to us. They include those who have no need to reincarnate. While they, for the most part, reveal themselves to the lower members of the hierarchy as outlined in silver or golden light, there are others without form who are either merely expressed in light or are the embodiment of it. These never reincarnate.

These embodiments of light, independent of outline or suggestion of form, are the archangels. Beyond the archangels is the directing energy of God. He is formless, nameless but still an entity. It is a sound principle of the Islamic and Jewish faiths to deplore the representation of God in painting or sculpture. This is simply because to do so is to endow Him with form. This is a kind of blasphemy but not so culpable as to theorise as to the nature of God. All statements that God wishes this or that of us are worse than blasphemous. They reveal the degree of our myopia and ignorance. In this world we are simply not equipped to speak of the nature, power, limitations or intentions of God. We should beware of those who, on earth, tell us what God requires of us. They are always speaking of themselves, expressing in veiled terms not what God, but they, require of us, which is always some form of homage. We have not a scrap of evidence that God requires from us any homage at all. Does the formless and nameless desire to exact reverence from us? This is an error in both logic and vision. God, so far as we can understand, is an energising force. He is the flooding of our nature with the energies of love and goodness. This is the true God and not the God of the Semitic scriptures. Even this God is not omnipotent. He could not claim to be and remain God. God is not concerned with power but love. Behind him is the still more nameless and anonymous and still more fecund something, the Tao, the Eternal Feminine of Goethe, the vibrationless node, the ultimate womb ready to release itself in an orgiastic energy of creation and goodness.

What this means is that, as we pass from the newly awakened discarnates in their world of colour for the higher strata of awareness, the more highly evolved the being the more he dispenses with form and with the impediment of matter.

From whence comes this information, this knowledge of the higher zones of awareness? From the minority in this life who have seen this pattern. It would be easier to say from those who have spoken with the discarnates but those of the latter with whom I have communicated have required of me, in these matters, that I saw things first for myself, after which I described what I had seen and what had been revealed to me and they verified that I had seen truly. There are a tiny, evolving handful in this world who have seen figures outlined in silver and gold usually seen only by those who have died. I was enabled to do so over a long period when I learnt of the significance of the figures outlined in silver and gold, and how the transformation of the former into the latter is the true meaning of alchemy because it signifies the transmutation of the psychic into the spiritual.

A highly developed sensitive is a person who, while still living on this earth, has the properties and powers of a discarnate. Each lives out of time. This is expressed in the sensitive by precognition, clairvoyance, telepathy and far memory. It is shown most of all by out of the body experiences in healing. What are these but a shedding of personality and matter analogous to what happens after death in the case of the discarnates? Similar properties are revealed by the discarnates who converse with us because they know our thoughts and fears, because they can tell us of past lives and can foresee and tell us, if they wish, the future. Beware of the discarnates who talk too much of the future. This is the prerogative of the fairground clairvoyant. Above all, the discarnate is seeing over a wide area from a timeless, spaceless point of vantage. (The last three words constitute a paradox but all great truths embody the paradox).

In the out-of-the-body experience as shown by the psychic healer, the latter is revealing a considerable emancipation from matter. People so gifted and those with far memory for several past incarnations, are showing in life the properties which the discarnates reveal after death. Such healers and sensitives have, in a sense, and without personal awareness of it, died to themselves in life. They are the stuff from which the discarnates who communicate with them are recruited, because even in this life they are partially discarnate. Those who speak with discarnates in this life are those who will speak with the living after death. There are exceptions to this rule. There are people sufficiently developed in this life who pass quickly to higher echelons than those occupied by the discarnates who regularly communicate with the living. This is inevitable because in any generation, there is a handful of people who have reincarnated from free choice and compassion. They may not choose to do so again or to maintain contact with this earth.

An interesting point arises about emancipation from form as we leave this world for the next. Strictly speaking, the discarnates we see are not basically visible to us, in terms of our five senses, otherwise we would see them all the time. What happens is that, when they wish to see us or when we have urgent need of them, they alter their system of vibrations, which is normally such as renders them invisible to us, in order that we may see them with our five senses. They can change and, in the broad sense of the term, solidify the atmosphere about them. All matter is inert spirit, just as all spirit is etherealised matter. The discarnate revealing himself to us is altering his system of vibrations so that his substance is temporarily less etherealised. The vibrating particles of matter of which he is composed become coarser than those in his normal state and are of a slower rhythm of vibration. In order that we may see him he has to alter his own system of vibrations and merge them with that of the atmosphere about him.

In many cases, the revenants, in communicating with us, choose to dispense with form. They may communicate verbally in which case the voice is as clearly heard as those of human beings. At other times they announce their presence by an odour characteristic of them. I know the presence of my particular mentor by the smell of balsam poplar. This preference of odour to form may be manifested when the living sensitive is not fully developed. It may be his first step in appreciation of the presence of discarnate entities. This, however, is not the whole story. The discarnate entity may announce his presence by his characteristic odour when it is inconvenient to communicate verbally with the sensitive because the latter may be surrounded by people. It may also be a form of message saying that someone known to the sensitive and on the same wavelength is in need of help. I have smelt the odour of balsam poplar myself when a highly psychic person known to me was taken ill. When I went along I found she was suffering from a severe coronary spasm.

Without certain experiences or special initiation even the highly developed sensitive cannot know with certainty what happens beyond the world of form in the regions of light. The latter is not just an irritatingly sentimental term to be used symbolically by the unstable. Light is primordial. It does not merely symbolise goodness but is goodness. This is true whether we go far back in history, or rather pre-history, or whether we mount high on the ladder of gnosis, of esoteric knowing, as distinct from knowledge. The latter can become an obscurantist occupation for the intellectual who fancies himself as an intuitive or psychic.

It is given to some still living to see and feel the presence of the archangels and even to be touched by them. The person to undergo such an experience may be warned by a discarnate that such a revelation is about to happen. Christ figures are always revealed in light, but are often replaced by a totally unearthly and indescribeable glow into which the shining outline of the archangel has become merged. This may occur in visions. For the less evolved, for those in the process of evolving or for those who have had other but different formative experiences, revelations may occur in what the individual feels to be a dream in which he has been transported to realms of light. What he remembers is a feeling of being transfigured and healed. He believes this to have occurred in a dream, but what happens in such cases is that the psyche takes the opportunity provided by sleep to slip away from the body and the personality in what is something more than a dream. The individual thinks of it as the latter because he cannot remember wholly what happened when his psyche and personality were separated from each other. Such partial visionary experiences occur when the individual is not sufficiently stabilized to support without ill effects full confrontation with the archangels.

It should be understood that, in our day, initiation must inevitably come from beyond this world. It must be done through the agency of the most evolved and proficient sensitive available. The latter will almost certainly be a woman. She will be acting the role of the female oracle of antiquity but with a difference. We must not ask or seek her services. Neither must she offer hers to us. In our time the initiative must always come from the discarnates themselves. What was the practice three or thousand years ago is no longer possible or desirable. In any modern community too many are concerned with the exercise of power over others and with the acquisition of wealth. This applies both to those seeking enlightenment and to sensitives themselves. So far as the acquisition of psychic powers is concerned, to seek such a goal should automatically exclude one from being trained for such purposes. Such frenetic seekers are almost all too tarnished to some degree by the materialism of the age we live in. It has seeped, without our knowing it, into the marrow of our bones. Unless any revelation given us is initiated from what is called the other side, we risk being contaminated by the will to power, which in the psychic sphere, is always diabolic. Anyone who hands himself over to an individual who has advertised his capacity to help is asking for trouble, most of all if we are promised quick results by opening up processes which leave us empty, defenceless and unable to resist the seven devils wishful of entering within us.

10.

The Survival of Individuality

We must now consider in more detail what happens to the psyche after death. The most important fact to consider is that it retains its individuality. This is the absolute contrary of what I would have expected. As a young man I rejected the existence of God or rather the kind of God my upbringing and education required me to venerate. I rejected Him because of the cruelties, punishments and injustices which He permitted to happen around me and which His admirers celebrated with considerable gusto in the Old Testament. As I was revolted by His punishments I did not wish to supplicate for His rewards. Among the latter I was sufficiently naive to reckon the gift of eternal life. With the passage of time I preferred the idea of total annihilation to the contrived hell and the inexplicable heaven we were left to shuttle between without much clear guidance from above or below.

Later in life I was interested, if not deeply drawn, to Buddhism because it seemed more reasonable and more clearly understandable and because it left wide open the nature of God. It gave us the opportunity if necessary to write a testimonial for Him rather than He for us. I was attracted by the brilliantly simple argument that life is suffering, that suffering comes from desire, and desire from attachment. I could see that peace came from self-annihilation, a phrase I became inordinately fond of. My cardinal error was that, however much I protested to the contrary, I was thinking always in terms of annihilation of the personality. The ultimate peace to me consisted in the drop melting in the ocean, of the last relics of personality dissolving in an indivisible consciousness common to all men and to all living things. It was a shock for me to discover that, with the death of the body and personality, the psyche still, from beyond the grave, maintained the interests and attachments of the human personality though the latter were manifested to a lesser degree.

We can understand this particular question best by limiting ourselves at first to a study of those discarnates who, after death, resume contact with us as soon as possible. I am here only speaking of those with creative and good intentions. As much as the good the evil discarnates are drawn back into this world but for different motives. Among those with whom one is now dealing one is struck first of all by the degree to which ordinary human love determines maintenance of contact. Here, again, is something I had never expected. Such a concept seemed too facile, too easy and too sentimental. I was also repelled by the reported banalities of many spiritualistic communications which possibly I did not study with adequate care.

The discarnates who speak to us soon after their death on this earth are recruited from those who, in this life, have developed the capacity to communicate with discarnate entities. It is as though they had crossed a barrier and were talking from the other side of the fence. It is impossible and foolish to define what one means by soon after death but this, in terms of our time, is a matter of months rather than years. My main mentor Braida de Montserver began to speak to her special woman friend a year to a day after her death. A still more evolved psyche, that of the woman who was Camillia in my Roman and Helis de Mazerolles in my Cathar reincarnations, returned to us in little more than two months.

The motives governing the speed of return after death are varied and more than one can operate in an individual case. Human love, interrupted at its height by death, is, provided those who love each other are both psychic, probably the quickest stimulus to resumed contact. I have known a case where the lovers were psychically rejoined inside less than two months. At the same time love of different varieties, particularly through several incarnations, can equally provoke a quick return. The aforesaid Camillia/Helis, whom I have known through six antecedent incarnations and whom I never met in this life, returned to her mother with a message for me inside two months after her death. In such a number of incarnations the love of sister for brother, of servant for master or mistress, is involved, but always there is a history of physical love and living together in at least one incarnation. This is again contrary to what I would have expected and what I previously thought but it is undeniably true. On reflection it makes good logic. How can one withdraw from matter and the urges of the flesh without having experienced the latter? To set up as a discarnate adviser without having known the ecstasies, agonies, disappointments and illnesses of the flesh would be altogether illogical. It would be a suitable background for raw, possibly eunachoid youths, approaching human agony by dogma picked up at the theological college, but it is not to be expected of those who have undergone the education of death as well as life.

The discarnates are interested in every aspect of the human lives of those with whom they are in contact. They said frankly that there were some for whom sexual activity was, if they were sensible, completely barred and those for whom it was a necessity. This is one of their most surprising revelations and is in complete opposition to the unreal and perverse duality of puritanical Protestant and Catholic Christianity which persists in seeing even our carnal life on this earth as a continual war between the flesh and the spirit. There was no doubt that the discarnates were on the side of the woman whom St. Augustine abandoned selfishly to save his soul. They had no time for self-imposed and willed mortifications of the flesh. The whole tenor of their thought in these matters was that love of any kind was important. In this they were taking the attitude Christ adopted to Mary Magdalene when he said her sins would be forgiven her because she had loved much. Their attitude to sexuality, at least to heterosexuality, of any kind was simple. 'Did it make them happier, and did they feel more relaxed?' They were insistent that sexual activity was no yardstick by which moral systems could be measured. They regarded the manufacture of sexual sins as the work of priesthoods of homosexual persuasion. Nevertheless they taught that human beings had to outlive the physical aspects of love but that they could only do so by its practice in a proportion of their incarnations. They were as positive about this as they were about the fact that the highly psychic, and those living at the level of the individualised spirit, had no need in this world for physical love and that they were ill-advised to indulge in it even to bring peace to others. In this, as in all things, wisdom was memory and the latter was in turn the summation of experience through several incarnations.

Where the discarnates are still concerned with human love and, in particular, with their love of those left behind, they will, if we are able to listen to them, continue to discourse with us. When there is no one left on earth to whom they have been bound by ties of affection they break contact with this planet. The former Camillia/Helis de Mazerolles said that I was her last tie with this earth and that when I died or ceased to have need of her, she would return no more. Some might find this difficult to follow because the discarnates have loved so often in this world, but this is to forget that they have so often loved the same person in different incarnations. I was loved by the woman of whom I was speaking as far back as 1250 BC or earlier. This really provides a long enough connection.

This means that the discarnates destined to keep contact with psychics still here on earth will for the most part return so long as there is a bond of personal love between them. At first sight this might imply that the ether would be choked with the voices of discarnates calling to those they have loved and left. It must not be forgotten that the discarnates who communicate with us for our instruction are only recruited from those who, in this life, have had the power to talk directly to the dead without the intermediary of a medium. This must necessarily reduce the number of such contacts. The individuals of whom I am speaking are to be distinguished from those who, deliberately and voluntarily, act as mediums to enable the bereaved to talk with their loved ones. Those functioning as oracles in this life have never qualified for the role of professional medium; it has descended upon them. Endowed with an inward passivity, often at variance with the active exterior they present to the world, the discarnates have spoken first to them and not they to the discarnates. Such people are distinguishable from professional mediums in that the discarnates who speak to them, and whose role they will assume in due course, are obvious agents of a cosmic purpose. The distinction is quite simple. The voices speaking through professional mediums are presumed to be acting for the comfort of individuals. The discarnates of whom I am speaking, and their human agents, are concerned with the benefit of mankind as a whole, with his destiny here and elsewhere, and with the unchanging truths of existence.

Of those who, psychics in this life, are destined to become discarnate entities communicating with us to further a cosmic purpose, those who have shown themselves capable of out-of-the-body experiences are the most likely candidates. This is easy to follow. In out-of-the-body experiences the psyche has, in this life, shown itself capable of detaching itself from the personality. It is therefore in life revealing aptitudes normally only revealed after death.

A person with the attributes of an oracle can act as a catalyst to another less capable of communicating with the discarnates when the latter wish to contact the less evolved subject in order to impart some constructive information. It may be a matter of instruction in healing or of help with the transmission of verbal or written truth. In such cases the oracle having direct contact with the instructing discarnates can be said to act in a mediumistic capacity. I have noticed that such persons detest the word medium. It seems that to them positive searching for communications from the next world is anathema. This distinction between passive hearing and acceptance of wisdom, and active searching and training for it, appears to constitute an unbridgeable gulf between the discarnates and their earthly contacts with whom I have been concerned and those operating in spiritualistic or allied circles. I do not say that the latter do not do good and provide comfort for many. I merely repeat what I have been so often told from the other side, that one only learns by unsought experience and passive waiting.

A few highly developed psychics have also the capacity to live and heal at the level of the spirit. There are those to whom in this life angelic and Christlike figures appear outlined in gold, and very rarely in the refined semblance of the human form. In the sphere of healing those who have such experiences have the capacity to build something of themselves into the nature of others. This process, contrary to the laws of modern psychiatry — are there any? — is an expression of the indivisibility of consciousness which occurs when we reach a high enough level. This intimate fusion with another can only take place at the level of the spirit. It is what the Buddhists mean when they speak of one mind and of the common essence, and analogous to what the dissemination of the Holy Spirit means to the Christian. Such people have often the capacity to take away completely the pains of others. They were especially active in periods of persecution when it was necessary for some to die for the faith often after, or under, torture. It is only natural that such people after death may not function as discarnates instructing the living. Having already attained something of the Christ status in life they may pass directly after death into the stratum from which they cannot reincarnate and which excludes them from regular, direct contact with this earth. Those who, in this life, manifest such qualities have been, prior to their contemporary incarnation, given the choice of reincarnating or no.

The discarnate instructors who remain sufficiently near to the earth to talk to us daily if they deem it necessary are still very much concerned with our lives on this earth. The fact that it is they who get in touch with us rather than we with them is revealed in their frequent question, "Is there anything else you want to know?" They talk clearly and lucidly and always in the vernacular. Each has his or her idiosyncratic approach as they would in life, but they are always lucid and practical. They talk prose and never poetry. I do not know any whose language is elevated. They prefer to deal with present or immediately future happenings rather than distant events. In present events their preference is always for the relief of suffering. In dealing with physical or mental illnesses they are more accessible than to questions as to what will happen today or tomorrow. They indicate what we should do to aleviate this or that symptom or situation. Even in dealing with illness they are diffident about answering questions about long-term prognosis. Occasionally they offer it themselves. This is not because they do not know but because they believe that, however much on this earth we may see into the future or remember the past, it is necessary for our own happiness and development that we should live a day at a time, better still a minute at a time. Also they are concerned that we should recognize that there is a pattern in life, not only in our life in this world but extending to the other worlds with which they are concerned. They emphasize that they cannot alter the basic pattern of existence but that they can amend some of its consequences. They cannot help a girl being possessed and intensely depressed after an agonising succession of illnesses. They can influence the mind of the surgeon who had recently performed a major operation on her so that he insisted that the psychiatrist called in should not be a Freudian. They cannot prevent, except rarely, malevolent living transmitters of evil or contaminated discarnates from causing depression, accidents and illnesses to those who are especially vulnerable targets in attracting the emanations of evil. But they can counteract the effects either by direct action on their part or by recruiting other psychics to rally to the aid of the afflicted, by offering treatment such as the laying on of hands according to specific Cathar or Celtic techniques. I myself tore a ligament in a hip. It was written in the book that I should do so. In spite of the intense pain and impairment of movement I staggered down the drive to be taken by car to a highly developed psychic. The logical course of action would have been to have stayed where I was and called in a doctor. While the benevolent discarnates could not prevent my fall, they could arrange that the woman to whom I was being driven and whom I had not telephoned previously was waiting at her doorstep to help me upstairs before giving me treatment.

It should be understood that the after death wisdom imparted by the discarnates was of two kinds. Firstly, they dealt with human problems, with the predicaments in which we on earth found ourselves. Secondly, they instructed us as to the history and symbolism of Dualism. Thirdly, they spoke of the eternal truths and of the future of man and this planet. In this chapter I will deal only with their attitude to day to day problems. They never call for the superhuman in man. They see us as we are and expect no more of us than we can give. In this they differ from more fanatical orthodox Christians. They are not out to train record breakers. Always there is the emphasis on happiness and simple personal enjoyment. This was surprising to me, not because what they say is unreasonable. I myself believe that joy is more educative than suffering. What astonished me at first was that such attitudes should be manifested by discarnates who had been Cathars. The latter have always been painted as impossibly ascetic and gloomy people. They have been so described both by the inquisitors and by rather embarrassed defenders of Catharism who felt that those to whom they were loyal were asking a little too much of human nature. Such people would have been comforted to hear many of the conversations I have had with the discarnates.

The reader must make allowance for the fact that all the discarnates with whom I have spoken were strongly Dualistic. To say that all discarnates are Dualist would be absurd. I am only saying that all I have contacted have been of this persuasion. I cannot do other than present the material as I received it. Not a lot of interpretation on my part has been necessary. Discarnates who are truly messengers of angels and archangels do not indulge in banalities. I have heard nothing of the 'Uncle Herbert still loves his gravy' level. The afterlife is never painted as an English picnic blessed with surprisingly good weather. 'Sweet of God to send us such a lovely day, dear.' Nothing of this nature has intruded in our conversations. At the same time I cannot say that what we said to each other was manifestly unearthly. It could not be because it was based on commonsense. But more than that, the revenants still in contact with the world retain a little of its prejudices. Braida herself said that of those remaining on this earth Miss Mills, the central character of two of my books, and her own daughter meant more to her than anyone. It did not prevent her from giving me completely disinterested advice. Camillia/Helis made no bones about it that I was her favourite and was constantly urging me not to expend too much energy on other members of the group and on people outside it. Braida de Montserver recognised that I would always listen to a female rather than a male discarnate and arranged things accordingly.

One discarnate to whom I talked admitted that he still hated his cousin. He described her as totally evil. This latter remark had a profound effect on me. It convinced me that that battle between good and evil goes on not in this world alone but throughout the universe except in the central vibrationless source of being from which the oeons emigrated at the Fall. I have for some time realised that the battle between good and evil cannot be confined to this planet alone. It is here where evil has its greatest victory but the next and higher zone of awareness is also saturated with evil. How otherwise could we have such phenomena as possession? Hades itself is not a hell of punishment but certainly a hell in that in it the light and dark entities are fighting after death for the possession of the psyches of those escaping from the flesh. The remark of this discarnate about his cousin enabled me to see that to conceive of this world as the most formidable battleground of Armageddon is erroneous. Here goodness is not being defeated. It is defeated already. The real Twilight of the Gods, the Ragnerok of truly Norse mythology, recognized this long ago. We are the fallout from Armageddon which has been conducted at a higher strata of awareness than we know in this planet.

I was interested to note to what degree the discarnates retain our feelings and emotions. I had originally credited them with none. I knew from the warmth of their voices that they were certainly not glacial. The discarnate who said he hated his cousin was almost devoid of the *emotion* of hate. In this life he had been totally selfless and considerate except towards his monstrous relative. What he really meant to convey was that he regarded her as hateful, as an instrument of evil and likely to remain so. Other discarnates have said they remain 'concerned' about what happens to those they love but that they no longer feel agony at their sufferings. They say that life is entirely changed for them. They do not use the word death but phrases like 'From on this side' or 'From where we see things'. They indicate that human agony is not possible for them because they are seeing as a whole what we call past, present and future. This is easy to understand because in this world our dreads and fears are directed mostly to the future. When confronted with a calamity we tend to suffer in the knife-edge present. Our regrets and depressions are often related to past actions or omissions. It is therefore easy to see that the relatively timeless state which follows death reduces enormously the discarnates' capacity to suffer. And very certainly they live in a world which to us is remarkably timeless. In talking to them they show no sense of chronological time.

That some suffering must be felt by the discarnates is surely self-evident. Why otherwise would they still be so occupied in relieving the agonies of those left on this earth? Here we must recognise a compassion so total that it can be painless and which differs from pity, which is an agonised state for he who pities as well as the pitied. I have felt this total compassion once in this life. I have no doubt it is what the creative revenants feel almost perpetually. I say 'almost' of intention because I have detected exhaustion in the voice of one of the revenants after she had moved from one to another of her proteges on earth who needed her support. I have heard Camillia/Helis reduced to faint exasperation by what she thought a recalcitrant attitude on my part.

What one must realise in dealing with the revenants is that they are only one step ahead of the most developed living psychics. They have often said to me, 'Go and talk to So and So. She is the same as us.' That is to say that So and So in this life has attained the same degree of wisdom as the discarnates.

One of the most telling of the simple maxims imparted to us is what is meant by imprisonment in matter, by being engulfed in the flesh. I had assumed originally that this referred to a considerable extent, though not to a preponderating degree, to the sensual pleasures of sex and food and drink. These are of little concern to the discarnates. To them the chief weapon of the flesh is the will to power, the desire to dominate over others.

This is implied in the very possession of personality because the body-personality complex is essentially competitive. The world is a jungle. There is in it every gradation between those who live like tigers and those who indulge in non-violence. The latter may be a form of self-indulgence because, unless other animals resist the tiger, the whole jungle falls under his dominion. To dominate does not mean to give orders and to see they are carried out. There are certain almost biological laws of nature which cannot be dispensed with. What the discarnates have in mind is the crime of revelling in domination which, beginning at the level of the personality, can dominate the psyche so that the latter remains after death tied to the world as a possessing entity or reincarnates as a transmitter of evil.

The individual acting as an intermediary between us and the discarnates regularly communicating with us is, if she is of the highest degree of psychic evolution possible to the living, able to do so without effort or amendment of consciousness. By the highest state of evolution one means a tiny minority who are given the choice as to whether or no they would reincarnate and chose to do so because of the intensity of their compassion. There are two discarnates with whom Miss Mills, whom I have described in some of my previous books, is in regular and effortless communication. She can see and talk to them every day without exhaustion or after effects. They act, indeed, as a tonic. There are others with whom she talks less frequently but equally effortlessly. These others are less versed in the higher truths than Braida and Dr. Charles, the constant mentors of Miss Mills. In talking with all four Miss Mills is fully conscious. She remains in this state and suffers no exhaustion. There is, however, one other discarnate who feels occasionally the need to communicate with me. This involves Miss Mills being taken over in a trance state. This is what she and the discarnates describe as a matter of vibrations. This particular discarnate Camillia/Helis, Betty in her life in this century, is of a higher level of evolution than the others. Here again, the latter phrase means that the discarnate in question may have no further need to reincarnate. She says that whether she does so or no depends on how I conduct myself in the last years of my life. As I have said she has indicated on more than one occasion that I am her last link with this earth. I cannot think that she means that it is impossible for me to escape the necessity of reincarnating again. I can only infer that she means that she can withdraw from contact with the earth if I show some evidence, at the end of my life, of being able to stand completely on my own two feet.

After talking to Camillia/Helis/Betty on my behalf, Miss Mills is for some hours disorientated in time and place and suffers from headache, giddiness and double vision. When I talk through her with the other four discarnates previously mentioned she suffers no symptoms. When, as happens very rarely, she acts as a medium to enable a non-psychic to talk with the discarnates she suffers from the above mentioned symptoms but more intensely and for a longer period. This, I think, is the cardinal difference between what I can only call a messenger of the discarnates like Miss Mills and an ordinary medium. The former has for the most part free, symptomless communication with the discarnates because the latter seek her rather than she them. It is for this reason that she communicates mostly in full waking consciousness and only goes into trance when she strays off the wavelength she shares with the discarnates. She never now goes into trance with me, as distinct from the days when we were reliving our past incarnations, because she and I are so much on the same wavelength, in having shared so many incarnations and in having been, to different degrees, intimately associated with each other in all of our previous lives.

The discarnates with whom I have spoken, mostly through the agency of highly evolved living psyches but occasionally directly, are relatively low in the hierarchy of communicating psyches but of course still to be distinguished from the mass of those who, after death, do not establish contact with us at all. There are higher beings who communicate with us under particular circumstances. They do not make direct contact with us, at least with people of my stage of development. They speak directly to such as Miss Mills. Even when she is present I cannot hear their voices as I can those of Braida and the other discarnates I have mentioned. One converses in a kind of celestial telepathy. One's mind switches off whichever subject it has been considering previously. One finds oneself speaking with confidence of subjects one has not hitherto understood. It seems as if one is asking questions and providing one's own answer, but the explanation is that our thinking processes at such times as these are taken over by the discarnate entity and that we are aware of the takeover. This has happened to me frequently with Guilbert de Castres, the most erudite of the Cathar bishops. There are two absolutely fundamental characteristics of these conversations. One is that they are only held with people who do not reincarnate. Guilbert de Castres has not done so since the thirteenth century. It is therefore necessary that they be approached through a lower stratum of discarnates because the latter are still in communication with us on earth. The second point is that such conversations are always initiated by the discarnate except in excessively rare cases where the living communicating with him are at the highest level of evolution possible in this world.

Discarnates of the level of Guilbert de Castres are interposed between those who communicate with us regularly and the angel or Christlike figures. They are usually only available at times of crisis or when some particularly complex point of philosophy requires elucidation. The angels or Christlike figures, described previously as outlined and embodied in light when seen from this earth, never speak to the living or even to the non-angelic discarnates, be the latter those who communicate regularly with us or people of higher philosophical status, of higher gnosis, like Guilbert de Castres. Just as form vanishes as we reach the higher echelons of the hierarchy so also does sound. If we recall that the lower discarnates are outlined in silver and the angelic or Christlike figures in gold it becomes clear that the old axiom that speech is silver and silence is golden has a deep esoteric significance.

Though form and voice vanish as we pass from the lower discarnates to those of higher philosophical pretensions the two are replaced by touch. It is not that the discarnates of any variety require to touch each other. I am here talking of our contact with them and what they achieve by touching us. Such touch is not to be conceived of as anything analogous to touch as a component of one of our five senses. The highest development of this faculty involves a form of contact far exceeding what is understood in this world by flesh meeting flesh, as in holding hands or in massage. Even on earth there are those who, by touch, can so release our psyches that we are enabled, usually through discarnates, to look back on past lives and to comprehend a little the acts of creation and the truths of the Cosmos. There are others who, still in this world, can give us deeper knowledge of worlds other than our own and of lives we have lived before by touch performed in out-of-the-body experiences. The touch of the lower discarnates, designed to heal our pains or comfort our afflictions, is felt as a layer of coolness a little distant from our skin. When we are touched by more than one discarnate we feel a feathery zone of coolness encircling our bodies. This is a healing effect which may last for days or weeks. It is not so potent as the rare touch of the angel or Christ figures, following which it is as though some permanent and untarnished goodness had been built into our nature. The wisdom of the lower discarnates who communicate with us is concerned largely with this world, but is intensely useful because from their point of vantage beyond time and space they see far more than we do from the cramped redoubt of our own personality. When they look upwards they see and comprehend as far as the angel or Christ figures. They are aware only of the existence but not of the nature of the archangels. But they know that the latter are what remains of the aeons which, at the Fall, remained drawn to the light from which they were derived and never succumbed to the allurements of matter. They know that the archangels are aeons like those which, descending into matter, form the prototype of man. They remain still products of the schism which occurred in the invisible harmony but are not contaminated by it.

As the discarnates cannot see or feel the realities of being beyond the state of the angels, this should enlighten us as to the ludicrous fallacy that we can from this earth talk directly to God. What may seem to be humility is monstrous pride. We cannot pray directly to God because to do so we would need an instrumentation beyond that which we achieve when we speak even to the higher philosophical discarnates like Guilbert de Castres or make brief contact, twice in a lifetime, with the Christ figures. All life, here and hereafter, is a question of attaining higher levels of awareness. In this world we have the added problem of synthesizing what we attain for moments and cannot sustain.

11.

The Fate of the Psyche

In the last chapter we studied the after death activities of those articulate psyches destined to remain in communication with us or to develop soon into members of the higher hierarchy.[1] What of the psyches who awaken from sleep and merely live an interterrestrial life before returning to the earth? As we have seen they are astounded and need to become habituated to the world of colours around them. The colours they see are realities and not sensations. They do not depend on the impact of light at different wavelengths on the retina because as discarnates they have learnt to dispense with such mechanisms as sensations. They see that their world is a reality. Compared with our world it is *the* reality of which our planet is merely the pale image. The scientists' theories of colour apply only to this world. In reality the green of the earth is a pale reflection of the emanation of the green of living and gigantic emerald pastures visible to those who have shed the burden of matter. The green and gold of the earth are shadowy distortions of their living equivalents transmitted through a distorting lens of matter.

Under the guidance of those attendant on them on waking from the sleep we call death they learn the reality of being rather than doing. They shed their cares and the labours of this world. All that was constructive and what they worked for below they see now without effort. In a word, with the shedding of personality, they perceive things clearly and without willed attention. In this world we are required to work for what we come to know. In the next we know what we have worked for. Perception in the next of the worlds takes the place of analysis, synthesis and willed learning. The

latter activities are necessary on earth because it takes a
number of lives to learn the limitations of intellectual
knowledge. Wandering in a world where the still
individualised being sees with his psyche he learns that he
has lived previously in a shadow world where ambition,
greed and love of power tried to create reality from transitory
abstractions. He sees that what is is and is not to be fought
for. "What is this life if full of care, we have no time to stand
and stare?" In the next world the psyche learns by
observation, based on merely being, what in this world the
personality failed to achieve by stress. In the next of the
worlds the psyche resumes its acquaintance with the psyches
of those it has known in this world. The idea that we take on
where we left off is not true. We do not necessarily resume
close contact with those nearest to us in the last of our lives
in this world. This may be a relief to many and a pain to
some. We stay in close contact with those we have known
well or been intimate with in the world if they have shared
many incarnations with us. The number of incarnations is
the factor deciding the company we will keep in the next
world. At this stage in psychic development wounds are not
necessarily healed or sins forgiven. The battle for the
ultimate freedom of the ultimate non-egocentric individuality
goes on throughout most of the layers of consciousness
which follow death. This is not as depressing as it seems. We
can describe it as a battle being fought throughout all
eternity but this is only an estimate of duration as seen from
this earth. We must remember that from the next of the
worlds and onwards time is a vortex of fused vibrations. Past,
present and future are in the whirlpool together. Words like
immortality and the instant cease to have meaning because
they are, in the higher zones, basically identical.

In the next world one does not avoid those who are one's
enemies on this earth or, worse still, run into our friends
with a glad start of surprise as at the commencement of a too
prolonged garden party. There is no neat arrangement by
which those who have been our enemies or with whom we
have been in considerable disharmony are placed in
proximity to us so that each can atone to the other in a
process of celestial disinfection. Neither we nor they atone
consciously for the wrongs we have done them. The next
world is not a branch office designed by those who believe

in karma. Such ideas arise from a complete misapprehension of the nature of the psyche, the consciousness of which is entirely different from that of the personality. It does not think in terms of likes and dislikes, of broken friendships or unforgotten wounds. Ultimately it is concerned with the overpowering energies of good and evil but its main function at this stage is to emit passively waves of radiation which draw towards it those it most needs in the higher lives we lead between our death on this earth and our subsequent rebirth. Guides to whom the psyche is entrusted after death are agents through which this magnetism is exercised.

If the guides are those the psyche has known through several incarnations the question is, do they go forward to higher planes or do they return to the earth? The latter is infinitely the commoner process. It is prepared for by the contacts made by the psyche in the next world. It spends much of its time in the company of psyches to which it must adjust its level of vibration. This is in order to fit it for its return to families it will enter on earth. It encounters in the world beyond ours members of these families and attunes its vibration to their level. Very often it does this as much for the benefit of the family it is drawn to enter as for its own. There is no element of choice in this question as to into whom the psyche will descend. This may seem cold and relentless but it is not so. There is equally no element of no choice. The psyche is not cast blindly into the world between its world and ours and enters without hope and in agony a new life. Certainly a child cries when it is born, and to enter into matter after the better world of the beyond is certainly calamity, but the child is only aware of the catastrophe as such after it has achieved human consciousness and the beginnings of personality. In the next world the psyche is beyond attractions and revulsions and desires and abhorrences. It moves like a young fish through sun and shade reflected in the water because both are necessary for its development. Remember that, even in the next of the worlds, the developing psyche is happier and more peaceful than we, locked up in our egocentric personalities, simply because it is not concerned deliberately with happiness and peace. It is passively fulfilling a destiny spread over many lives on earth and in many psychic existences between our lives on this planet. As an agent of destiny, in the psychic

world between our lives on this earth, it feels little pain.
When it descends here below it pays full measure for its
temporary immunity.

Does the psyche continue after death its earthly
occupations? There is a naive and sentimental idea that
somehow we continue to go to the office, which in some
mysterious way has inevitably become well loved since our
death, and that we go on as before but in a nicer way. This is
impossible. The next world is not an Orwellian nightmare
packed with offices and consulting rooms. More than this
such activities are attributes of personality, something which,
in the next world, we have outgrown. What happens is that
the psyche sees the past played back like a film in reverse.
Commonly it sees its past incarnations. Even the
undeveloped see a number of these. Even after death only
the very developed see several. What all see is a flashback of
our last life on earth. They undergo, but in a more extensive
and prolonged way, what happens to drowning sailors.[2] The
difference between the flashback and real life is similar but
far more intensive and comparable to what we would see if,
every day, we could see recorded a film and view
dispassionately the events of the day and our reaction to
them.

The cosmic aim of this process is to enable us to assess
the enormous emotional wastage which accompanies our
actions and to estimate the colossal loss of energy we
expend in the hates and prejudices which we manage to
weave into the pattern of our day's work. This process is a
slow, even, protracted and painless abreaction, far more
useful than what is achieved in the world by drugs precisely
because it is a natural, inevitable process which is part of the
pattern of our destiny and not a surgically brutal shortcut.
The experience of seeing our past lives recorded prepares us
for our return to earth. There comes a point at which not the
will but the magnetic impulse to return becomes imperative.
The psyche does not say to itself, 'It is time I had another
try.' It is drawn back into a cosmic whirlpool which returns it
to earth.

What I have said applies to the generality of psyches.
Those more evolved engage in what they call study. There is
no doubt whatever about the philosophical nature of the
latter. It is always said of any prophet worth his salt that his

fundamental message is simple, that is to say not metaphysical or philosophical. What this means is that, *in this world*, there is always a straightforward exoteric message for the untutored. Any Christian can understand at its simplest level what is meant by 'God is love' and 'Thou shalt love thy neighbour as thyself'. Buddhist peasants can understand that life is suffering and that the latter comes from desire and attachment. There is, however, no doubt whatever about the philosophical preoccupations of the developing discarnates. Among the subjects studied are the nature of light and the creation of life on this planet. This is because exoteric communication, including exhortations, prohibitions and the Ten Commandments, are addressed to the personality. The revenants have indicated that to try to understand transcendental philosophy with the intellect, the weapon of personality, is a cardinal error. (This, incidentally, disposes of most European philosophy with a single blow). It is only through the psyche that we can achieve sufficiently piercing insight to comprehend the nature of truth. When evolving discarnates 'study' they are indulging in a higher development of perception, of seeing things as they are. The difficulty I have found in the past in describing their thoughts on paper is that I was trying to understand rather than to see. What such discarnates are aiming at is an ultimate esoteric simplicity as easy to comprehend as the statement that God is love. We see this in the frequency with which they study 'the nature of light'. This is because light is the first canalisation of the energy of goodness. Goodness itself is, with evil, the first fission product of the Fall. It is in returning to simplicities such as these that the discarnates continue their studies.

Special consideration must now be given to the post history of violent deaths such as occur in accidents, crime, in war and in what, significantly enough, are called acts of God such as earthquakes and lightning. As we have seen it takes the psyche three days to leave the body. In a soldier killed in war the psyche is expelled from the body too quickly. It is not prepared for its flight as are those who succumb at the end of an illness in which a fatal issue could be anticipated. It may be argued that the same problem occurs where a person dies in his first coronary attack or stroke but the circumstances are by no means similar because, below the surface, and not erupting through consciousness in the form of symptoms, the tissues have been preparing for days or weeks for these cardiovascular catastrophes. Many patients doomed to perish under such circumstances have premonitions, without any concrete reason, that the end is near. Some of these premonitions may be psychic but others are substitute quasi-symptoms through which the tissues are predicting the end.

The psyches of people meeting violent ends have difficulty in reconciling themselves to the fact that they are dead. They wander about in a no-man's land between this world and the next. They do not enter into the sleep which follows death. They may remain in this state for what in our time extends to weeks or even months, as in the case of a woman who perished in a fire in a building to which she had re-entered to see if there were any victims still left inside. Such people, when they finally fall asleep, sleep late.

Psyches which remain especially disturbed and disorientated are those where death results from violent explosions, including shell-bursts, in which the body is shattered or disintegrates. Here the wandering in no-man's land can be desperate, disorientated and very protracted. This is because every organ and cell in the body has an etheric equivalent of its physical form. The whole is joined together in an insubstantial harmony. This etheric harmony, normally ready to take over in natural death, is completely shattered by, say a bomb bursting and blowing the victim to pieces. It takes time before the synthesis of the etheric equivalent of the whole man can be achieved. In addition, in death from violent explosions, the psyche is expelled suddenly from the body and denied the three days allotted for the process. A minor version of this catastrophe can occur when the patient does not die. In his story "Now I Lay Me Down", Hemingway records how, when a shell burst near him, he felt that his soul had vacated his body and implies distinctly that the insomnia which followed was due to this cause. In this insomnia he was translating to the level of the earth the sleepless, disorientated wanderings he would have suffered in Hades had he been killed by the shell.

NOTES

1. Words necessarily exposing time and duration to us on earth are wholly inapplicable in the next of the worlds. We have to use them because they are the approximate equivalents to meanings we try to convey.

2. An ex-sailor patient torpedoed in the last war left me in no doubt of the reality of this phenomenon which, once underway, was viewed with detachment.

12.

From Death to Life

We can write of the psyche's return to earth to reincarnate again simply because we are of the earth and are more aware of what goes on in the zones of consciousness nearest our own. The evolving discarnates who communicate with us and largely reincarnate may, however, aspire to the state of the higher gnosis in which they do not reincarnate but are still able to speak with us through lower discarnates functioning at the level they have just vacated. Those capable of the higher gnosis, like Guilbert de Castres, ascend in their turn to the angel strata and beyond it to the archangels. In doing so their adoption of form diminishes to vanishing point in the angel figures and when it occurs is expressed in gold. The archangels are always invisible. What we know of what occurs from the archangelic state onwards I will deal with in a later section, but the last stages of our ascent are inevitably less clear to us than the more accessible phenomenon of our return to earth in order to reincarnate.

When preparing to return to earth the psyche is drawn towards the influence of the planets. The vibrations of the latter are attuned to different degrees of development of different psyches. The degree of evolution of the psyche is not the only consideration. In the next world the psyche maintains the same interests as its accompanying personality has had during its life on this earth. It has the same bias in favour of the visual or literary arts as the case may be. It has the same intoxication with beauty or the same preoccupation with ethics. The difference is that in the next world these interests are pursued passively, without the individual wishing to gain from them or acquire proficiency in them. He has no need for proficiency because the beauty he sees in the next world is greater than he can accomplish in this and there is therefore no need to strive for it. When the time comes to reincarnate, the psyche moves within the vibrational orbit of those planets associated with its particular interests as well as its level of consciousness. The exodus is seasonal. Different times of the year on earth have a rhythm and amplitude of vibrations suited to the reception of certain varieties of psyches. The metaphysical, the mystical, the lovers of order, the ardently creative and the psychic are drawn into the particular vortex of vibrations generated by the earth for their reception. It is for such reasons that we associate with people born in different months with different traits of character.

A descending psyche is subject to another cross-fire of vibrations which accompanies those which are of seasonal inception. It is pulled to the earth by the latter but as it comes nearer to the mechanisms of matter it is influenced also by the vibrations of the family to which it has been drawn. My wife and my own family must serve as a single example of what I mean. My eldest daughter was born on December 14th. Her two first cousins appeared on the same day and her aunt on the 15th. Her husband saw the light on the 18th and her paternal grandmother on the 20th. My wife was born on January 25th, her second daughter on the 24th and her sister's son on the 26th. This kind of experience is commonplace.

This descent into families supplies the psyche on the point of reincarnating with the workaday requirements for its career on earth. It is through these connections that it learns the necessity of living with people and that it needs must, in certain directions, develop through the personality which it inhabits in its life on this earth.

This tendency for birthdays to be grouped together is only shown where one or two members in the family are evolving at a significant rate. Otherwise the birthdays are scattered more haphazardly through the year. The psyches of those evolving rapidly or already considerably developed are subject to another magnetic compulsion. They are drawn towards those types who will most facilitate their psychic development. The influence of the family which they will enter is, as I have said, primarily concerned with the development of personality. It is for this reason that in their new incarnation they show a tendency to be drawn towards those themselves born under certain signs of the Zodiac. It is astonishing in my life how so many who have meant so much to me have been born in September. It seems that it was essential for me to consort with those born under Virgo or Libra. The most developed psyches I have met had birthdays in the first half of September. It seems that it is part of the pattern that those closest to me physically and spiritually should be born in September or early October.

The last mentioned phenomenon is one of the most basic influences inducing group incarnation. In this latter process there are two other factors of equal importance. Those who have known and loved us in past incarnations may actually share the same birthday or be born within a day or two of either oneself or members of one's family. For example, a woman who was a friend of mine as far back as two thousand BC, has a birthday on January the 23rd, lining up with my eldest daughter, wife and nephew. Another man friend shares the same birthday as myself.

Where group reincarnation is a major consideration these temporal factors exert a stronger compulsion. This is to enable us to see the importance and purpose of our return in groups. This goes as far as to reveal itself in members of a group, or fringe members or relatives, being born on historical dates important in the history of the group. I have said more than once that the Cathar was my dominant incarnation. The massacre at Avignonet occurred on May 29th 1242.[1] This was my father's birthday. The horrifying massacre at Beziers with which the crusade against the Cathar Languedoc got thoroughly underway was on July 22nd 1209. This is the birthday of my son and also that of the only child of a friend of mine in a previous incarnation. The psyche reincarnates on dates important in world history, as well as for familial considerations, in order to emphasize the element of purpose in group reincarnation. It is realised that we on this earth are inescapably caught up in the clutches of time. We cannot estimate the importance of this or that historical movement without attention to dates. Equally we cannot see clearly for what purpose a group has been brought together throughout history without knowing its connections in time with certain historical periods. In short, the Cosmos uses the scientific materialistic evidence we can understand, in order to

convince us that we have a more serious role to play. Once
this has been proved we are free to contemplate the higher
aspect of the purposes for which we were born.

The element of place determines also the geography of our
return. This does not commonly apply to developing psyches.
To be rivetted to one particular place on earth is more the
fate of malign possessing entities or of psyches of
individuals who have come to violent ends. Among
developing psyches the element of place operates under
different sets of circumstances. Members of a group may be
born in, or gravitate towards, the site of a past incarnation
not because they were necessarily happy there but because
the place in question was an especially powerful centre of
healing and other psychic attributes. This certainly happened
in the Bassenthwaite and Loweswater areas in Cumberland in
this incarnation. I was born in Cumberland and walked the
roads and tracks I had followed assiduously thirteen
centuries previously. Other members in this life were
irresistably drawn towards Bassenthwaite and felt they had to
visit it.[2]

The vibrations of place operate in another manner not
connected with the past. Why, in the twentieth century, were
a group of Cathars either born, educated, chose to make their
living or to settle down within fifteen miles of Bristol? The
latter is not a notable power centre. What happens in such
cases is that the agglomeration of psyches forms into a
group, as it were, in transit. They are, by confluence of their
vibrations, drawn towards each other on their way to this
planet. This illustrates a cardinal point. A reincarnating group
formed before birth, as all reincarnating groups must
inevitably be, is in total contradistinction to psychic groups
organizing themselves together in this world. The aims of the
latter may be frankly nefarious or the aim may be good and
its realisation bad. This is because the descent of a group of
psyches ready to reincarnate in Tottenham or Timbuktu is
already passively the subject of a cosmic purpose. The latter
is positive because it is not conceived by the will, but
passively comes into being. This is always the gulf between
what is willessly contrived in the beyond and what we
organize here.

What we have dealt with so far is the descent into matter,
prior to the next incarnation, of either the evolving or the

run of the mill psyche with a lot of incarnations to come. These terms are relative. The huge majority of psyches are evolving because in the end most return to what Christians call the Father, but which is a long way beyond the Father or, for that matter, the Mother Goddess. When we come to consider the matter of the psyches who remain, in close proximity to the earth or return from the next world to Hades but continue to circulate within its frontiers, we are up against an entirely different question.

There are, as it were, psyches who never 'take off'. After death they remain in close contact with the world. This is what is meant by living in Hades. It has nothing to do with a hell devised by a punishing god. It does not even imply an anteroom to it. The classical writers who spoke of the shades and the crossing of Lethe had infinitely more sense than the Christians with their lakes of fire and brimstone and their angelic agents, or were they devils, who kept the flames well stoked. The classical writers referred to Hades as a place but this was allegorical. Hell has been described by modernist Christians as a state of mind. The idea of reward and punishment is still there but has been refined down by sheer necessity imposed by the pressure of public opinion. Hell is a word which is best not used in the present context. People may suffer hell in Hades but the latter is to be seen more as a region of disorientating shadows, neither good nor bad in itself, but where the war between good and evil is conducted at particular intensity, where battles for the soul literally occur, but where the main tension is the struggle of the psyche to emancipate itself from matter.

There are psyches which depart with reluctance from the earth. I am not referring here to those retained by the obligations imposed by a great love but to those who in life have been securely embedded in matter. There are those in whom the love of power, of domination and of riches are so compelling that, even after death, they feel the magnetic compulsion of the world. These vices are usually attributes of personality. We all have them to some extent but in some the degree of development is inordinate and spills over so that it contaminates the psyche. This is what is meant by the iron entering the soul. Most such souls pass through Hades and achieve, after delay, the prolonged sleep which follows death. In this they resemble those who have died by violence. In a way they have, seeing that they have lived beyond the normal limits of aggression and acquisitiveness manifested by the human personality.

There is, however, a grosser variety of those who have lived in error, where the impulse to dominate and acquire has been located primarily in the psyche and where the personality has been a kind of ragged camp follower of a thoroughly corrupted soul. By corrupted one means primarily those who wish to possess the souls of others. One is not talking of those sergeant majors of both sexes whose function it appears to be to mechanise other peoples' lives. These are merely insightless and unconscious puppets who love to bellow, literally or figuratively, but who are not basically rotten. They are themselves insecure people with no insight into their insecurity, only arrogance with which they compensate for it. The evil psyche, heavy and reluctant in its passage through Hades, is that in which the individual has not only exercised and loved power but has had insight into his need for power and has never attempted to curb it.

Another variety of psyche which is reluctant to quit the earth and traverse no-man's land is that of the person who has faithfully followed rigid intellectual systems designed for the salvation of the soul. The latter is quite simply best occupied in communicating with others. This is how it learns best because it is born for active communication. Passivity lies in our hushing our personalities to permit the free action of the psyche. But there are fanatical priests, inquisitors and the like for whom salvation consists in a constantly watchful, second-to-second rigid adherence to systems of belief. There is a type of ecclesiastic for whom ordinary decency and good nature count for little beside frantic subservience to articles of faith. This came out clearly in former ages in trials for heresy and depositions made before the Inquisition. In these the goodness and the sanctity of the accused's life was often not questioned by his interrogators because, to them, it counted for nothing compared with their frantic fidelity to fabricated articles of faith. Indeed it often counted against him as hypocrisy. Was it not evil to be loving and charitable if one did not believe in Transubstantiation or the doctrine of redemption by grace? Such attitudes parch the soul like a desert. They are less evident now than they were because the Church, certainly the Anglican variety, will do anything in its power, be it never so servile and accommodating, to win back its lost authority. Nevertheless, the frenzied practitioner of ritual is still amongst us. In our time there are still those who defend the Inquisition. It only burnt the body to save the soul. The idea of a soul being a kind of fritter left over after the cooking process is quaint and appealing.

In spite of their ironbound faith in their salvation in another world, people of this make up are reluctant to leave this planet. One of the most striking remarks I ever heard was made by one of the best general practitioners I have ever encountered. He was of another generation and infinitely wise. He said that in his time he had been at the deathbeds of many patients. Those were the days when doctors took seriously the dying and their suffering relatives. The old doctor said that the vast majority of deaths were peaceful, that, in the end, the average man was glad to go. He said that among those who were terrified of dying, priests constituted an enormous majority. The support of cast-iron theological systems is a good enough weapon for the contaminated psyche to belabour the recalcitrant blessed or endowed with ordinary good nature. It is the ultimate diabolism to believe and teach that the simple qualities of the heart count for nothing beside Church observance, ritual and subservience to theological systems, men manufactured and men administered, designed to enable priesthoods to ration grace and maintain themselves in positions of power by so doing. All this is less evident in the mild, apologetic, untrained social worker priest of today, but men adapt to the age they live in and there is nothing in the ecclesiastical mentality to lead us to believe that, given the opportunity, the enticement of power would not again prove irresistible. At the last, in the blinding clarity which so often precedes death, and which comes even to the demented as well as to the vicious, the dominating ecclesiastic sees that his kingdom is on *this* earth. He reinforces the magnetic attraction of the latter by his own passionate clinging to it. It is for this reason that many of the revenants seen in hauntings are priests and monks, very often described as austere and sorrowing. Austere they may well be. They are continuing after death the self-mutilation which meant so much to them in this world and which was necessary for the mutilation of others. As for sorrowing, even in Hades they

are regretting their lost dominion. Most of us are glad to
shed with age the burden of what power we have
accumulated. Those who go through Hades with a light load
will see early the living colours of the next world and will
learn more quickly that knowing is more than the
accumulation of knowledge and that love can be full and
nevertheless painless.

There are those in this world who have acted as
transmitters of the force of evil. I am not talking of what I
call sinners because to sin is of our very nature. In a sense
we descend to the earth to learn how to sin with profit, not
in the acquisitive sense but in such a way that we are able to
shrug off the burden of the errors imposed on us by the
possession of a personality necessary to us in the jungle of
existence. One is not talking at all of the so-called sins of the
flesh. If God who created this world gave men desires, and above
all desires which ensure the continuation of the species, the
responsibility is clearly His. Sexual sins are among the
manufactured products which have proved most profitable to
the Church. We should buy in another market and, apropos
this particular manifestation of what is called sin, cease to
call ourselves miserable sinners. Evil is a primeval force little
related to the summation of our earthly sins. The latter are
chiefly destructive to ourselves. Evil, often a gift of the
naturally and even eminently respectable, is an unrecognized
and destructive contagion whose purpose it is to kill or maim
by inducing disease, depression, accident or violence. Some
of those who transmit this force are unaware that they are so
doing. Others act of deliberate intention and, in so doing,
perpetrate the worst horror the world can achieve, the
reinforcement of a capacity for evil by an act of will. When
such people die they enter Hades but never get beyond its
limits. In the cosmic sense of the word they do not sleep at
all. They wander as black shadows in the grey
insubstantiality of the shades, waiting for an opportunity to
return quickly to the world. Some of those who reincarnate
soon are of this nature. They return to their former metier as
transmitters of evil. Those who were passive and
unconscious transmitters in their last life may gain
promotion to the rank of active and conscious transmitters of
evil. Some may, by acts of will, and by consorting with those
of similar make up, become almost generators of evil. This

rapid reincarnation of psyches drenched with evil occurs when civilisations are in a state of decomposition. This is happening with growing intensity at the present time.

Such psyches as I have described remain in Hades, what I have on occasion called the no-man's land between this world and the next, because Hades is essentially a battleground in which the psyches of these transmitters of evil hover constantly like unsleeping bats, to possess the souls of those embarking for the next of the worlds. This is what I mean when I say that the war between good and evil is not only conducted in this world. We can say that, at times like the present, evil triumphs in this world. We cannot laugh off Hitler, Stalin, hijackings, kidnapping and pointless murders as playful variations of the daily round. But certainly in Hades, in the interim between our world and the next, the battle is intensified. The evil entities waiting to reincarnate quickly seek to pervert the vulnerable psyches moving to the next of the worlds and to ensure their return to the earth as satellites of evil. These perverted souls, when they return, are usually normal and happy children at birth and in early infancy, but, with increasing years, there is a tendency to be shut in which has nothing in common with the withdrawn state of the schizophrenic. Theirs is a deliberate, disciplined, conscious withdrawal. They are open to instructions and learn quickly. A number are very gifted. They are resistant to affection but demand it of others and turn it to subservience. 'Shut in' does not mean for them a refusal to learn to acquire. They do these things all too quickly. While passing muster, on superficial observation, as normal and contributing members of the community, they resist all creative contacts, all love, all charity and all the ties of the heart. They are not dead souls because their psyches are alive but only in a negative non-creative sense. They are, in fact, acutely perceptive but use their telepathy to sense the vulnerable moments of their victims. They are often highly psychic but their gifts are contaminated. They are serpents who choose unerringly the moment to strike. They are essentially psyches arrested by others more depraved than themselves who haunt the long colonnades of Hades.

There are some psyches which remain more or less permanently in Hades. Theirs is a two-way recruitment. They include those we have mentioned who have exercised excessive power on earth through their psyches. They include others arriving, as it were, from a reverse direction.[3] Some are psyches which have inhabited Hades since the Fall of man. They have never descended to incarnate in matter because though the latter is from some points of view an impediment, it is infused with the spirit and the memory of the light from which it came. The psyches which never descend further than Hades are the successors of the fallen oeons, who preferred to remain in Hades, in the shadow of matter than in its full substance, because in Hades they could exhibit greater power and reap greater havoc. The construction of matter was, after all, an act of creation. To descend from the light and to haunt Hades perpetually is to be bent on pure destruction.

Those who have redescended into hell include the Furies and other diabolic entities we pass off for our own convenience as mythological but which have been a menace to us since the beginning of time.

To descend into Hades, rather than to enter it from this world, is also the route chosen by those who have, after death, reached the next of the worlds but have gained very little from entry into it. Still drawn by the magnetism of matter, most of all by the compulsion of evil, they redescend and re-enter the shades and take up permanent habitation there. It is from this mid zone between this world and the next that our worst troubles and horrors derive. It harbours the possessing entities which are active at the time of the winter solstice, because at this season the slow vibrations and torpor of the earth and the atmosphere around it, favour the entry of possessing entities into vulnerable psyches on this planet. The malignant discarnates may soften up over years the unstable, and sometimes not so unstable, psychics who are taken over by these malign influences at different times of the year. This occurs through the combined effects of the possessing entity and constellations hostile at certain fixed and limited periods in the calendar. These disaster periods can be very terrifying not only for the possessed but for those close to them, on the same psychic wavelength, and with whom they have shared previous incarnations. Possession varies in intensity but at its worst is aimed at the death of the victim by suicide or that of others by inciting the victim to homicidal frenzies. The old and enfeebled are not spared. Old women may take to self-destruction and old men to the motiveless slaughter of others. At a lesser intensity but spread over a wider sphere of influence these possessing entities are constantly hovering close to the young child's consciousness, seeking opportunities to effect entry and achieve possession, as when the psyche is 'floating' in childhood, when, in the delirium of high fever or concussion, it separates itself from the personality. These effects produce such conditions as night terrors, somnambulism, epilepsy and asthma.

The question arises as to whether the permanent residents of Hades can ever be redeemed. The question is a contradiction in terms because permanence implies non-redemption. Our error in looking at these matters is to think in terms of redemption, of salvation or damnation. The answer is that those once caught up in the central and intoxicating rhythm of Hades stay there forever. This is a horrifying picture to us. Firstly, the phrase forever has a more than ominous note but once again we are thinking in terms of time as it is measured on this planet. In Hades the time factor still exists because how otherwise would the possessing entities come within the pull of the time governed earth in order to take over the innocent but sometimes vulnerable psychics? How otherwise would those who return to earth from the after death sleep and traverse Hades be enabled to do so if they were not sensitive to the attraction of the timebound earth. Nevertheless allowing for these exceptions, the permanent residents of Hades, the furtive guides who are there to meet and seduce the disorientated victims of violent deaths, are largely emancipated from time. They are not condemned to a hell of unending duration. It should also be remembered that there is here no question of torture. They receive what they want, just as, in the end, the evolving psyche reaches a state of bliss. We can say they enjoy hell as others enjoy Heaven. Here again, while we must always accept the reality of the forces of good and evil, above all the latter because it is positively harmful not to do so and makes the inroads of evil easier, we must never think too much in terms of good and evil when we speak of the destiny of the individual. If we do we sink again into the metaphysical morass imposed on us by accepting that there are rewards for good and punishments for evil. There are no rewards and punishments. There is only knowing and being, and in the higher grades of each we see, what we have learnt from our own past lives, most of all from the higher sensitivity we are granted between our lives on this earth, that peace comes from the final surrender of all we have recognized as individuality. Here again we are faced with a paradox. With the disappearance of the said individuality we have left within us something which is supremely but non-egotistically individual and which enables us to know when we are passing through the more heavenly regions.

This idea that all souls cannot be saved may be repellent to good Christians and, indeed, to many right thinking persons of different sectarian allegiances or merely to the civilised. To such people it may smell too much of the Calvanistic doctrine of predestination, of pre-arranged salvation for the chosen few. Have not the Cathars said that in the end all souls, even that of the devil, will be redeemed? But Catharism varied a good deal according to the area in which it is practised, which is perhaps another way of saying according to the degree of culture of its main practitioners. For myself the whole question of saving souls is an anachronism. Once the psyche has passed the rigid time barrier of the world and the partial time barrier of Hades, it it is circulating more or less within its own orbit like a spacecraft cut off from connection with the earth, and fulfilling the laws of nature applicable to it. It is neither damned nor saved. It is merely arranged, in the pattern of the universe, that it continues.

We have to accept that, from the moment of conception to the time we spend level with higher discarnates, we are engaged in a continuous battle between good and evil. Emphatically it is not limited to this earth. To a large extent the battle for good is fought by psyches, actively living in this world, but part way extended to another. These highly evolved people have in fact some of the attributes of the beneficent discarnates. Living psyches of this type are especially vulnerable to the onslaughts of evil, particularly if their capacity to emanate goodness is outstanding. Sometimes creative discarnates intervene on behalf of those who have suffered from the carriers of the plague of evil, be they living or discarnate. A creative discarnate working for good may divert evil to some extent from its target. It may by its influence substitute less malignant symptoms than those extended by the agents of evil. It may apply by discarnate hands measures which reduce the pain of disease or accident. But never can these entities favourable to us alter the total pattern of our destiny. It is indeed part of their function, without telling us over much which will frighten us, to give us some inkling of what is in store for us. (Beware the discarnate who constantly tells you freely, accurately, what will happen to you and yours, without requiring some patient labour of verification on your part).

Sometimes there is a war between the discarnates working for us in moments of crisis and those who wish to hurt us more deeply than they have already. The beneficent discarnates are by no means always successful. There are envenomed interventions on the part of malignant entities designed to poison our relationship both with discarnates who have helped us and with our living friends on the same wavelength. The voices of such evil entities can often be heard breaking into conversations we have had with the creative discarnates. Sometimes they imitate the latter's intonations. They are always freely aware of the subject under discussion and it is difficult to say how one recognizes their intervention. One can say that there is a sudden spitting of venom in the middle of much that was helpful and kind. Sometimes the interjection is so subtle that one is only aware of it afterwards. It has, in my experience, one salient characteristic. It is seldom prolonged. It does not shake one's faith in, or loyalty to, discarnates who when they lived on this earth, one knew through several incarnations. It does not separate us from the living with whom again we have shared a common purpose in previous lives. Nevertheless it is such results as these which malignant entities hope to achieve. What they desire to produce is a horrifying feeling of apartness, of being alone in the world, a dark night of the soul in which one feels one is friendless in this world and the next, and that only the forces of darkness speak the truth, which is often disguised in the form of ethics.

We are not only confronted with the intervention of malign entities in our affairs in this world. The battle for our souls goes on in Hades. It is not a case of the weak-kneed requiring strengthening by the discarnates who watch over us for our benefit. This is true but it is not the whole of the story. There are, in Hades and in this world, those who by their tremendous emanatory capacity to radiate goodness are a special target for evil. Anyone involved in these matters and with eyes to see, though most eyes are sealed, will recognize that this happens in this world. It happens, too, in Hades but here the power of the good discarnates is enormously enhanced by their being not only freed from matter but moving, or destined to move, steadily away from it. This gives them an enormous advantage over the dark discarnates who are still drawn to the slower and earthbound rhythm of matter.

When the evil discarnates, still traversing or lurking in Hades, seek to possess the psyches of the living their magnetic attachment to matter gives them an advantage so that the psyches of the living can be overwhelmed and possessed by them. The picture is changed when good and bad discarnates meet in the relatively immaterial world of Hades. There, those who are concerned with our protection, have an enormous advantage over those bent on our destruction because they have overcome the magnetism of the earth's substance.

The battle between good and evil continues beyond Hades and permeates also to the level of the discarnates who communicate regularly with us. In this last case the battle is only partial. The lower creative discarnates who communicate regularly with us, only encounter the evil entities when they, the former, are engaged in helping the living or the recently dead. In helping the living they are not always successful in preserving them from disease or disaster. They are triumphant in helping those of the newly dead who are due to evolve and benefit by their existence in the next world. This is because the newly dead, moving through Hades, are adjusting their level of vibration to that of the merciful discarnates descending towards them.

So far we have only discussed discarnates tethered to the world by their addiction to the power and the glory and motivated by psychic evil. We must now consider the psyches who, through no fault of their own, find it difficult to elude the pull of this planet. These include the victims of violent death, particularly those who succumb in war or through crime. What these individuals suffer from is an inability to resynthesise a psyche the total harmony of which has been disrupted by violent death and by the absence of the three days needed by the psyche to co-ordinate itself after natural death. They have been denied the smooth, psychic cohesion which accompanies the molecular death of the individual cells in the three days following cessation of the heartbeat and breathing. These victims may appeal to the living, either as forms or voices or approaching footsteps. They are asking to be released from their bondage from this earth. This is achieved by their encountering some person with the capacity to emanate goodness, someone who, in this world, has achieved the degree of psychic perception which, for the most part, is only achieved after death. Such victimised souls, tethered painfully to earth, are released by living beings capable of the perception of discarnates, who receive them in a friendly manner. It is important that such victims should be treated without fear and as though they were still living. They can also be released from their torture by benevolent discarnates assuming form for that purpose. A lot of the harmless 'ghosts' seen by many people are not tied to this earth by their being victims of death by violence or because they are consumed by unassuaged love. The explanation is in fact the exact opposite. Such discarnate entities often come to free those still riveted to the earth.

It may seem a monstrous perversion of justice that those who have been slaughtered in war or brutally murdered should continue to suffer in Hades and should extend to us imploring arms from the shades in order to ensure their release. This, in biblical phraseology, is a hard saying. We must always remember that, once again, we are looking at the phenomenon from the ultimate, shrivelled periphery occupied by our personality on this planet. It may seem to us that such souls suffer for years or even decades from the memory and the continuing horror of their end. But in terms of their own wanderings in Hades this is but a moment. There is no foundation whatever, be it psychological, philosophical or anything you please, for the Christian idea of perpetual hell. Hades is a transit station not a base camp. It is moreover a transit station where movement can be rapid. What to us may seem a decade long haunting is, in Hades, no more than the blinking of an eye. Without a proper understanding of the nature of time we cannot understand anything.

Finally, what are the curses inherited from one generation to another where the victims are innocent and come to untimely ends? What of the families where the eldest son never inherits? Are these fictional or are they no more than an average to be expected by the professional statistician? But are the latter to be listened to in these matters? Are inherited curses one of the norms with which statisticians are usually associated? Let those who prefer comfort to truth dismiss this paragraph as fiction. To me the explanation is evident. We have seen that there are, to certain psyches, danger periods in the year when all manners of disasters and diseases can happen to psychic individuals and their friends. In some cases the menace is intense and covers only a period of a few days during which the attacking malevolent entities are at the height of their powers. (All such acute disaster periods are examples of possession.) Psychic factors are commonly inherited. With their inheritance goes, all too often, an increased vulnerability at certain periods of the year. If discarnate entities, year after year, can attack vulnerable psychics on exactly the same date, what is there to prevent, time having no real existence on the psychic and spiritual planes, a malevolent entity repeating these attacks generation after generation? For the lifting of such curses it is necessary for a threatened member of the family to meet someone who, in this life, is so transcendentally good, in the emanatory sense of the word, and so highly developed psychically, that he or she has reached, in this world, a degree of development equal to that of the communicating discarnate.

NOTES

1. I have said elsewhere, and it has been confirmed by the revenants, that the 28th, as given in the history books, is not a possible day.

2. See *The Lake And the Castle.*

3. Words like direction are purely relative. One cannot dispense with them but fundamentally they have little or no meaning.

13.

Reincarnation

I have written enough elsewhere of the evidence for reincarnation. On evidence such as I have received it would be impossible for me to doubt its reality. It is now necessary to discuss its general nature and purpose.

First of all one rejects altogether the argument that reincarnation is a reality because it is a reasonable and just conception, in a word, that it makes sense. People accept with great comfort the idea of reincarnation because it explains and corrects the injustices of this world. The man drunk with the exercise of power in his last incarnation becomes a kitchen porter in his next life. He who, last time round, was a glutton cannot, in this life, eat his food with comfort because of his gastric ulcer. The Casanova of the eighteenth century is impotent in this. It all sounds very neat and reasonable, above all it answers, or seems to answer, the appalling question as to why a so-called merciful God permits so many injustices to happen to individuals, and why so many of the latter seem to start life under grievous and undeserved handicaps. We can understand a little better, and perhaps rekindle a spark of faith, if we feel that this poor wretch born with a withered arm once exercised it in the application of torture in a past life, or if this victim of club foot habitually kicked his servants in a past existence.

These arguments, that reincarnation fills a need and is reasonable, count for nothing. Are our needs signposts to veracity? To say that reincarnation is reasonable is to presuppose that the universe is reasonable. This is a monstrous assumption. From our viewpoint in this world it seems often the apotheosis of unreason and cruelty. Why should we comfort ourselves, without evidence, that the

Cosmos is benignly ordered? Great writers have rejected totally the concept of a reasonable universe. Let us ponder the sonorous passage towards the end of Hardy's *Tess of the D'Urbervilles*, "Justice was done and the President of the Immortals, in Aeschylean phrase, had ended his sport with Tess." Faith, as an indefineable reaction of the whole man, is one thing. As a blind, senseless soporific to dull our pains in our darker moments it is quite another. It is childish to believe in reincarnation because it makes sense.

I have known people who have approached matters such as reincarnation, possession and survival after death as what they call working hypotheses. This is often the attitude and method of the scientist. I don't know what it means unless it implies that one takes out a temporary and partial option on the theory in the hope that a new fact will adhere in due course like an encrustation of barnacles on an old ship. Reincarnation is without meaning unless there is evidence for it. I would remind the scientists and pseudo-scientists that the correct order is facts first and belief afterwards.

I cannot reproduce or even summarise the enormous evidence for reincarnation I have supplied in my four[1] books and many articles. The point I would make in directing the reader to the evidence of my books is that the first two were epics of scientific and historical verification in which I showed myself addicted to factual truth in the materialistic sense of the word. In the last two books I acted as a vehicle of revealed truth through psychic synchronisation, co-operation with the discarnates and direct and unsullied far memory. Either one believes in revealed truth or not. The main purpose of this present book is to bear witness that there are some to whom the ultimate and cosmic truths of life are revealed. What I am saying in these pages is not my voice alone but what has been told me by the lower and higher echelons of the discarnate hierarchy. Misbelieve them if you will but, to be logical, you have also to disbelieve the evidence of those who saw Christ on the road to Emmaus, the vision of St. Paul and the Transfiguration on the Mount because, whether or no it seems blasphemous, my mentors on this earth and from the next had, in some cases, the attributes of Christ figures even though they would never have claimed to be the sons of God. What is evident from my books is that the Cosmos is divinely and therefore reasonably ordered. I state this as a fact on the evidence presented. I do not ask any tired laboratory technician, doctor of science or modern metaphysician to accept it as a working hypothesis.

What is the purpose of reincarnation? It is commonly said that it is to purify the psyche until the latter has no need to reincarnate. Such expressions as these appear to me to be merely paraphrases of the word reincarnation itself. What do we mean when we talk of purifying the psyche? With our Christian heritage it suggests a long battle with ourselves throughout not only one but many incarnations. This is indeed a gloomy prospect. At the other end of the scale we find hedonistic agnostics, attracted to the idea because, if we fail in this incarnation, and indulge ourselves however we please, we have always several chances. This is certainly a cosier conception than the rigid, Christian, one life one chance school, but both are fallacious.

Both these points of view over-emphasize the element of battle, the one accentuating it and the other deferring it. However much we exercise our will the whole ensemble of our many lives will constitute a pattern over which we have less control than we think. In each life we add, or subtract from, the number of stitches in the fabric. The whole design is already contrived. I use the last word deliberately to avoid the inaccurate use of words like predestination.

If we believe in reincarnation it is only natural that we should think sometimes in terms of preparing ourselves for our next incarnation. With some it is more than a question of the thought crossing their minds. They are prepared to devote their life to this end. Such attitudes forget one thing. If the pattern is already laid down there is a limit to what one can do. What is more important is that reincarnation has become associated in the minds of people in this country and Western civilisation generally with the necessity of raising one's level of awareness. This is often held to stand one in good stead for one's next incarnation. I am the last person in the world to decry the effect of individual methods of meditation, chosen to meet the requirements of individual people and directed by experts such as Tibetan Lamas, but the effect of mass produced and mass administered transcendental meditation is to heighten not merely one's level of self awareness but one's degree of self consciousness. The end result is often the spiritual athlete, weighing every movement or thought against the background of a hypothetical perfection, trained to a whisker for his next incarnation, never behaving naturally or spontaneously but always measuring his thoughts and actions in terms of progress and never radiating anything of value to anybody. I have known people so morbidly preoccupied with reincarnation and, above all, with lives impending in the future, that the sterility they achieved in this world amounted almost to a death in life with, as their single interest, their own salvation.

The idea of karma looms large in any discussion on reincarnation. This is because, till our day, our ideas have been influenced by Oriental literature. The latter attracted the attention of Schopenhauer but since his day many of lesser stature and culture have endeavoured to translate, and often to transmute, Oriental wisdom for our benefit. For some there is always a star rising in the East. The idea of karma is that we reap as we have sown. I have exposed the fallacy of this view in what I wrote earlier in this book on the falsity of the idea that we create our own hells. The doctrine of karma, applied to reincarnation, specifically implies that what we do in one incarnation leaves, or should leave, its imprint on the next. If I was an alcoholic on my last appearance I should be abstinent or teatotal in this life. If I fail to do so I am creating a grave gap in my personal evolution. If this example is too specific for some, it cannot be denied that the more obsessional Western exponents of karma expect continuous progress from one incarnation to the next. These people simply fail to make allowance for human frailty. If, with the passage of time, our youthful standards become tarnished, is it to be surprised at if, in later incarnations, we appeared at times to fall from a grace we have attained in earlier lives? Such an analogy is perfectly justifiable because we must always look at these matters against a timeless background. The fluctuations in our development in a single life on this earth are an expression in microcosm of the fluctuations which will occur in the pattern of our many lives before we cease to incarnate.

I have met those who have been puzzled by the fact that I was a priest in two successive incarnations and returned in my last, mostly in the first half of the nineteenth century, as a sailor and a spy. I have met those who would be prepared to reject my views on karma for this reason alone. The fact that I may have been a better man as a sailor than a priest is by no means irrelevant.

There is no foundation for the idea that any incarnation is centred round the need to correct some flaw shown conspicuously in a previous life. This is a neat, semi-mathematical attitude to the Cosmos but there is absolutely nothing to be said for it. The Cosmos simply does not work like that. Because a tree bears little fruit one year one cannot guarantee a bumper crop the next. Some people even lose faith in reincarnation because of this lack of arithmetical progression. A great deal depends on what people mean by improvement. I am quite serious when I say that some expect a gradual progress through many incarnations to what are called higher callings. It is expected to us that we do not come near our last incarnations until we have become recognizeable as priests or sages. This is equivalent to the idea that a doctor does more good to people because he is a doctor than a girl serving at a counter in a grocer's shop. The doctor may be a semi-educated rabbit interested in disease and not in human beings. The girl behind the counter may have the gift of radiating happiness to people for two hours. One does not need to ask which is performing the higher function.

It is significant that the doctrine of karma originates in the East where monotheism is not a theological feature of either Hinduism or Buddhism. What might be logical to a Hindu or Buddhist does not make sense against the background of our belief in what the faithful regard as an all powerful and all merciful God. If God is love, how can He connive at or permit our pain in this life for sins we have committed in another? This may be logical on the part of the Almighty but it is lacking in charity. In making points like these one has to be careful not to be too logical oneself. I do not wish to contradict myself in insisting that logic is not the way to truth. One cannot criticise Thomas Aquinas and at the same time use his method. Nevertheless it is necessary to talk to people in the language they understand and Western man is a reasoning if not a reasonable animal.

Because, in passing through our various lifetimes, we do not exhibit a steady improvement from one life to another this is not to say that we must make no effort. Those we make should be as passive and unpretentious as possible. They should be totally unconnected with our coming incarnations. Incidentally, what is the point of preparing for what some of us can see already? Because an awareness of future lives is less common than remembrance of past lives does not say that it does not exist. As far as possible, in governing our lives, we should refuse to allow ourselves to be influenced one way or another by past or future incarnations. To do so is to interfere with our pattern of destiny. This is not only a useless but a dangerous proceeding. In so doing we may become either power addicts or psychiatric casualties. One should live a day at a time. This is one thing on which all the discarnates are agreed. Better still we should live an hour or a minute at a time. We prepare ourselves all the more rapidly and efficiently for the time when we will have no need to reincarnate by being as spontaneous as possible. How is this achieved? This is another hard saying. The best answer I can offer is that we should never try to be spontaneous. We are ultimately taken back whence we came by an unremitting if attenuated love. This resides in our psyche. It is what is left of the primary goodness which occurred with the great Schism and the Fall of Man. We can go back even further and say that it is what remains to us of the universal harmony which existed before the division into light and darkness and good and evil. All this is remembered, sometimes at a deep, sometimes at a more superficial level, by our psyche. The latter carries with it the memory of the light and what preceded the light. We therefore have within us the spirit of love, no matter how tightly it is tethered. Since our salvation lies within us, is it not wise that we should be passive and allow the seed to germinate quietly within us? Do not all self-conscious efforts to develop, like transcendental meditation and yoga, provide us with artificial targets which do not facilitate by one jot or tittle the radiance which is, in this world, so largely obscured within us?

If we must think of ourselves, and whether we are good or bad and how we might improve, we should all the more leave alone the thought of reincarnation. The latter is a fact. Let us leave it at that. It is something that happens to us. It is not necessarily something we can contribute to. We are wiser to think in simple terms of the forces of good and evil. By this I do not mean that we should waste our time on the metaphysical, and worst of all, psychological examination of our motives for so doing, and above all, for thinking this and that. What I mean is that we should realise there are two circuits, good and evil, into which we can switch. Every loving or tender thought has an endless and measureless emanation. It is like a tide the last waves of which end soundlessly on invisible shores. Similarly every access of hate adds hostile vibrations to the world. How otherwise can human dowsers detect in an instant that a violent quarrel has just taken place in a room they enter? But it is of extreme importance to see good and evil as forces, and not be too tied up with the ethical nature and repercussions of our actions. Certainly there are basic rules of conduct we must all observe. These are not difficult to define and resemble each other in divergent civilisations. Apart from this we should avoid too much study of the sociological consequences of our acts. Any kind of love or spontaneous charity is better than the self-conscious enlightenment of those who spend their lives looking round to find the oppressed in order to create tension by relieving their oppression.

It is useless struggling too much to be other than we are, because the psyches we inherit are drawn in to our personalities at conception by some kind of electromagnetic process the nature of which we cannot understand on this earth. Also, as the psyche chooses us rather than we it, is it logical that we should try to alter radically our character and with it our prospects in future incarnations? We are beyond doubt governed by our psyche. All we achieve which is truly creative is attributable to it. If we manufactured our psyche for ourselves, if we were not born with a full and complete psyche and contributed to it lavishly by the efforts of our own personalities, there would be something to be said for an all out effort to change our nature and disposition. This we cannot do because in all the realities of life our psyche is dominant. It plays the leading role in our psychic and spiritual communications, in religious experience and in any inspired art we may produce. Any doctor of experience will agree that it is impossible to change man's basic nature. The best we can hope for is to get the best out of each particular kind of make-up. Above all, we must accept the fate brought on us by our psyche at the moment of conception. In performing this act of acceptance we submit without resistance to whatever incarnations are in store for us. We do not jump the gun by seeking to alter their nature.

It is superficial to regard this as a hopeless proposition. Firstly, as soon as we recognize deep in our hearts that we cannot change basically we *do* change. This is another example of the fact that truth is wrapped up in paradox. Always what we are dealing with is that the *personality* does not change. It is the antenna we are given with which to make contact with reality. The artist remains the artist, the bureaucrat the bureaucrat and the logician the logician. By recognizing this, deep in his heart as well as his brain, the individual acquires a peace in which his psyche is more free to operate. The free operation of his psyche leaves him incidentally with the same kind of personality. To accept that we retain our personality is to surrender peacefully to its claims. The reduction of tension which ensues facilitates the freer operation of the psyche. Basically we may appear unchanged but we emanate more. The psyche grows from our silence of acceptance. Such results can rarely be achieved by the practice of meditation because here, however much we talk in psychic or spiritual terms, our approach is based on stifling the personality. This we attempt to do by using its own methods. 'Try to concentrate.' This for Westerners practically always involves an effort of will. This is vigorously denied by many yogis but is nonetheless true. To *try* to empty one's mind is a positive willed action. It is the direct opposite of the mind emptying itself. The psyche cannot be forced to function by a forced annihilation of the personality. It can only flower if we realise that the personality is its instrument and if, within limits, we let the latter have its head.

Is there, then, nothing constant and nothing of purpose vouchsafed to us when those who remember past lives look back at them dispassionately. Understand that here I am talking simply of the reincarnation of the individual and not of a group. In the latter the element of purpose is obvious. It seems one develops *not* by shedding or curbing special attributes of personality but by developing and expressing those which press most constantly on us. These tendencies may not necessarily be those we most want to fulfil. It is more a case of doing what we have to do. As a schoolboy my favourite subjects were English and History. To tell the truth they were the only ones I could support with comfort. When the urge came upon me in my early teens to be a doctor it was necessary for me, when I had reached School Certificate level, to take up for Higher Certificate literally all my worst subjects in order to qualify as a medical student. This was part of an impulse to heal which I had manifested in five previous incarnations. This impulse was something I simply could not get out of my system. I see now that this was the way I was destined to learn. Even as a sailor and spy in my Napoleonic incarnations I was still preoccupied with healing herbs and made a concoction from them for my employer, sick with bronchitis, when I was a prisoner of war on parole.

My impulse to heal has been shared with several incarnations by others particularly Miss Mills and Annette whom I have mentioned often in previous books. The former was a healer in an incarnation round about 1750 BC and also in her Celtic and Cathar incarnations.

Another constant trait in all my lives has been my love of beauty, particularly of nature. I can safely say this was firmly embedded within me in my early childhood. I loved the countryside in my Napoleonic incarnation and was forever wandering the woods in my life as a Cathar. This love of nature has always been my solace as well as my instructor. When I look back from the next world I shall turn more towards the countryside round Montségur, the Dordogne, West Cumberland and the Botanical Gardens in Bath than elsewhere and this not from the influence of past incarnations, but simply because of their beauty. Looking effortlessly at landscapes, gardens and flowers for the sheer pleasure they give me is the form of meditation which had been chosen for me. It is sensory rather than highly spiritual. To me it is none the worse for that.

I have always been intensely preoccupied with the truth. In this life as a child of four I refused absolutely to listen to fairy tales. I have been regarded as cynical because I could not always accept without proof other people's high estimation of their own motives. In my Napoleonic incarnation, which extended to the return of the Bourbons and ultimately to Louis Philippe, I was an indefatigable lecturer and pamphleteer, disseminating what I regarded as the truth, often at considerable risk to myself. I was, as in my Cathar incarnation and my present life, intensely preoccupied with the nature of time. In my Cathar incarnation I wrote a philosophic work in which the nature of time figured largely. The manuscript was lost in the course of ages.

There are certain guiding motives which persist in people through several incarnations. One has indeed little evidence of complete changes in basic character. In this I am speaking of the broad foundations of character exemplified in people with far memory whom I have myself known well. Few of these I have known, with a detailed memory for past incarnations, fluctuated violently in their basic make-up. There were indeed some fundamental common denominators which have characterised those I have known. All are intensely practical people. All judge people and policies by results. If I describe myself as interested in the nature of time this is not to say that I am not practical. I think most of the doctors who sent me patients would agree that I acted more quickly and confined myself more to practical issues than the average psychiatrist. All the others I have known with memories of past incarnations were markedly extroverted. This was at first sight surprising to me but it was unmistakably true. I see now that to be able to ignite others psychically, so that they remember past incarnations and develop powers of psychic healing, is the most intense form of communication known to man. It can be regarded, in fact, as the supreme form of extroversion, if the latter can, as it should be, considered in terms of the capacity to communicate.

A curious example of fidelity not only to nature but to metier is provided by one of my reincarnated group. This was a man who was associated with financial administration through four incarnations. In this life he made his living as an accountant, he was concerned with the handling of money in the Roman incarnation and, as the bishop, Bertrand Marty, in the Cathar incarnation, he is often mentioned in connection with payments, financial deals and the practical administration of the affairs of the Cathar Church.

None of those I have encountered with far memory were intellectuals, that is to say they were not submerged by the worship of ideas. They were completely uninterested in sociology or the science of politics. Their intelligence was pragmatic. They had the capacity of seeing immediately to the heart of a problem and discarding the irrelevant details. They could always see the wood *and* the trees. They were uninterested in metaphysics and philosophy. They had a profound understanding of the meaning of life and the destiny of man, but this they had obviously been born with. What they had discovered by their innate endowments was reinforced later by a deepening degree of insight and, in some, by the capacity they developed to communicate with the discarnates. Their knowledge of the truth was communicated directly and not an intellectual process. Though non-intellectual they exhibited on the whole a higher than average feeling for culture. They appreciated the arts but I would not say that their cultural level was outstanding. All had a profound sense of atmospheres and a sharp nose for evil and tension in places or persons. To sum up, they were perceivers and feelers rather than thinkers. But this is not to say that they were precipitate or fallacious in their judgment of situations and people. The truth was absolutely to the contrary. Ninety-nine times out of a hundred I would back their judgment in practical issues against that of the average lawyer, schoolmaster or scientist. This is quite simply because their judgment was uncontaminated by theory. It was based on their five senses plus an additional one.

It is characteristic of all people with detailed far memory for several incarnations that they are also clairvoyant, precognitive and telepathic. I do not know a single exception to this rule. A number have the gift of healing, but this is not so universal as the other gifts mentioned.

Another interesting point arises. Those who remember past incarnations are for the most part athletic types, using the adjective in the typological sense of the word as laid down by Kretschmer. Pyknic means broad in relation to height. Asthenic is its willowy opposite and athletic is somewhere between the two. Most of those remembering past incarnations are well muscled people, usually a little more than average height — I fall short in this — who, in their middle and later years, tend to put on weight. Some people who remember their past incarnations go beyond the athletic category. They tend to be stocky pyknics. The lean, refined asthenics seldom, in my experience, recall past lives.

Of course this is not to say that there are not wild fluctuations in behaviour exhibited by the same people in different incarnations. I have merely been concerned with the fact that the basic aims, interests and tendencies of the individual remain the same through several lives. Behaviour obviously varies because the same tendencies may be utilised well or badly. As for more secondary items of character, these manifestations of mood vary enormously. A woman remembered her life as a sailor, a prisoner of war, on the top floor of the keep at Portchester Castle in Hampshire. At this stage in her career she spent her whole time gambling, sometimes losing the clothes off his/her back in the process. She went to the dogs in a big way and was scruffy and unkempt. In this life she had a positive horror of gambling, was always neatly and tastefully attired and always offered to clean other people's walls, carpets or ceilings if she thought them in any way stained. It is fluctuations in character such as these that are seized upon by exponents of karma as evidence of the truth of their theory. This is totally erroneous. The woman in question remembered in detail her discreditable life as a prisoner of war who had completely let himself go. That first memory must have been at the near conscious level but in early middle age became completely conscious. Nor can one call such examples as this evidence of the deep urges of personality I have mentioned earlier in this chapter. Going to the dogs in her last incarnation, pulling herself together in this (she did so in the last after the prisoner of war episode) are not as primordial as the impulse to heal or an intense preoccupation with the truth. Also, in the case quoted, the variations in behaviour in successive incarnations were two different aspects of the same story. A naturally clean person, her letting herself go in her Napoleonic incarnation was a grave sign of deterioration. In this life her aversion to gambling and her fastidiousness was another aspect of the same trait.

A woman doctor, normally reticent and completely self-reliant, became agitated and self-accusatory when she remembered the part she had played in a massacre of Inquisitors seven centuries previously. She showed the same reaction when it registered fully with her that she had allowed a comrade, involved with her in her escape from the prison camp at Portchester, to be beaten up and tortured by his captors without any protest or intervention on her behalf. Here again one would say at first sight that this was karma with a vengance. It was no such thing. The signs she showed in this century could have been reactions to any discreditable episode in her present lifetime. They were engendered by guilt for what she clearly remembered.

There is further evidence of the fallacy of the doctrine of karma. Here on this earth we reach our lowest level of sensibility. Put at its lowest the colours in the next world are brighter and with a greater living reality than here. At a higher level we, from the next world, can see round corners. We are not just limited to looking at one person in one place and then travelling a hundred miles to see another. Space is annihilated to the degree that we can, if we are communicating discarnates, inform the living of how their friends are faring a hundred or a thousand miles off. (Be it noted that space is not entirely annihilated. Sometimes the discarnates with whom we are talking disappear suddenly to minister to someone in need). At its highest the discarnates, even those lowest in the hierarchy, can look back to past lives. This latter capacity is only given to a small minority in this world. The doctrine of karma implies that, in earthlife No. 2 we take on where we left off in earthlife No. 1 and try to build better on its foundations. This is to neglect the far more formative existence we experience between our deaths on this planet. Karma cannot be adjusted to our degree of development in the next world.

The doctrine of karma plays a large role in Hindu and Buddhist philosophy. Some of it is contaminated with folklore and superstition as, for example, the idea that we may return as animals, that if we have been unnaturally cunning we may come back as foxes or, if unpleasantly furtive, as reptiles. This is nonsensical. Once we have attained the privilege or burden of human consciousness, have it which way you will, there is no going back. Animals may certainly reincarnate as men but once we have achieved this we are tied irretrievably to the wheel of existence. All consciousness is indestructible. Human consciousness is also incapable of forgetting or being made to forget. If, however, we accept it as karmic that we should revert to the animal or reptilian state as a punishment for past sins, can we seriously argue that we are promoting the animal to the human status as a natural development of his past virtues? Can we even say with certainty that man is a nobler creation than a dog or cat? The former is capable of endless fidelity no matter how he is treated. The cat has the sacred virtue of having no herd instinct. Wild animals as a rule kill only to eat. Man kills in the exercise of power, from hate or merely for pleasure. To Schopenhauer man was the "animal mechant par excellence". How, then, can we believe, if we regard it as karmic that we are turned into rattlesnakes, a reasonable enough idea if you weigh it up, that the converse is true and that humanity with its enormous capacity for evil is a karmic reward for the innocent goodness of a domestic animal? Animals like dogs reincarnate as men because they long to do so and identify themselves with those they have loved. It is part of their creative evolution and has nothing to do with the law of karma.

It is possible that the doctrine of karma has been inserted into Hindu and Buddhist teaching as a means of enhancing the power of the leaders of each faith. Did they introduce karma into the doctrine in the same way as ecclesiastics perverted the simplicity of Christianity by the corrupting doctrine of redemption by grace and by the sacrifice of Christ? Certainly Hinduism does not lend itself as much to organized perversion as Christianity. It lacks a complicated ecclesiastical hierarchy. It is replaced by a reverence for holy men. This sounds better because it reveals preoccupation with the nature of man rather than with questions as to the soundness of his theology and his religious orthodoxy. But are holy men inevitably holy? Some of those who have transported themselves to the West seem suited to its decline and to be frankly corrupt. I doubt if they are as dangerous as the gurus who believe too much in the santity of their mission and achieve something of the ascendance over their adherents as is acquired all too often by the Freudian analyst. All this is not to deride the truly saintly gurus produced by Hinduism or Buddhism. By saintly I mean those who influence by emanation, example and compassion rather than by disquisition or verbal guidance. One must always remember that Western man is doomed to translate everything in terms of obsessional definition. We should never condemn any Eastern doctrine because of what we have seen of its Western exponents. Karma appeals to the latter intensely because of its seemingly crystalline logic. There is no room for mathematically precise doctrines such as this in the history of human evolution. The more mathematically precise they are the less they apply to anything so variable and fallible as man. Be that as it may many of the Western believers in karma will cling to their doctrine, albeit regarding themselves as enlightened, with equal ferocity to that displayed by the average ritualistic Christian believer in Transubstantiation and Redemption.

The doctrine of karma is a total misrepresentation of the meaning of reincarnation. It is self-contradictory. It denies the background from which it came. Constantly we are told in Hindu and Buddhist philosophy, particularly the former, that we should be beyond good and evil. (As Jung pointed out it would have been a great deal better for the inhabitants of Eastern civilisations had their leaders and guides paid a litt'e more attention to these two forces). But how can one reconcile the insistence of Oriental philosophy, that we should be beyond the dualism of opposites, like good and evil and beauty and ugliness, with the doctrine of karma? The latter is full to bursting with the preoccupation with good and evil. You do a specific bad deed in one incarnation and need to repair it with a specific good one in the next. You pay through a former incarnation or incarnations for a single bad act. To me it sounds a little like the Christian hell. You may not be directly punished by an avenging god but you are paying all the same. Karma is a diluted version of hell but with the saving grace that it is located in this world. One can say, defensively, that karma operates on several different planes but so many such arguments are pretentious intellectualisation of theories based on false premises.

What, then, is the point of reincarnation if it does not involve the deliberate correction of mistakes and errors we have made in past incarnations? But how can we correct these errors if we are unaware of them? After all, only a tiny fragment of the community are consciously aware of their past lives. Do we correct our errors sub-consciously? It is possible. It is our psyche which remembers when our personality has forgotten. Is our psyche directing us from well below the conscious level? But what directs our psyche? Certainly we have to reject the idea of a managing God pushing psyches here and there like pieces on a chess board. Any progress we make is made slowly by our contact with those strata of the hierarchy above our own. As we have seen previously we cannot make contact direct with God.

The psyche is drawn to the personality and family in which it needs not necessarily to develop but to learn. It gravitates in the necessary direction in virtue of magnetic forces we cannot comprehend on this planet. But does it move towards a particular personality or family merely to eradicate a single fault, weakness, or attitude of mind? Is it not that it has to see and face life in all its aspects? In each incarnation it is drawn to this or that new personality to experience rather than to improve. It is for this reason that we do not see, in successive incarnations, that steady progression from holiness to holiness which is required of us by so many. It is because, after each incarnation, the psyche is drawn in zig-zag fashion from personality to personality that we see so many fluctuations in our degree of development in different incarnations, as in my own series of lives when I was a priest twice and returned last time as a sailor and a spy.

What we have to face here is that our development through several incarnations is basically a matter of simple experience rather than the progressive correction of this or that weakness or sin. This involves inevitably the number of incarnations we have undergone. The old soul is a colloquialism which has been used for centuries. It describes a psyche which has seen and understood much which, indeed, has had many lives. "She is older than the rocks among which she sits; like the vampire she has been dead many times, and learnt the secrets of the grave." An old soul is simply one who has been here many times and will not be required, if it so chooses, to reincarnate much longer. It has seen through life and not sought to transcend it. It transcends it automatically, without effort, because it has seen through it. It asks no questions because it knows the answers. But before it draws to the end of its cycle of lives and is exempt from the necessity to reincarnate it has to remember a number of its past incarnations. This is because wisdom rises from memory when, by the latter, we mean the recollection of the lives we have lived before.

The psyche may remember in many ways. It may begin by

déja vu phenomena, by the feeling of intense familiarity with a place it has never visited previously in its present life. In the beginning far memory may not be completely conscious. In the *déja vu* phenomenon familiarity is absolute but the place or event recalled cannot be named. The psyche may also remember by an intense emotional reaction to places. Here we must be careful because there are sentimentalists so suggestible and over-imaginative that they cannot cross the fields of Culloden and Waterloo without believing themselves to have been either Bonnie Prince Charlie or Napoleon. This is a different phenomenon altogether to that displayed by my friend who, as Raymond de Perella, owned the castle of Montségur at the time of the great siege by the French Royalists in 1243 to 1244. Before she knew, due to my discarnate contacts and my own perceptions, that she had been the said Raymond she visited Queribus, a neighbouring chateau also involved in the Albigensian wars and indeed the last to surrender. She only visited the last named chateau once because she passed into such a state of collapse that the friend who had taken her there was agitated and concerned about her violent reaction.

Recollection of past incarnations may ferment, still below the conscious level, in recurrent nightmares, in obsessions, phobias and depressions which originate in past lives and reverberate particularly on the anniversaries of disasters in previous incarnations. Nearer the conscious level we have the remembrance and reliving of past lives often in a state of trance. At the conscious level we hear voices from past incarnations which do not tell us directly what happened in past lives but instigate our recall of them. Finally we have pure and unadulterated far memory. All these mechanisms I have dealt with in previous books.

NOTE

1. *The Cathars and Reincarnation, We Are One Another, The Lake And the Castle* and *The Island*. All Neville Spearman.

14.

Group Reincarnation

The old soul near the end of its cycle of lives has another phenomenon to experience. This is that of group reincarnation. The individual encounters others he has met before in past lives. Here he encounters a phenomenon so simple that he fails to take notice of it because it seems hardly credible. He recognizes people he has met before because certain features of their face, colouring and stature have changed little. One person has the same luminous eyes in all the incarnations recalled. Another has auburn hair and greenish eyes in more than one previous life. Another has Roman features, a prominent nose and the same blue eyes in two or three incarnations. We spoke of the way the individual's most basic characters and aims do not change through several incarnations. When we begin to partake in group reincarnation, the same applies to a remarkable extent to physical characteristics. It will be understood that this of course does not apply to all the individual's previous incarnations. It is only applicable when he is approaching a comprehension of the reality of group incarnation. The number of incarnations through which physical characteristics may be retained is about half a dozen but there are cases where the same face crops up, unchanged, after millennia. I know one woman of completely British origin whose face is identical in its classical Greek perfection with what it was about 1700 BC. This likeness of feature is provided to enable people to recognize their friends from past ages, and to comprehend more clearly the reality of group incarnation. The latter becomes still more evident when the individual realises that reincarnation in the same family can occur. A mother and daughter in the twentieth century were brothers in a Napoleonic incarnation. People meeting in contemporary existence could have belonged to the same family in a past life. In my series of lives I married the same woman three times, twice in the centuries before Christ and once in the seventh century AD. In this incarnation she is the central member of the group to which I belong. Three of the characters added to this group which has extended over years were actually our children in the Celtic incarnation.

The question arises as to whether there is such a thing as a group soul. This is certainly true. It shows itself in two ways. The telepathy exhibited between members of a group, though separated by thousands of miles, is so intense that it is as though they were one person. This accounts also for their capacity to pick up each other's symptoms the moment the original patient has acquired them. Telepathy manifested to such a degree is the sign of a group soul. A second related phenomena is where there seems to be a complete fusion of psyches. Two couples known to me have used, on innumerable occasions, the identical words and rare metaphors in giving opinions on different subjects to third persons.

This fusion of pysches for reincarnation is certainly not haphazard. There is no such thing as coincidence. It is impossible to think that the expanding number of people I have met belonging to our Dualist group are part of a gigantic inexplicable hazard. Can it be that people ignite each other at a distance and are so drawn together? This is possible but the seemingly magical way I have encountered fringe members of the group can only be explained on the grounds that such meetings were ordained. But what does ordained mean? It does not imply predestination in the ordinary meaning of the word. What it demonstrates is that, in returning to earth, there is a fusion of psyches, a meeting of the messengers in their descent from the next world to this. In the process of reincarnation they are joined together. Such group reincarnation is always creative and a manifestation of the light. A group soul is not possible in this world or the next in the case of contaminated psyches bent on the establishment of power over others because such aims are manifestations of apartness. If they seem to join together, as in the case of the Furies in Hades, this is not a true union but a utilisation on the part of a number of contaminated psyches of the reinforcing power of evil. They are activated by the beams of evil like motes in a sunbeam. Certainly willed groups of living people exist in order to bring evil and disaster to the good, but such circles are the product of will and organization in this world and cannot cohere in the descent through Hades of returning psyches.

What is the purpose of group reincarnation? This was clearly stated to me by my chief living mentor as described in *We Are One Another.* I was instructed to talk and write as much as possible about Catharism. The reason given was that the world was engulfed in materialism, that we were not, as I myself had said, approaching the Dark Ages but already living in them. It was evident that Catharism was regarded as an antidote to materialism. I found it difficult at first to reconcile myself to the idea that, much as I sympathised with it, it was justifiable to allow a single philosophy to occupy so exclusively my attention. All this became clearer when I recognized, as I could not fail to do on the evidence presented[1], the reality of group incarnation. It was then pointed out by one of the discarnates that there were other groups, not necessarily Cathar, forming up and down the world. It was necessary to be aware of their existence even if one did not make contact with them. Then the matter became clearer still. The other groups of which the revenants spoke were also Dualist, even though they may not be recognized, or recognize themselves, as such. Then it became noticeable that the revenant ceased to use the word Catharism and simply to speak of the truth. This means the truth of reincarnation, of the existence of two energies of good and evil in the universe and that the world was created by a lower entity.

There is another aspect of purpose in group reincarnation. I have always taken a passive attitude towards individual psychic phenomena. If they happen to me they happen, and I have no doubt that in pain and happiness alike they are contributing to my development, in which I have ceased to have much personal interest. It was therefore not easy to see myself missionising for any particular cause, even for something which had haunted me for years before it was revealed. It was then put to me that such an attitude as mine was justified in normal times and so far as my personal

experiences were concerned, but that, at the end of
civilisations, such as we are witnessing at the moment, it is
necessary to sow the seeds of truth as widespread as
possible, not in the childish hope of saving the world by a
dramatic last minute rally, but to ensure that, through the
Dark Ages, at least a thread of light will be kept alive. It was
for this reason that our group had met together, at least so
far as its principal members were concerned, in five
incarnations and that in all we had lived at the end of a
civilisation and adhered to some form of Dualism. In the
Roman incarnation several among our number had followed
the cult of Mithras. In the Celtic we had served the Dualist
Christian Church, we had testified to the same faith in the
Middle Ages in the Languedoc of the Cathars and had
certainly been Dualists in our obscure masonic practices in
the early nineteenth century. The periods in which we lived
saw the end of Roman civilisation, the end of primitive
Christianity in Britain during its Romanisation in the seventh
century, the end of the enlightened civilisation in Provence
in the Languedoc in the thirteenth century, the changed
world that came with the Revolution and Napoleon and now
the death of a civilisation surrendering to materialistic
totalitarianism in different quarters of the globe.

What I have said of group reincarnations certainly implies
that the members of such groups as I have mentioned are
special beings whose function is to enlighten others. This
smacks of elitism. Must we argue in favour of a kind of
analogy to the nauseating doctrine of predestination, as
preached by Calvin, that only a preselected elite can be
saved? There is no such analogy. If people choose to regard
the members of such groups as specially selected people
with special gifts they are at liberty to do so. They can never
know how embarassing and fatiguing it is to be put on a
pedestal or to be used as a talisman or lucky charm. The
attitude that members of this group are a kind of elite is
certainly a threadbare justification if we are thinking only in
terms of one life in this world. Spread over the millennia it is
merely a question of who qualifies by seniority of psyche.
Our psychic gifts themselves are only an expression of
memory, because the development of a full and intensive
range of such attributes only comes with an equally full and
intensive range of far memory. In speaking of memory in this

way one is not talking of any capacity to bore weevil-like into the ultimate substance of being. True memory is merely freeing ourselves from the blinding veil of matter and enabling us to see what others cannot because we have seen and remember it all before. Aeons on, others now psychically and spiritually myopic, will be members of groups similar to ours in some other civilisation possibly on some other planet.

It may seem to the reader that what I am saying involves an attitude so passive that it amounts to determinism spiced with the rather tepid sauce of 'everything comes to him who waits'. I speak of our inability to alter the cosmic pattern. Does this involve determinism and the denial of free will? In a way I deny the existence of both. Once again the answer depends on from what point of vantage we are examining the question. If we look at it from this time-bound world one would certainly seem to incline towards determinism. The discarnates tell us, and I believe and know, that nothing can alter our role in the great cosmic pattern. At the same time they say that they, and we too, can repair some of the damage inflicted on the victims of destiny. This allows us a modicum of free will. But in the world of the psyche, be it operated in this world by the intensely psychic or manifested in the next world by members of the hierarchy, neither free will nor determinism exists because time vanishes as we move from the level of personality to that of the psyche and spirit. Determinism expresses belief in a future. What will be, will be, but in the future. Free will implies the capacity to mould our destiny, again in the future. What we will today will be accomplished tomorrow. But how can either of these suppositions be valid in a real world where there is neither future, nor past or present? This is why I have so carefully avoided the word preordained in speaking of the cosmic pattern. Such a description implies something planned in the past or present for fruition in the future. No such process occurs. When we reach the very hub of reality we are living in a world of being where no effort is required of us, and where we know because we are, and where we are because we have outlived the illusions imposed on us by the pressure of matter.

All this is emphatically not to say that we twiddle our thumbs in this world and wait for our incarnations to pass as effortlessly as possible. We cannot escape our destiny in this world because the pain and the pleasure we experience in it are already laid down and are inescapable. It is an inevitable fact that all the developed psychics I have met have been intensely active people. They have done their duty and more than their duty and have been constantly occupied in acts of charity. Say if you like that it was their destiny to work while other people idled. Certainly the effects of what they know of the inability to change the pattern have not been debilitating. They have, on the contrary, been highly tonic compared with the absolutions of the ritualistic churches which have a comforting but enervating effect on many of their exponents.

I have spoken of the undesirability and the danger of preparing for future incarnations. Any attempt to accelerate the wheels of the cosmos by special techniques is always dangerous. Even if, by artificial means, one is stimulated to see accurately into the future, no good will come of it because vision will have outrun development. In any case the problem is less important than that posed by the social implications of far memory, because the latter is more common than the anticipation of future lives. The question inevitably arises, to what extent do these loves and loyalties arising in past lives interfere with one's harmonious relations in the present, particularly with those who play no significant role in the group to which one belongs. First let it be stated that far memory must certainly put a strain on the young and vulnerable psychics who have loved someone in a past incarnation and find him or her comfortably and happily married in this. I have never known one who tried to cash in on such circumstances. This is not to say that they did not suffer from being presented again with an old love in the middle of their contemporary obligations, but in the end what they gained paid many times over for what they suffered. They learnt that it is possible to love totally without desire and totally without any impulse to possess. They acquired the capacity to love so impersonally that they never forced themselves on each other's company and could love as much in absence and without pain as when the other was present. What they achieved was to be the agents of love as a power. This love did not arise within themselves as it does when a man or woman have a face, figure and personality which attract each other. They were instruments of a force bigger than themselves, just as a person who emanates goodness is an instrument and just as a healer is a transmitter of a power channelled from the main stream of goodness. This is not to say that one or two cases may not have passed through a remarkably brief period of special attachment which they were able to abandon with a curious absence of pain. The people in the group in which I was associated used the word love easily and naturally and expressed freely their love for each other. This practice was used more between the women because of the lesser number of men involved in their contemporary incarnation. It is quite obvious that they were using the word love in the early Christian and Cathar sense of the term. Love was regarded as an expression of psychic fusion. It was merely their shorthand term for the fact of being totally on the same wavelength.

The idea of anything sexual entering into the proceedings was out of the question. This was not because the individuals concerned were repressed. I do not think I have met any collection of people so open and spontaneous. It was merely because they were a different kind of being to the average. With their capacity for psychic communication they had little need to communicate by way of the flesh. In this life the women were often unmarried or, if they had embarked on Holy Matrimony, none had produced more than one child.

What was at times a problem was their deep concern for each other. If one was ill or depressed, or in any way in trouble, the others were intensely worried about her. There was no question of serene detachment. The revenants said quite simply that, if you cared for somebody and they were ill and in trouble, you suffered with them and there was no way round it. That, they averred, was hell. It was something to be got through and there were no nostrums. This concern for the health and safety for others sometimes approached the obsessional. This was easy to understand. It was noticeable that it was more evident in younger people discovering those who had been their parents and elders in previous incarnations.

For anyone with far memory one of the main necessities of life is to harmonise and absorb what was lived in previous existences. This involves the need to live in the here and now more than ordinary people. This is sometimes easier said than done. When a woman encounters a man she has loved in a previous incarnation the shock, if recognition is immediate, can be such that she is left bewildered, particularly if, as sometimes happens, her old feelings waken for a time with recognition. The recognition by a girl of someone in this life as having been her father in a previous existence can be both a delight, an emotional trauma or both. A suddenly blinding certainty on the part of a man that he has recognized a girl after centuries as an old comrade in a past life, may waken in him undesirable pangs of feeling, of timelessness and of yearning which he can easily mistake for love. This can happen even if the girl in his company was a man when he knew her last. Such situations and feelings can cause pain and problems, usually of a transitory nature, to developed psychics with experience of several incarnations. It can be imagined that they can cause disruption among the inexperienced and unstable. What it really amounts to is that people on the fringe of psychic experience are more likely to develop messy and immature relationships based on acquaintances in past incarnations than those with deep and detailed far memory. A good deal of trouble can arise from a compound of instability and sentimentality. The idea that one has met someone in a previous incarnation is attractive to the romantic. Very often such people associate themselves with eminent and colourful historical characters or their entourage. Under such circumstances interest in reincarnation can become a preoccupation of the debilitated romantic.

It follows that a number of those who build insecure relationships or make dirty weather of contacts from past incarnations are people in whom far memory is fragmentary and sometimes a product of the imagination. They wish to inject a little colour into contemporary contacts which seem drab and unsatisfying. The more full the remembrance of the past incarnations, the more completely the latter have been relived, the less likely is the individual to form ridiculous, stultifying and absurd attachments. What arises between those with detailed far memory for several incarnations is a mutual and effortless unity of opinion and outlook. It is not a question of one person leaning on another or being devoured by passion for the other. It is merely a case of two people acting as one.

While the romantic exploiters of past incarnations are concerned with those they have loved and who have loved them in the past, they are often little bothered with those who have been their enemies and do not realise that the latter may reincarnate in this life. If one meets a person who has harried and persecuted one in a past life is one's reaction likely to be hostile, suspicious or painful? Human nature being what it is this is only to be expected of some, but again only of those who have not realised that reincarnation is a matter of the psyche's development and not of the individual's comfort. To recoil from, or beware of, someone because they have persecuted you in a past incarnation is infantile. An unreasoning dislike of a person can be justified in the case of those who do not realise they are in the company of someone who tortured them in the past and, possibly, would even do so in the present if the chance were afforded. Once recollection has reached the conscious level there is no justification for such attitudes. It is not a question of forgiving one's enemies or deriving a morbid satisfaction from turning the other cheek. It is sheer absence of sense to hate the inquisitor who grilled one centuries ago because he or she may be the person who, in this life, bandaged one's wounds and showed one the fullness of compassion. I have known one case of a man who treated a woman brutally in a past incarnation and with great chivalry in this. The more extensive knowledge of our past incarnations the more it should enable us to live completely and fully in this, estimating others by what they are in the present and not by what they have been in the past and will be in the future.

The question arises as to what will happen to our psyches if this planet is destroyed by earthquake and by tidal waves, by atomic warfare or if it simply burns itself out. The answer is that we reincarnate elsewhere on other planets. This has happened before. All those who deplore the facts of life and shun the question of the death of our world should realise that the existence of dead stars which once supported life has been known to astronomers for centuries. Perhaps our nervous fibre, and with it our capacity to face facts, is a little depleted in the twentieth century. The living beings who have inhabited now dead planets have already reincarnated elsewhere.

We are indeed already prepared for reincarnation elsewhere than this world by the fact that every psyche after death, passing from the level of angels and archangels, is drawn within the orbit of influence of different planets. The latter send out different waves of vibration corresponding to those of the different level of consciousness the psyche has attained. This is the reverse process to what occurred at conception. When the psyche descends to earth before birth it passes from the zone of the highest and farthest planets until its vibration is slowed up and attuned to what is necessary for conception on this earth. It still carries with it the memory of its divine origin in and beyond the farthest stars. It is drawn towards its earthly home by the fused vibrations attributable to the position of the constellations at conception and birth.

After death the reverse process occurs. The psyche ascends from matter and through Hades and is drawn again by the same vibrational processes it encountered in its descent into the orbit of the planet or planets where it will develop most. If it has learnt a good deal in its last life on earth its quickened vibrations will lead it into the range of influence of a farther planet. The latter determines the level at which the psyche resides after death and whether or no it passes from that of those destined to reincarnate or whether it goes onwards through the lower and higher discarnates to the angels and archangels. It is quite clear, from the threat to this planet, from the growing evidence of interplanetary communication, from the increasing revulsion in a rapidly growing minority to the materialism of this earth, that the next stage in cosmic evolution is to provide us with a higher basis on which we may reincarnate and in which we may live more in our etheric and less in our material bodies. The destruction or partial destruction of this planet may evoke the return to a state of being like that possessed by the Atlanteans.

Why is the psyche drawn to the same planetary zone in its descent into, as in its ascent from, matter? This is because the psyche is exposed, like every organ in the body, like the body itself, to a dual mechanism. This applies not only to the psyche but to the Cosmos itself. It is what we mean when we say that man, even chained in matter, is an expression in microcosm of the macrocosm. In birth we have uterine contractions expelling the child into the world. In pathological inertia of the womb we have a contrary wave of contractions seeking to retain the child in the uterus. The peristaltic movement of the intestines are designed to expel waste matter from the body. In intestinal obstruction there are antiperistaltic movements designed to obstruct the passage of waste matter. There is the systole and diastole of the heart, the pumping of the blood through the body and the relative pause for the heart to refill the same purpose. There is the universal diurnal variation between sleep and waking. The psyche has also this dual purpose of descending to remind us of the light from which we came and ascending, sometimes in life itself, but mostly after death, to remind us of the divine sources from which we derive. The psyche, by virtue of its two-way mechanism, operates always timelessly but enters time in its descent through the influence of the stars which determine the moment and place of birth on this planet. The psyche is confronted with time again when it pauses, in its ascent, at the planetary level attuned to its further development.

NOTE

1. See *We Are One Another.*

15.

Arguments Against Reincarnation

In this chapter it is necessary to consider the arguments against reincarnation. While belief in a cycle of lives arouses increasing interest in Western civilisation there is still a majority for whom it is not reality. Many of these latter are recruited from those who never develop at all, who only accept what they were brought up to believe or who, lacking even the vitality for this, cease to believe anything at all. There are others, said to be scientific, for whom reincarnation is not true because it cannot be proved, that is to say measured and others, equally scientific, who preserve what is called an open mind, a synonym for closing one's eyes to evidence.

In assessing reincarnation against a European background one has to consider the case under two headings. Firstly, do we believe in an immortal psyche? Secondly, does it reincarnate? So far as the first question is concerned it is remarkable how many reject the existence of a psyche. This is largely because we have allowed ourselves to be dominated by bureaucrats who do not merit the name of scientists. Such people do not believe in anything they cannot explain. No reasoned or logical argument can pierce the armourplate they manufacture for themselves in their laboratories, which are often cocoonlike evasions of reality. The psyche exists because psychic phenomena are its symptoms in action. Psychic phenomena occur against a timeless background. In clairvoyance and precognition we see or feel things, pleasant or unpleasant, before they happen. The psyche is immortal precisely because it is emancipated from time. I cannot repeat myself here for the benefit of those who still deny the existence of psychic phenomena or, which is the same thing, believe that extrasensory perception can be explained other than by postulating the existence of a psyche. One is not postulating anything. One learns more by perceiving, seeing and hearing the psyche in action, as I have described in several previous books.

It is very necessary to note that, under the aegis of the technocrats, in denying the existence of a psyche we are being misled by views which only achieved eminence in the last two centuries. In discussing these matters we should limit ourselves to our European and possibly Middle Eastern sources, the latter because Christianity originated there. Limiting ourselves in this way is necessary because our cultural background, mass unconscious and ancestral memory differ from those of Orientals and Africans. Since at least 2000 BC practitioners of the Mysteries in the Balkan peninsular, as at Eleusis in Greece, have believed in an immortal soul which purifies itself by reincarnation. This was revealed to practitioners of the Mysteries. It was preached more openly by Pythagorus in the sixth century BC. In the third century BC Plato stated also his belief in the immortality of the soul and in reincarnation.

The whole basis of Christianity rests on the immortality of the soul. Where Christ was unique among the great prophets was in the immediacy of His resurrection. It is not possible that the early Christians believed in the resurrection of the physical body as it is stated baldly in the Creeds. Those who had been present at the Transfiguration on the Mount must have known that they were dealing with some kind of spirit body. Be that as it may, no adherents of any religion were, with the empty tomb and the appearance on the road to Emmaus, ever presented so immediately and so conclusively with the evidence of an immortal component in man. It is not our business to waste ink over what actually reincarnates. Buddhist theology is, on this point, as exasperating as anything produced by Christianity. What I am concerned with is simply that in each individual there is a real I, as distinct from the transitory ego of personality, which persists throughout what the Christians call all eternity. The doctrine of an immortal soul persisted through the wide confines of the Christian world, be it Catholic or Protestant, until the French Enlightenment of the mid-eighteenth century which started man off on what was to become the most damaging of all beliefs, that he is merely a product of his environment. In orthodox Christianity, as distinct from the beliefs held in classical antiquity, the soul is not strictly immortal. It is planted within us as a seed at birth, germinates with growing consciousness, achieves some kind of fruition in life, goes into a state of suspended animation after death and is brusquely reawakened at the day of judgement. This is not the same as the ancient belief, inherited from classical antiquity and still justifiably extant, that a complete psyche with a memory for past incarnations enters matter at conception, accompanies the personality throughout life, resists and survives the dissolution of the latter and lives in a state of heightened awareness between reincarnations. Nevertheless, in two thousand years of Christianity, its adherents have believed in an immortal psyche of one kind or another. Even since the eighteenth century the mass of people, until the last three or four decades, retained their faith in an immortal soul. Agnosticism and atheism in the last century in England were primarily products, perhaps the only ones, of the intelligentsia.

It is strange that man should have preferred the evidence of the last two centuries to that of the last four millennia. Has the last two hundred years produced such notable philosophy? Isn't it possible to say that a good deal of our thinking in the last two centuries is not merely a cause but a sign of the crack up? Doesn't a good deal of the ghastly errors in our thinking and feeling attitudes stem from the naive idea that progress is synonymous with the passage of time and that, except for an occasional nasty skid on the black ice of evolution, man gets better and better as time goes on. The argument runs that a hundred years ago cock fighting was widespread. Haven't we come on since then? Certainly. There is always Auschwitz, Buchenwald and Katyn. Western educational systems, in scattering so much seed to so many and being indifferent as to the quality of the fruit, cannot afford to emphasize that there have been periods in past history of far higher culture and sophistication than our own, and that the evidence for the existence of an immortal psyche is, over the millennia, far greater than that against it.

As to the length of time during which man has believed in

reincarnation this belief is not only revealed in the Mysteries
and was taught by Pythagorus and Plato, but was also one of
the items of faith in the cult of Mithras which continued
until at least as late as the fourth century AD in the Roman
Empire. It is often argued that one of the articles of faith in
primitive Christianity was belief in reincarnation but that it
was expunged from the records at the council at Nicea in
AD 325. The evidence produced has never seemed to me
conclusive. It is time the Old Testament rather than the New
was scrupulously searched for references to reincarnation.
What one can say with certainty is that the so-called Dualist
heresies, certainly rooted in primitive Christianity, believed
without exception in the cycle of lives. These included
Manicheism, the spread of which was, in its day — it began
in the third century AD — more rapid and widespread than
that of Christianity, the Paulicians and Bogomils in the
Balkan peninsular and the Cathars and Patarini in France and
Northern Italy. As well as these there is evidence that, away
from the Mediterranean basin, on the Western fringe of
Europe, there were centres of the Celtic Church which were
certainly Dualist and believed in reincarnation.[1] The order of
the Temple was also Dualist as were the working masons of
the Middle Ages.

One quotes these European sources to show that, far from
dying altogether, belief in reincarnation has at times been
widespread and determined in Western civilisation and has
never wholly died. It was revived quite vigorously in the last
century and the early years of this by the Theosophist
movement, but it is not accurate to regard this revival as in
the direct line of European culture. Like Schopenhauer at an
earlier date the Theosophists sought for their evidence in
Eastern rather than Western sources. This is a point to be
noted. Surely the exponents of the far Eastern religions,
Buddhism and Hinduism, at least equal the number of
practising Christians. The former believe in reincarnation.
Generally speaking, it is an inevitable accompaniment of Far
Eastern faiths. It seems to arouse the antipathy of the more
legalistic religions of Middle Eastern origin, be they
Christian, Judaic or Islamic. The latter seem obsessionally
preoccupied with the need to define. The Far Eastern
religions stress the necessity of feeling. One can say with
confidence that half of the world which has retained any

kind of religious faith believes in reincarnation. For this reason alone it should not be necessary for Western believers in a cycle of lives to take the precaution of acquiring first a certificate of sanity.

It is claimed that phenomena pointing to reincarnation are in fact due to cryptamnesia. This implies that the mind recalls out of its deepest recesses something it appears to have long forgotten but which it is actually remembering. In short the mind forgets that it remembers. This is a palpably crude attitude. The use of this word implies that those who use it have not studied the evidence. It is a convenient condemnation attractive to the mind of materialistic psychiatrists, in the same way as the word medium once meant to the *bien pensant* black magic and the darker aspects of the occult. The last two decades has also seen the emergence of the strange hybrid called the Christian psychiatrist, an astonishing evolutionary aberration. The function of any kind of doctor is to utilise compassion and knowledge against a non-sectarian background. A number of these gentlemen cannot support the idea of reincarnation. Certainly some people may inadvertently fuse what they have read in a book with what they have genuinely remembered from a past life. But nobody could possibly attribute the evidence which has come my way to cryptamnesia. When I am recalling the existence of obscure characters appearing in no textbooks in any language and where my information was derived from depositions in Latin translated by my friend Duvernoy into French and done by me into English. For the comfort of the professional, as distinct from the natural, sceptic I was, at school, kicked out of the Latin class as ineducable.

Cryptamnesia is also a completely superfluous suggestion when, in group reincarnation, one finds the memories of several people tallying with complete accuracy. It does not come into the picture when recollection of past lives does not depend on memory in the strict and direct sense of the word but on the type of psychic synchronisation described in *The Lake And The Castle* through which I was aided enormously in recalling my Celtic and Napoleonic incarnations. Nor cannot it apply to the co-operation of the discarnates who contributed also to my remembering not only the immediately aforementioned incarnations but also

my life in Rome in the fourth century AD. Cryptomnesia is
another of those umbrella diagnoses we use to dismiss what
we are ignorant of or have failed to discover. It goes into the
rag bag of discarded diagnoses with expressions like over
suggestibility and mass illusion. Having known people
dismissed as hysterics who have gone blind from cerebral
tumour I am all the more on guard against terms used not to
describe cases and facts but the investigator's attitude. At the
present time the word cryptomnesia tells us more about
people who use it than about those to whom it is applied.

Another kind of memory is sometimes postulated to
account for past lives and, in so doing, to dispose of the
necessity for reincarnation. Have some people, it is asked, a
built-in ability to look back hundreds or thousands of years?
Are they gifted with some kind of special memory which
enables them to reverberate to events which occurred six or
seven centuries ago? Is it something transmitted by the
genes? I am perfectly prepared to believe that people with far
memory have a genetic equipment different from others.
Have not I laboured the fact that psychic attributes in
general are often inherited? More important than this, have I
not said that everything which happens on earth from coitus
to cosmic consciousness must have a mechanism, and that
the latter functions in many aspects including physiological,
genetic, biochemical, psychological and psychic factors. But
the possible possession of a genetic tendency to remember
the past has nothing to do with the fact of reincarnation. If
we remember a past life five hundred years ago and another
a thousand years ago in virtue of genetic memory we are
talking only of the isolated recollection of past lives. We are
still left with the question, what links these lives together?
We are still only dealing with another possible mechanism
involved in reincarnation and not with the latter itself.

Another argument used against the existence of
reincarnation is that what people may sincerely believe is the
recollection of past lives is actually only the results of
telepathy. It is said that by such means a person may derive
from an erudite student of, say, Egyptology, enough data to
make him believe that he himself has had a past incarnation,
in that country and preferably in one of its heroic periods.
This is indeed possible, which is precisely why I am so
opposed to regression by hypnosis to enable individuals to

recall past lives. In the highly suggestible state induced by hypnosis the person hypnotised may acquire all sorts of information from the mind of the therapist. If the latter is knowledgeable about medieval masonry, a patient, his brain suddenly inundated by all manner of signs and symbols, may honestly believe himself to have lived in the Middle Ages.

No such element of telepathy has entered into the cases with which I have been associated. I have sometimes been asked whether, owing to what has been described as my considerable knowledge of Catharism, Mrs. Smith and Miss Mills, the central characters in my books, could have acquired from me by telepathy their own knowledge of Catharism. This is totally impossible. I learnt all of what I know about Catharism by verifying their statements to me. Before I knew Mrs. Smith I did not know the three basic tenets of Dualism. Besides, at the time I wrote *The Cathars And Reincarnation*, I did not myself consciously remember my life as a Cathar. It was proved to me by Mrs. Smith. The latter, until she learnt it from me, did not even know the name of the heresy she had remembered as a schoolgirl. Miss Mills, when I first met her, was totally ignorant of the words Albigensian or Cathar.

It has been said that much of what is taken to be evidence for reincarnation is the work of discarnate entities. Presumably what is meant is that for a discarnate to talk to one about a past life does not in itself contribute proof of reincarnation. Such an attitude is justifiable but to say that because a discarnate enters into the proceeding, this offers a differential diagnosis to reincarnation, is the wildest folly. What is not realised is that communication from discarnates is one of the common mechanism whereby we obtain evidence as to the reality of past lives. If a discarnate appeared and gave us an illuminating discourse on life in the Holy Roman Empire and said that she and the hearer had lived together at that time one would be justified in thinking that not just the lower grade of discarnates but a truly lower entity was playing tricks. This is simply not the way that the true discarnates guide us on the subject of reincarnation. Positive statements are not made and positive questions not answered. One is given clues, verbal or in writing, and is expected to verify them. In the presence of the discarnates, once one has achieved the capacity to vibrate on their wavelength if only temporarily, one shares their capacity to see into past lives. When, by such means, the story has been strung together and one has told it oneself, then and then only, the discarnates confirm that one has spoken the truth.

The argument that much material described as contributing to belief in reincarnation is actually due to clairaudience can be answered in the same way. Certainly this faculty plays a part in some cases of reincarnation. Naturally not all clairaudient material is evidence of reincarnation but, to take the matter further and say that because clairaudience enters into the picture we are not dealing with reincarnation is plainly ridiculous. I do not see how Mrs. Smith could have taken down her poetry in medieval language if it had not been dictated to her in a state of clairaudience. The statement that So and So hears voices seems to terrify some people beyond measure. This is not the place to labour the fact that I am a psychiatrist and that it is not difficult to distinguish between clairaudience and schizoid auditory hallucinations.

The point to recognize above all others in dealing with reincarnation is that the individual is made ready to receive evidence of it beforehand and also that it never appears as an isolated phenomenon. Acceptance of the reality of reincarnation is the attribute of a special kind of individual. The latter may be prepared for it at birth. He or she may be born with scars, deformities or birthmarks originating in previous lives. These may be followed in childhood by recurrent dreams also originating in past lives. They may be *déja vu* phenomena, discarnate voices from the past, similar voices indicating where one should search for evidence, and what seem at first occurrence to be remarkable coincidences but which are revealed later as psychic synchronisations, together with a multitude of other manifestations such as I have recorded previously in the four books which deal with my past incarnations. What strikes the individual who is being prepared for the truth of reincarnation is that he lives through what I have called open periods in which he finds himself, and often those about him, unaccountably telepathic and clairvoyant and involved in situations in which he has only to think of a person, not seen for years, to meet him in the street and in which he has only to search for a quotation for some stranger to supply him with the immediate answer.

The processes I have just described constitute a kind of initiation not recognized as such because there is no named hierarchy, no organization with a semi-mystical title and no official directing guru. (Certainly the discarnates act as our mentors but they do not advertise themselves as such). As is expected of initiations, those who undergo them are transformed. It is this process of transformation which indicates the reality of reincarnation more than does any single item. Those enabled have a detailed knowledge of more than one incarnation are unmistakeably changed and developed. I mention with intention more than one previous life because, in group reincarnation, it is the usual rule that the central members of any one group remember more than one incarnation. How otherwise could they be aware of their existence as a continuing group? As for their transformation this involves, if they have not manifested such gifts before, the rapid development of telepathy, precognition and clairvoyance. If they have had these gifts before they are dramatically intensified. Most of all they acquire the gift of healing. I know of no case with the memory of several incarnations without some capacity to heal. The latter gift may be lavish and may be manifested in the laying on of hands or in out-of-the-body visitations or in the healer taking the patient's symptoms.

Such total transformation of an individual is the best evidence that he has truly remembered past incarnations. Expressed in simple terms he has undergone an experience of revealed truth. But as well as this there is another important sign which accompanies utterly valid experiences of reincarnation. This is the revelation of purpose. It was evident from the start in my own group. We were told that because the world was rapidly darkening it was necessary to illuminate it a little by means of Catharism. This evidence of purpose is of course clearer in group reincarnation than in isolated examples of a person remembering a single previous life. This is because it is only through a group keeping together through several incarnations that the element of purpose can be properly disclosed. This is achieved with the help of discarnates. It is quite impossible for the phenomenon of group incarnation to occur without their help. Discarnates are the artificers making the chain which joins together the links with separate incarnations. Those who refer to talking to discarnates as an alternative diagnosis to reincarnation have missed the point entirely, certainly so far as group reincarnation is concerned.

I have never encountered outright fraud in the sphere of reincarnation, that is to say I have never met individuals who have manufactured past lives to impress others or to be associated with what may well become a popular preoccupation. I have, however, met numbers of those who have snatched at visualised scraps of the past and have thought themselves into *déja vu* experiences and have succeeded in convincing themselves they have had previous lives. So they have, but the question is, do they remember them? Many of these are earnest camp followers of reincarnation rather than living examples of its truth. They regard it as a romantic and comforting conception and are unaware of its pains. Even the more sober, who confine themselves to statements that it explains things reasonably and fills a need, have no idea of the pain and anguish it brings in its wake. If one looks back on a single lifetime it includes enough sorrow without embarrassing oneself with several. Many of the suggestible romantics are distinguishable by a preoccupation with eminent names. They prefer to have been the Queen of Sheba rather than a servant in a squalid inn. Another habit of the romantic, in looking back on supposed incarnations, is to go far back in time. Atlantis is more telling than Wigan and the uncertain but eager acolytes are only too happy to opt for the former. The recall of distant incarnations is usually accompanied by great depression and tension. I do not see regularly signs of such disasters on the faces of those who have been mistresses of Rameses the Second of Egypt. Few such people have detailed and continuous knowledge of a past incarnation. Their recollections are fragmentary or non-existent. I do not say that such people are dishonest or even that they do not remember bits and pieces of distant incarnations. What I do say is that their heightened suggestibility exceeds their memory.

I am puzzled by the number of people who claim to have had Oriental incarnations, some of these at distant epochs. In discussing these one can, to some extent, use the same arguments as one has employed in the foregoing paragraph, but so far as Hindu and Buddhist incarnations are concerned those who claim to have had them do not plunge so far into the past as those faithful to Egyptian and Atlantean culture. Here we are up against a different proposition. Certainly the number of those claiming Hindu and Buddhist incarnations could be whittled down with profit. Nevertheless there are those who have had, say, two Oriental incarnations in the course of two millennia. In their other incarnations they have been of European origin. Such people are often completely true bills but tend to be mentally unstable and subject to severe attacks of depression.

In Britain twenty years ago reincarnation was a subject for cranks. Now it is in danger of becoming the in thing. Is this enormously increased interest a passing mode? Is it even slightly morbid? I do not think so. Certainly there are people who would take up reincarnation as they would skittles because they would take up anything. Certainly we are living through the end of a civilisation when those caught up in its decay will grab in all directions for salvation, even plunging their tentacles into the cultures of people they formerly despised. I do not think these precautionary views need depress us too much. The interest of many people in reincarnation is healthy and reasonable enough. Here again mere interest in a subject need not concern us too much. The cardinal question is always, "Is it true?" I myself know this to be true but I do not expect others to believe what they have not experienced. Not all can be inundated with data as I was. But during my last years of practice I noted a steep increase, beginning perhaps in the early 1960s, in people admitting to experiences of telepathy, clairvoyance and clairaudience. Many of these people, mostly English working class, were totally out of the current of European thought in believing in a positive force of evil. Many had an acute nose for it and a strongly developed sense of atmospheres. They believed equally in the force of goodness. A surprising number believed or were interested in reincarnation. Most of these people had limited culture as well as modest origin. What they had derived was from experience.

It seems to me that there has been, beginning two decades ago, a sharp rise in the level of awareness of a minority in the community. These people, with their growing precognition and clairvoyance, showed that increase of perception which accompanies the awakening of far memory. What is more, they had that belief in the power of evil which, with belief in reincarnation, provides two of the three basic tenets of the Dualist philosophy which has persisted relatively unamended throughout recorded history. Is it possible that the symptoms shown by many of these patients were due to the repression of far memory? I can recall a positive number in whom this could have been a factor. Certainly their symptoms cleared up when they accepted that reincarnation was true or when they themselves had fragments of recall which consoled them as to the solidity of their convictions.

What is the use of reincarnation if the majority do not remember their lives? This is one of the commonest objections raised to belief in reincarnation. We can, if you wish, dismiss the matter by saying that here is another example of refusing to believe what one does not understand. Why should we hope on this earth to comprehend thoroughly any cosmic process like birth or death when we lack the instrumentation for so doing? But we can offer a more specific answer to this problem. Our life on this earth is our lowest level of sensibility. Those who have died stress the greater reality of the life between our lives. Also, in developing after death, we acquire knowledge of our past incarnations. What is common in the beyond is what a few achieve on this planet. The acid test of development on earth is that we learn to remember our past lives. This bridges the gulf between life, in this world, and death. If the mark of the old soul is that, on earth, he remembers his past incarnations, it is obviously intended that all should do so in due course, since the highest wisdom and the uttermost evolution we can attain to is due to the age of our psyches. The answer to those who see no purpose in reincarnation is therefore to wait until they see for themselves. They will be submitted to the same processes and atmospheres which enable the old souls of the present day to look back on several incarnations. In the gaps between our lives we learn more than we do on earth. Even here below it is evident that more are remembering than even half a century ago. In the end, with few exceptions, we all catch up with each other.

One is sometimes asked, how is it possible, with so many souls waiting to reincarnate, to find accommodation for all the permitted number of personalities on this planet? I never think questions of this kind are worth answering. They are shuttlecocks to be thrown about between imperceptive intellectuals. I once heard this particular one answered with such brilliance that I forgot the explanation immediately.

NOTE

1. See *The Lake And The Castle.*

16.

Good and Evil

In this chapter I am concerned with the extent of the battle between good and evil. This is not simply a question of metaphysics or ethics and if it were I would not touch it. Watching and hearing the antics of contemporary philosophers on the television and radio has limited my philosophical aspirations. Philosophy to me is only valid if it is based on revealed phenomena. What passes for the art is an intellectual dissection of situations in which all the time available is consumed by defining raw materials, often called norms, which it is clear the pundits have manufactured themselves. This chopping out of images of truth by intellects which their possessors imagine to be rapiers and which are used as cudgels began, admittedly, in a more refined form with Plato. That I am tired of it is of no importance to anyone, not even to me. That the world has gained little from it is of greater moment. Plato is only truly the philosopher when he is in touch with his daemon. True philosophy is a record of our conversations with our discarnate guides. One is allowed a few intuitive leaps, themselves presided over by the same sources, to ensure that the river of truth runs smoothly.

To waste time defining the nature of evil in sociological terms is not my intention. This is because I believe that the contemporary sociological and psychological approach to the subject is itself evil. The latter as a power does not exist for the majority of psychiatrists. We are either social or anti-social, group adjusted or maladjusted. In other words our goodness is measured by our cohesion to the group. Our sin is to be outside it. Under the heading of scientific progress we are relegated to a kind of spiritual Buchenwald. This classifying us as good according to the degree we fuse with and submit to society is diabolic. Society itself may run amok, *vide* Hitler, Stalin and the rest. The greatest and most damning achievement of modern psychiatry and the subordinate studies into which it has percolated to their detriment, is the abolition of evil. Its practitioners have persuaded us that the latter as a force does not exist and is a pathological aberration produced by faulty environment. This unawareness of the nature of the force of evil makes us all the more vulnerable to it.

Evil, like psychic activity generally, is less easy to define than to see in action. This is why the intellectual metaphysicians fail with such touching fidelity. They have been rendered myopic by too little use of their visual apparatus. Some were merely born blind. I do not propose here to deal with the evidence for evil in action. My attitude is similar to that I adopt towards disbelievers in extrasensory perception. The evidence is there and, if it cannot be accepted, there is nothing more I can do about it. I have written of the effects of evil in inducing tangible physical and mental disease in my book *The Psyche In Medicine* and in several monographs. There is nothing more tangible than vomiting, migraine, Meniere's syndrome, accident proneness, severe allergies and cancer. All these can, without any doubt, be attributed to the force of evil or the influence of its transmitters.

Life is essentially a battle between good and evil. This, translated in a superficial sense, is possibly the most trite observation ever made. It could be used by any politician applying a little ethical varnish to his next lie. It could be used by any bishop exhorting us to do our best in a short, one-life sprint when what we are faced with is an interminable cross country course with a diversity of obstacles. Do we appreciate properly the width and depth of the battle between these two forces? Firstly the combat begins within ourselves. Any orthodox Christian will support this view with fervour but in this book we are not dealing with ethical conflicts and heart-searching choices as to this or that line of conduct. What we are concerned with is a confrontation which penetrates through every layer of being, from the philosophical origins of evil to its electromagnetic influence in causing certain cancers.

On the subject of the evil we inherit at birth Christian
doctrine is incomprehensible. It seems we are born in sin.
The Roman Catholic service of baptism makes no bones
about the necessity of expelling the devil as soon as
possible. At the same time, in orthodox Christianity, we are
not credited at birth with the presence of a mature psyche.
Our soul grows with consciousness and is a kind of
quintessence of a vague entity called our better self. What
are we then expelling at birth? How can the devil drive out
anything other than our psyche? It is not worth his while,
any more than it is worth God's, to expel a mere promising
seedling soul. God and the devil both want the soul in its
entirety or nothing. The doctrine of original sin is infinitely
mysterious, an immortal tribute to man's genius for
confusing himself. The idea that a child, the product of
copulation, and to that extent coming into the world through
no choice of his own, is born in sin, is repulsive. A good deal
of this mist-enveloped theology is tied up with the subject of
sex. There are even last ditch moralists for whom the sin of
Adam and Eve was the discovery of coitus. If, however, we
go a little deeper into the matter, there is a hidden logic in
the notion of original sin. Applied to the individual child it is
disgusting. Considered in relation to creation as a whole it
makes more sense because it is by assuming form and
entering matter that our psyche, saturated already by contact
with matter, descends again from its higher state in the next
world to inherit once again the evil that comes with the
presence of form and matter. With the acquisition at
conception of a mature psyche the individual is exposed to
the vibrations of the mass unconscious. As we have
indicated the psyche's activities are two-directional. In its
darker aspects it absorbs the reverberations of the herd.
These mob emotions extend from gregarious prejudices to
tribal frenzies. Their influence is always bad because they
subject us to a debased form of communication which
impedes the contact of our psyche, in its lighter aspects, with
the individualised spirit which is what remains to us of the
light from whence we came.

This subjugation to the mass unconscious may take the
chronic form of providing us with targets for tribal hates.
Under the influence of persuasive paranoics the Jew and the
Freemason become objects of hate in Catholic countries.

This is dying away but in places dying hard. Similarly the Catholic is a moveable target in some Protestant communities, *vide* the Ku Klux Klan. People like Hitler, who play on the crowd so that the latter clamours for satisfaction and domination like a passionate woman, are possessed or given over consciously to the generalised force of evil. In the case of Hitler the latter description is more likely. It is doubtful if possession alone could have sustained him through the years of mass murder.

This has been, in the carnage of its wars, in its slaughter of millions, sadistic on the part of the Nazis, scientifically cold-blooded on that of the Communists, surely the darkest age of European civilisation. Though the Inquisition was a model for the Bolshevic interrogators, it never achieved, in mass murder, the proportions of a great pandemic. Intellectuals who still believe in regular progress with the passage of time must be lacking in head as well as heart. Since the war the evil represented by murder in the concentration camps, with carnage on the battlefield a very poor second, has been expressed in a cult of violence revealed in kidnappings, brutal and pointless murders, rapes, vandalism and hijackings.

What happens in such an age is that the number of malignant discarnates is intensified. There is a thickening in the atmosphere of Hades caused by a greater accumulation of hostile entities. Those responsible for mass murders remain still in Hades, lured by the delicious proximity of the earth on which they have perpetrated so much crime. They return again, not directed and organized as in the Gestapo, Ogpu and the S.S. but as isolated savages repeating in the formerly quiet provincial towns of Western Europe what they formerly performed in Dachau. Some of their victims return with them. The disorientation of violent death, which prevents the after death sleep, and the continuing mystery and terror associated with their violent end, draw some back to the earth so that they never traverse the whole width of Hades. They are guided back to the earth by malignant entities similar to those responsible for their end on this earth. In some cases on return to the earth the killed become the killers. Here again we seem confronted with an appalling injustice. Must the innocent suffer because they were victims? They do not suffer because they were victims but because, for them, further suffering was part of the pattern. Remember that the pattern itself is in part imposed by evil. All the threads in the cosmic design, as seen from this earth are not healthy and beautiful. The bad is inwoven with the good. Remember also that the sojourn in Hades is not perpetual. In relation to our own chronology it may be miniscule.

Great horrors such as we have known this century result in many psyches never getting beyond the confines of Hades. As these contaminated psyches cannot progress further the result is a congestion in Hades which is relieved by the return to earth, often after an unusually brief sojourn in the shades, of a number of psyches still contaminated by the exercise or memory of violence. Others may not reincarnate and become the thugs of the next generation but may hover in close proximity to our planet and possess as many souls as possible. The latter act as transmitters of evil. This influence may be constant or epidemic. There is also a regular wave of malignant discarnates hanging on the fringe of the consciousness of those who inhabit this planet. After a particular great wave of bestiality, the flood waters issuing from it are naturally intensified and the world is tortured by an increased wave of violence attributable to the raised number of those either totally possessed or acting as passive transmitters of evil. The distinction between possession and being a passive transmitter has been dealt with in other books of mine and will not be amplified here. Possession involves the complete taking over of the psyche of the individual by discarnate entities. The personality of the victim is totally changed. He either becomes the hopeless instrument of the discarnate or the tortured, partially articulate victim who struggles with the dark invader and attempts to expel him by compulsive movements[1].

It may seem to us here below that the great battle between good and evil is fought on this earth because we cannot envisage anything worse than the horrors of genocide or the mass slaughter of people because they are cultivated and have lifted themselves a little above the level of brute creation. This is not so. Our destiny is decided in the next zone of consciousness, in the Hades of the ancients. Discarnate evil is stronger than the incarnate variety because its scope is greater. Its victim is the psyche whereas in this world the effect of evil may be expended in disrupting the ordinary human personality. Only those who have seen people possessed can appreciate the truth of these statements. The possessed themselves cannot because, except for the realisation that they were taken over by something nameless, their detailed memory is mercifully obliterated. Only the observer, provided he appreciates that he is concerned with possession, can be aware of the horrifying sense of isolation, of being utterly lost, which afflicts these people, who are often conspicuously good because, as one cannot say often enough, it is those who emanate goodness who offer the most seductive targets for the forces and agents of evil. People thus possessed are literally in Hades. They have passed from the workaday hell of this world to one of the darkest facets of Hades where they stand alone and are battered by the force of evil. In this life they are beyond death. It is they who offer us the best picture of the Armageddon between good and evil which occurs in Hades.

Is this Armageddon continually being fought? Seen from the level of the psyche, from Hades itself, seen by the possessed transposed in this life from earth to Hades, it is always on. But there can be no doubt that, to our eyes and in terms of our time, we are living at the moment an intensifying Armageddon. This is because we are living not only in a disintegrating civilisation but in the disintegration of all civilisations. We cannot see this because we are blindfolded by the luxuries and appurtenances of what we call culture. With our cars and colour televisions it is harder for us to realise than it was for starving, disease-ridden serfs in the Middle Ages. Such a state as we are living at the moment has occurred before. We must meditate not on the minor deaths of civilisations which have occurred in recorded history like Rome and the Holy Roman Empire, but on those civilisations of which we know little or nothing which have disappeared from our planet leaving scarcely a trace.

The result of Armageddon may well, once again expressed in terms of our life on this planet, be against us. We may relive another true Gotterdämmerung, a Ragnarok where the good gods failed to control the outpouring of the victorious dark forces from the chasms of the earth. Is it not for these reasons that it will be necessary for us to reincarnate on other planets? We exemplify this in an exoteric and misguided way by our preoccupation with space travel and putting satellites into space. With our usual brutish insensitivity we must actively investigate from this earth the other regions of the Cosmos instead of waiting for those messages which are beginning to be emitted by them. It is better to listen than to break down doors.

In the Armageddon being fought in Hades the forces of light are well represented. Their guardian angels are constantly active in the zone of consciousness between this world and the next. Some are concerned in piloting a proportion of lost and bewildered psyches to the next level of awareness where they may learn to sleep. Others, of whose activities we here can be aware, help protect us from harm. When our attention is so misdirected by malignant discarnates that we are exposed to danger by our inattention, our guardian angel may steer us on a safer course. Even when we have an accident, as when we fall, as in those cases of Meniere's syndrome precipitated by evil, we are often spared serious damage by the guardian angel's intervention. It is sometimes difficult to understand why, if the guardian angels are able to protect us, that at times they fail to do so. Once again we cannot alter the cosmic pattern because the evil entities are, at certain levels of operation, contributing to it.

The guardian angels are creative and good discarnates who remain in Hades and partly within the orbit of the earth's magnetism. They do so for completely different reasons to those which impel the evil discarnates to lurk in no-man's land to possess and inflict evil on troubled psyches and to hurry back to this planet those destined to do evil. The guardian angels are a permanent light in the grey obscurity of Hades. They constitute a layer of the hierarchy between ourselves and the accessible discarnates which communicate with us freely. It is possible but incredibly rare for a living being to act as a guardian angel of another. For this to happen it is necessary for the individual to be as highly developed in this life as the lower discarnates. The person protected must also have known him or her intimately through several incarnations. The only living guardian angels are women.

Guardian angels do not make themselves known to us as do the communicating discarnates. They do not tell us verbally to avoid this or that danger. They often feed us with hunches which enable us to do so. They are recruited from beings still tied to the earth by bonds of love. They have neither the capacity nor the wish to free themselves from those they have loved on earth often with an ordinary human love. Some people are aware of the presence of their guardian angels. Some claim permanent contact with them but this is erroneous. Their prolonged

presence is responsible for what is called the Doppelgänger
phenomenon, of a sense of another self almost identical with
one's own, being present. Sometimes the individual can feel the
departure of the guardian angel from him. This usually occurs
either late in life or when the person concerned, after a troubled
existence, passes for some years into smoother waters.

Ultimately the guardian angels pass on to become the kind of
discarnates who communicate with us verbally and visually.
One can regard their subtle and unspoken communication with
us as guardian angels as a preparation for their more obvious
role.

Though Armageddon is at its most intense in the zone
between this world and the next there are increased invasions of
evil in the world we live in. This is shown perhaps most
significantly in popular music. I am not speaking of the wailing
invocations to love and to one's own sufferings which pass,
among the elect, as the Sermon on the Mount set to music. I am
referring to the constantly repeating tribal rhythms in which the
music is accompanied by shuffling, repetitive movements never
built up into a whole and resembling compulsive rituals. The
difference between ordinary obsessional acts, such as occur in
the neurosis of that name, and the rituals of which I am speaking
is that the former are designed as a protection against evil and
the latter are a response to it. It should also be observed that
ordinary neurotic compulsive ritual is practised by the individual
alone. With the obsessive rythms of which I am speaking
practised by crowds, the result is entirely different. In the case of
the solitary obsessional patient the intention of the compulsive
act is to ward off evil, whereas the ritualistic chants and
movements are designed to break down the resistance of the
personality and open the psyche to the floodgate of evil. It
astonishes me that the likeness of these activities to jungle
rhythms has been so little commented on. The aim, not
necessarily conscious, is to break down resistance and facilitate
orgiastic frenzies of violence and sex. It is significant that so
many people attracted by this form of entertainment are also
addicted to drugs. It is still more significant that many bandleaders
who preside at these disintegrating sessions openly admit their
usage of drugs. The use of the latter is designed for the same
purpose as the chants themselves, to change the level of
awareness of the individual so that they are more vulnerable to
the invasion of evil.

There is no doubt that these tribal chants often presage outbursts of violence. Certainly they have grown up alongside the cult of violence. It should be noted that people's responses to these rhythms vary and the effect is not necessarily to induce antisocial behaviour. I myself feel unbearably strung up by such rhythms and, if I am forced to endure them for more than a few minutes, physically exhausted. This is in part a matter of discordant wavelengths and in part because I know the significance and intention of these pathological repetitions, designed as they are to open the sluices to the flood waters of evil.

One cannot here expand on the subject of modern art. Matters of individual taste enter too much into the question. One cannot forget that Chopin, over seductive and even, for some, a little over sweet, was once regarded as barbaric because of his use of discords. One recalls that the Impressionists were described as indecent not because of the subjects they chose, which were mostly landscapes, but because of their methods of painting. I most particularly cannot forget that, what to me is one of the most perfect books ever written, Madame Bovary, was the subject of a trial for obscenity. This surely earns a gold medal in any competition for crimes committed by the Establishment. Nevertheless there are discordances in modern music, as distinct from the pop variety, which seem to me to symbolise and emanate evil. Possibly my view is prejudiced by the particular effect of such music on me. The reader may regard such opinions as the foibles of the neurotic and senile. To do so is short sighted. It is recognized that certain visual patterns are basically evil. A Tibetan Lama of great culture was horrified to discover such evocative arrangements in a shop in Oxford. I know of hospitals the outward designs of which make me shudder before I enter their portals, and this in spite of the fact that I have been used to going into hospitals for forty odd years. From time immemorial arrangements of lines, numbers and notes in music have been regarded not by the superstitious or ingenuous but by the sophisticated and enlightened as good or evil. It is no use dismissing out of hand my statement that there are passages in Stravinsky which make my flesh creep or, what is more important, that the same reactions are experienced by people far more evolved than myself and with an acute flair for detecting evil in places, persons and situations.

So far as the visual arts are concerned some sculpture which seems to me laughably obscene, not in any sexual sense of the word but in its perversity of form, is reverenced by a self-proclaimed *avant garde* which asks, or demands, if one fails altogether to see the likeness between what modern sculptors have produced and this or that variety of primitive art. I do see the likeness. That is the whole trouble. Leonardo, Michaelangelo, Raphael, Titian, Rembrandt, Caravaggio, Constable and the Norfolk school stand between me and the primitive to which I do not wish to return, preferring Ruysdael and Hobbema's landscapes to pieces of bent wire said to reveal the significance of the void.

I cannot but feel that in much modern art, be it musical or visual, the conflict between good and evil reveals itself, in a different form, as the battle between beauty and ugliness. This latter is perhaps a subtler expression of the struggle between good and evil because beauty is an ultimate harmony beyond both these forces. The perversion of art may indeed in the long run have a more deadly effect in inducing decadence, violence and destruction because a culture may represent the permanent quintessence of a civilisation doomed to deteriorate.

In making these suggestions about modern art I should make it quite clear that I am in no sense tainted by the horrible puritanical tendency to judge a work of art by its subject matter. To many Victorians a novel became automatically evil because it dealt with adultery. If a novel is related at all to life it must inevitably be concerned with adultery because the latter is a common enough episode in the relations between men and women. Another sort of puritanism is equally repulsive. To the Nihilist critics who subjected the Russian liberal intelligentsia to a more severe censorship than did the Tsarist bureaucracy, a book had no merit if it dealt with the sorrows of a beautiful woman rather than the construction of a workers' factory. I firmly believe that all human activities from incest to censer swinging, from the cultivation of sugarbeet to sodomy, are fit subjects for literature and that 'le traitement est tout'. Even allowing for this I believe that the battle between good and evil is fought in art as anywhere else. It would be surprising if this were otherwise since it is inherent in wild nature as well as in our nature as men. We may rhapsodize about primroses and violets in the coverts in Spring but we can hear beneath the same trees the cry of the rabbit as it is seized by the stoat. No less than Goethe took what to many readers may seem an ingenuous view of art. In later life he feared that his own work *Werther* had had an unhealthy effect on German youth.

I am not in any way talking of the artist as a corruptor of morals. The latter are not constants but variables according to the type of environment and the degree of civilisation of those who inhabit it. Besides the phrase 'to corrupt morals' is usually applied to so-called sexual delinquences. I cannot accept that the latter should ever be incorporated into moral systems, except in cases where the young are coerced into sexual activities before they have reached an age where they can choose for themselves.

The question arises, does the battle between good and evil go on perpetually or are we ultimately gathered into the bosom of the Father or, more accurately, the Mother? The answer depends once again on the viewpoint from which we are contemplating the question. We are here situated in time. We are looking principally at a war conducted in Hades, that is to say the zone between death and life. We think of Hades as expressed in time and distinguish between the transitory nature of this our life and whatever happens to us after death. What may seem endless to us here below, basing as we do, and ever increasingly, our ideas of Hades on the Christian hell, is actually almost without duration because in Hades we are living in the world of the psyche. But because it is in this still psychic sphere that the war continues we are bound to consider that it lasts perpetually because in the zone of awareness of which we are speaking there is no beginning and no end. The act of creation was not something which happened in the past. It is a continuing moment of constant vibration. What we can say is that the battle in the universe between good and evil goes on in this earth and in Hades and impinges a little in the zone occupied by the discarnates who communicate with us. This infringement is inevitable because, in speaking with the lower among the communicating discarnates, we are again brushing the fringes of time. The universe, so far as the battle between good and evil is concerned, extends therefore from this world to that of the lowest beneficent discarnates in the hierarchy. Beyond the latter level we are emancipated from time and there is no more battle between good and evil because in being beyond time we are beyond doing. We are merely being and in this there is no evil because, in non-doing, there is no more impulse to dominate.

Are all souls saved in the end? This is an academic question. Merely to pose it shows lack of comprehension. Again, it is a question of the point from which one is viewing the situation.

Seen from this world of time the dark entities remaining in Hades must stay there because, in being there, they are already beyond time. We cannot understand the problems at this level until we cease to think of time as duration and see it as a kind of expanded moment. To do this we have to understand more of the nature of creation, of the great sound the reverberations of which created matter and light and which, in our time, are still continuing but which, in reality, have neither beginning nor end but are instigated by a kind of supreme pang of consciousness. This is the meaning of the term, "I am the Alpha and the Omega, the beginning and the end, the first and the last". The I in this phrase refers not to a personal god but to a supreme impulse which expressed itself, and remained, beyond chronology.

Another question naturally arises. Does the Devil exist or is he a merely picturesque allegory? One can make out a far better case for the Devil than for a personalised god simply because personalisation is itself an evil. To see personalised represent-ations of evil is very common in the night terrors of children. The gargoyle-like features so often described by the young as having nasty grinning evil faces are certainly endowed with form. A child of the same age rarely sees beneficent discarnates. He may feel their presence, he may talk with them by clairaudience but he rarely perceives their form. This is not to say that children do not sometimes see benign presences. What is evident is that this latter phenomenon is far less common than the manifestations of evil we call night terrors.

In malignant possession by invading entities the victim is aware that he is possessed by an evil something, as much an entity as a human being but infinitely more malignant. Such evil entities produce blinding attacks of depression in which the individual feels utterly and indescribably alone. In other words he has a terrifying sense of apartness. The latter may be intensified to the degree that the patient attempts or commits suicide, the supreme act of separation, at the instigation of these malignant discarnates.

Now in benign possession we see a diametrically opposite process at work. In one of its forms the individual may be taken over by a benign entity to transmit some message to another person for the latter's benefit. This happened to me when I heard the voice of a deceased colleague, talking over that of a surgeon who was talking to me on the phone and, through the latter, telling me that I needed to have my electrocardiogram repeated.

Another form of benign possession is when an entity takes over a psychic and relays through them intricate and detailed items of past incarnations. (This is an entirely different process from remembering or reliving the past in trance.) The point at issue is that those undergoing benign possession are unaware that anything has happened. They do not know that anything so personalised as a discarnate entity has taken them over. Of course when one talks to the good, creative discarnates low in the hierarchy one is aware of their more than reality, and that they have preserved an often idiosyncratic individuality, but there is no feeling of positive personalisation of people laying down the law or of entities forcing one into courses of action one does not approve of. One is advised and not pressed or menaced. Such entities appear in form to many. The higher up the hierarchy, except for excessively rare visitations of Christlike figures, the less one is aware of form and the more the element of personalisation is diminished[2]. In the course of initiation I saw Guilbert de Castres, very high in the hierarchy, as a round-faced, heavily built, stocky individual but afterwards he was only a voice answering philosophic questions which had confused me.

The longer individuality with aggressive and dominating features persists after death the more we are dealing with the diabolic. Those dark entities still circulating in Hades are elements of darkness rather than light precisely because they demonstrate, on the psychic plane, the worst attributes of egocentric personality but with a greatly amplified malevolence. This is what St. Paul meant when he spoke of us fighting evil in high places. By the latter phrase we mean higher in the Cosmos than this world. When Christ was tempted in the wilderness and offered the kingdoms of this world the scriptures attribute his temptation to the Devil. We can see from what we know already that Christ may have been attacked by a possessing entity who promised him dominion and power over things, just as similar entities in our own day seek to corrupt those they consider their enemies by inducing them to commit evil or to act as passive transmitters of it. But the trouble is that the Devil is referred to specifically as the prince of this world. Is this just picturesque phraseology on the part of people less instructed than ourselves? To adopt such an attitude is dangerous. It is always a mistake to credit ourselves with great philosophic discoveries. Of its very nature truth is something we rediscover after it has been lost. How could truth be changeless if we truly rediscover it every two thousand years? I think it possible that there is a presiding daemon in the zone of consciousness between this world and the next. It is possible that different entities assume the supreme diabolic role at different times. Is it so far-fetched to think of a personalised Devil, of someone still so attracted by the lure of matter and earthly dominion that he has dominion in Hades over other malevolent psyches? I do not think so, because the essential feature of the Fall was the separation off from a total harmony beyond good and evil of entities which were œons both in terms of physics and metaphysics. These œons gave rise to matter and ultimately to human life and form.

What we call the Devil may be a descendant of a prominent œon responsible more than any other for the creation of the world. Such a creator, seeing the horrors which have been perpetrated on the innocent on this planet, surely qualifies more for the title of Devil than God. To the Dualist certainly the creator of the world was a devil rather than a benign deity. When Voltaire said that God created man in his own image and that man immediately returned the compliment he surely referred, rather than to God, to a dominating being with all the attributes of a Devil. For my own part I think the Prince of Darkness and the creator of the world are separate entities. The former is the senior and superior of the latter. He presides over the dark corrupting forces in Hades. He is, at it were, wholly evil. The creator of this world is certainly a lower entity but not so low as the Prince of Darkness because he still retains in his substance the memory of the light he shared before the schism between good and evil.

The existence of a Prince of Darkness is the weakness, the Achilles heel of evil. This is because he is a personalised entity containing all too human characteristics. He has all the malevolence of a vicious human ego multiplied by thousands. It is his supreme crime that at the psychic level he retains all the vices of personality. He is unable to evolve because he cannot transcend the intoxication of his own power. He remains the lord of the dark forces in Hades against which the guardian angels protect us. He reinforces from the shades the power of evil in this world and the activities of its main agents, be they passive or conscious. It is his weakness that he cannot permeate deeply or for any prolonged duration even the lower order of discarnates. He can interfere with their good actions and even mimic their voices to mislead us but in the end he is unable to triumph over them. His battleground is this world, Hades and the first zones of the next world. After that his dominion ceases. At this level the influence also of the god who created this world has its end. He stands at the crossroads where light and darkness diverge as good and evil. This is why he is only partly committed to this earth. He is half angelic and half emanated by the darkness of matter.

Combat between good and evil depends on the nature of matter. The latter should never be thought of as inevitably gross and therefore weighing down the wings of the psyche. All depends on the degree of concentration of matter and on the rate of vibration of the particles of which it is composed. Most things which seem to us to be irrevocably material are also inert spirit. At the other end of the scale spirit itself is etherealised matter. We carry within us always, whatever the level of awareness at which we exist, this duality of matter and spirit. This is inevitable because at all the levels of our existence on this planet and after death we are living the drama of the creation.

In this world large particles of slow vibration form the main inanimate objects around us. We ourselves are composed of less inert and smaller particles of quicker vibrations. Our psyches, which seem relatively immaterial, are nevertheless composed of matter in less substantial form, and vibrating at a higher rhythm. As we pass from the psyche to the level of our individualised spirit the matter within us is partly dispersed and expressed in light. The light is moving once again on the surface of the waters. Even in the angel state matter is still present, suspended in light like motes in a sunbeam. This is because the angels have separate existence and recall the departure from the indivisible and total harmony from which all things sprang. After the angels and archangels the existence of the Mother Goddess is still expressed in the ultimate refinements of matter. Were it not so she would not be recognizeable as our mother. In her immaterial substance matter, as we know it, terminates in the circulation at immense speed of infinitely tiny particles. Beyond this is a whirlpool of the eternal feminine principle, more fecund, more total than the Mother herself. This principle is entirely mute and works in silence. The whirlpool leads to the vibrationless node of being. In all these higher echelons of existence we experience an increasing refinement of matter. The latter itself is divine. What we see in this earth is matter in its most contaminated version.

NOTES

1. I am speaking here only of malignant possession. Benign possession occurs and this may involve no more than the interruption of consciousness, the switching over to another era and the individual adopting the accent and mannerisms of the possessing entity.

2. When I speak of personalisation I am referring not to the egocentric human personality but to the revelation, chiefly through form, of separate individualilty.

Conclusion

The first chapters of this book have been in my mind for decades. They are an expression of my basic nature. In my attitude to organized religion I could not have felt other than I did. It was all in the marrow of my bones. In the first chapters I make my case for revealed truth. Afterwards I divulge its contents. I learnt what I have divulged by a process of initiation in which I learnt the symbols through which psychic and spiritual men have communicated with each other through centuries. When I achieved the capacity to talk to the discarnates at differnt degrees I acquired an understanding of what would formerly have been incomprehensible to me. Sometimes what they communicated was so difficult that I only understood it while I was actually speaking with them and had to write it down in order not to forget it. I have excluded such matter from this book which contains nothing which is not now clear to me at the conscious level.

It may seem to some that I have stressed too much the virtues of passivity, that I have spoken too much of knowing rather than being and doing. When I speak of passivity I am describing an inner attitude and not an outward demeanour. The last thing I wish to convey is that the truth is the prerogative of a self-elected immobile elite. I have met these people who, sitting with folded arms, seek to impress by claiming special insights and exuding a self-conscious serenity. It is not a pleasant sight. All of us are born to occupy different action stations in this life. We cannot escape our destiny. But let it be said with resounding emphasis that our destiny is also our duty. We are here to work, whatever the outcome, and to express those traits of personality which we have developed in past lives and which must be evolved further. They are the mechanisms by which we learn.

If this world is a battleground between good and evil it is not enough to recognize this and remain neutral. Certainly benevolent neutrality towards ourselves is better than a protracted puritanical brawl between the spirit and the flesh. We must accept that we ourselves are an expression in miniature of the battle in the macrocosm. If we hate and castigate ourselves too much for our own failings we increase our tension and with it our sense of apartness and this is a great evil. We must recognize that we live in a world of emanation. Our own good acts are not our own. We do not generate love but are possessed by it. The evils which afflict us, the very diseases from which we suffer, are rarely self-inflicted. In them we are overborn by the power of evil. This is where an understanding of the nature of the Cosmos is so vital to our well being. It helps us to accept that we are interconnected molecules in nature and not lords of creation. To accept that we are enveloped in waves of good and evil enables us to live naturally and to avoid being trapped in ethical systems. The moralists are all too often the persecutors.

We are here to accept ourselves as we are and other people as they are. This is not fatalism but commonsense. Fatalism implies doom and is only logical to those who think in terms of this world only. What we have to accept is the certainty of defeat in this world, but this is no tragedy if we are partakers in a continuing evolution in which we recognize the world as the lowest rung of the ladder. But what happens even in this world is that acceptance, in the deepest recesses of our hearts, of our own limitations and of those of the world about us, enables us to change. As soon as we recognize that we cannot change we *are* changed, because to recognize that we cannot change is an abnegation of the cult of personality and when this dies the wings of our psyche are unfolded and we are reborn in this life. We pass from the world of social and ethical standards to that of emanation. We emit light rather than explanations.